# Ceremony and Ritual in Japan

# The Nissan Institute/Routledge Japanese Studies Series

# Ceremony and Ritual in Japan

Religious Practices in an
Industrialized Society

Edited by Jan van Bremen
and D.P. Martinez

London and New York

First published 1995
by Routledge
11 New Fetter Lane, London EC4P 4EE

Simultaneously published in the USA and Canada
by Routledge
29 West 35th Street, New York, NY 10001

Reprinted 1996, 1997

© 1995 Jan van Bremen and D.P. Martinez; individual chapters:
the contributors

Typeset in Times by
Ponting–Green Publishing Services, Chesham, Bucks

Printed and bound in Great Britain by
George Over Limited, London and Rugby

*British Library Cataloguing in Publication Data*
A catalogue record for this book is available from the
British Library

*Library of Congress Cataloging in Publication Data*
A catalogue record for this book is available from the Library
of Congress

ISBN 0-415-11663-5

# Contents

# Illustrations

## TABLE

# Contributors

**Jane M. Bachnik** is a Professor at the Institute of Multimedia Education, the Ministry of Education in Chiba, Japan. Her research interests focus on pragmatic/indexical meaning and include Japanese family, self, society and small business organization. Her publications include *Situated Meaning: Inside and Outside in Japanese Self, Society and Language* (with Charles J. Quinn, Jr) and *Family, Self and Society in Contemporary Japan.*

**Augustin Berque** is Professor of Geography and Head of the Centre de recherches sur le Japon contemporain at the Ecole des hautes études en sciences sociales in Paris. His recent publications include *Du Geste à la cité: formes urbain et lien social au Japon* (Japanese translation forthcoming) and *Miburi kara machizukuri e* (Cosmology of the city).

**Jan van Bremen** is Associate Professor at the Centre for Japanese and Korean Studies, University of Leiden and Co-founder and Liaison Officer of the Japan Anthropology Workshop. His interests focus on the anthropology and intellectual history of Japan and he has published widely in these fields.

**Jane Cobbi** is Research Fellow at CNRS and a Lecturer at the Ecole des hautes études en sciences sociales, Paris. As a result of much fieldwork she has published work on, among other things, material culture, food habits and the anthropology of work.

**Sylvie Guichard-Anguis** is affiliated to the National Scientific Centre of Research in France. She is currently a Lecturer in the UFR of Geography at the Sorbonne and the Institut Catholique in Paris. She has published several articles on urban geography in Japan.

**Joy Hendry** is Professor of Social Anthropology at Oxford Brookes University. Her current areas of interest are politeness and other forms of indirect communication in contemporary Japan. Her most recent books are *Wrapping Culture: Politeness, Power and Presentation in*

*Japan and other Societies* and *Understanding Japanese Society* (second edition forthcoming).

**Arne Kalland** is Senior Research Associate at the Centre for Development and the Environment, University of Oslo. His publications include *Shingū: A Study of a Japanese Fishing Community.*

**Sepp Linhart** is Professor of Japanology at the University of Vienna. With research interests in the sociology and social history of modern Japan, he recently co-edited with S. Formanek *Japanese Biographies: Life Histories, Life Cycles, Life Stages* and is author of *Japanologie Heute: Zustände – Umstände*, a collection of essays on the state of Japanese Studies today.

**D.P. Martinez** Lecturer in Anthropology with reference to Japan at the School of African and Asian Studies, University of London. Her recently published work includes 'Women and Religion in Japan' in Holm and Bowker (eds) *Women and Religion*. She is currently editing a book on Japanese popular culture and rewriting her D.Phil. thesis for publication.

**Hirochika Nakamaki** is an Associate Professor of the National Museum of Ethnography, Japan. He specializes in the anthropology of religion with reference to Japan and Brazil and has published several works in related fields.

**Ian Reader** holds a Readership in Japanese Studies at the University of Stirling. He has published articles about various aspects of popular religion in Japan and is author of *Religion in Contemporary Japan* and co-editor of *Pilgrimage in Popular Culture*. He is currently writing a book on pilgrimage in Japan.

**Robert J. Smith** is Goldwin Smith Professor of Anthropology and Asian Studies at Cornell University in Ithaca, New York, where he has taught since 1953. He is Past President of the Association of Asian Studies, and in 1993 the Government of Japan conferred on him the Order of the Rising Sun in recognition of his contribution to Japanese studies.

**Halldór Stefánsson** is Professor of Anthropology, Department of International Studies, Osaka Gakuin University, Japan. His research interests focus on the anthropology of death and death rituals in Japan, on which he has published several articles. He has been engaged in fieldwork related to such topics in various parts of Japan, Taiwan and South Korea since 1982.

# Series editor's preface

It remains unfortunately true, halfway through the 1990s, that Japan is an underreported country. Despite significant increases in the amount of information available, it is still the case that few aspects of Japan and its people are discussed in comparable depth, or with similar assumptions about familiarity, to discussion of the United States, Britain or other major countries. Differences of language and culture of course constitute a barrier, though less so than in the past. As the patterns of our post-Cold War world gradually consolidate, it is more than ever clear that the regional and global importance of Japan is increasing, often in ways more subtle than blatant. To borrow a phrase from Ronald Dore, we really should start 'taking Japan seriously'.

The Nissan Institute/Routledge Japanese Studies Series seeks to foster an informed and balanced, but not uncritical, understanding of Japan. One aim of the series is to show the depth and variety of Japanese institutions, practices and ideas. Another is, by using comparison, to see what lessons, positive and negative, can be drawn for other countries. The tendency in commentary on Japan to resort to outdated, ill-informed or sensational stereotypes still remains, and needs to be combated.

Japan has one of the most advanced economies in the world, and the bulk of her population enjoy a high standard of living. Contemporary Japanese civilization is materialistic and people's attitudes highly pragmatic. Scientific thinking is the predominate paradigm. The Japanese are a modern, or 'postmodern' people. By no stretch of the imagination can Japan be regarded as a theocracy, nor are the Japanese particularly religious, in the most commonly accepted senses of the word. Yet ceremony and ritual flourish, to the point, it might seem, of addiction. Is this just a peculiar Japanese trait, of the kind that inspired Western books ninety years ago with titles like *More Queer Things about Japan?* Or is it a culturally conditioned set of responses to the general human condition in advanced societies at the end of the twentieth century? Jan van Bremen, D.P. Martinez and their collaborators in this fascinating book do much to illuminate and suggest answers to this conundrum.

J.A.A. Stockwin

# Acknowledgements

This volume owes its origins to the fifth meeting of the Japan Anthropology Workshop which was held in March 1990 at the University of Leiden in the Netherlands. The workshop was made possible through the generous financial assistance of the Stichting Isaac Alfred Ailion Foundation and the Faculty of Arts in the University of Leiden. The editors would like to thank the Stichting Leids Universiteits-Fonds and the School for Oriental and African Studies for their financial support in the preparation of this volume. Our warmest thanks go to Ans Smit for her work as an exemplary editorial assistant; to Dr Roger Goodman for his sound advice; to Professor Arthur Stockwin, our patient general editor, for his careful reading of the text; and to Dr Marcus Banks for his help with a key figure. This book would not have been possible without the support and input of Keiko Itō and David Gellner. At Routledge our thanks go to Peter Sowden, Gordon Smith, James Whiting and Diane Stafford for their encouragement and support.

# Introduction

## The myth of the secularization of industrialized societies

*Jan van Bremen*[1]

### RELIGIOUS PRACTICES IN INDUSTRIALIZED SOCIETIES[2]

The studies collected in this volume are by anthropologists from a number of different countries and backgrounds. They are about ceremonies and rites in Japan, one of the most urbanized and industrialized countries in the world today. It has widely been asserted that progessive secularization is innate to industrialized societies. It is thought that in an unholy alliance, urbanization, industrialization, and secularization cause the attrition of rites, but research (see Boissevain 1992) contradicts this notion. As rites disappear, in rural as well as in urban areas, others are seen to take their place, reflecting new levels of competition and integration such as those shown in the development of the nation-state. Meanwhile some of the older local rites are being maintained or revitalized in communities that enjoy economic prosperity in the Americas, Europe, and in Asia, in countries like Japan, Korea and Taiwan.[3] The re-emergence of the *Dainenbutsu* teams described by Halldór Stafánsson (in this volume) illustrates this point, as does Joy Hendry's analysis of gift exchange (in this volume).

Actually, rites are seen to be a part of the very establishments that were said to cause their loss. Religious rites are regularly held in Japanese factories, where they play an important role. David Lewis concludes:

> [The] secularization hypotheses predicated on an assumption that the non-religious aspects of industrial society are essentially antagonistic or contradictory to religiosity break down in the light of this kind of data from Japan. Rather than declining in an urban industrial context, it is clear that in Japan religious rites have not only survived but may have even increased in both number and variety through factors such as fires and other disasters in the industrial context.
>
> (Lewis 1986:274)

Ceremonies and rites do flourish on a large scale in industrialized societies and Japan is not an exception.

Post-war surveys in Japan about attitudes towards death and belief in the other-world showed an increase in spirit belief in the 1980s, particularly among young urbanites (Wöss 1992:91–5). Inhabitants of Okinawa held periodic rites for their dead in the 1980s, some costing several tens or even hundreds of thousands of yen to perform (Namihira 1991:219). Also in the 1980s, megapolitans had rites performed for the appeasement of the souls of their aborted foetuses (*mizuko kuyō*) on a large scale (LaFleur 1992). Namihira (1991:240) explains this practice by the belief that the aborted foetuses have the power to curse (*mizuko tatari*).[4] There is ample evidence from folklore that people believe in the power of the dead not only to curse but also to bless and protect the living. The living and the departed remain in close proximity and share experiences and concerns in Japan (Namihira 1991:223–37).

Whilst it may be that ceremonies and rites are very much alive in industrialized societies and are even growing in scale, some scholars maintain that the religious elements are in decline or are lacking altogether. This claim is based on the assumption that social life, always and everywhere, divides into two separate and essentially different domains. According to this view, social activities occur in either the domain of the sacred, or else in what is seen as the secular sphere. Life in non-industrialized societies is thought to partake more of the sacred, while life in industrialized societies is deemed to take place for the most part in the province of the profane.

The view that this particular distinction is valid and should be maintained has been defended by Max Gluckman (Gluckman and Gluckman 1977) at a time when other anthropologists were changing their thinking on the matter. In what was to be his last delivery, Gluckman said that he would describe as 'ceremonious' those actions and words which do not involve beliefs in occult power, and as 'ritual' those which do involve such beliefs. In his view, to call all formality and ceremonial 'ritual' is to blur the distinction between formal activities that address and move the spirit world (which Gluckman maintains should be called 'ritual') and formal activities that do not.[5]

Nonetheless, the bipartite division of society into sacred and secular domains is progressively being abandoned by anthropologists studying industrialized as well as non-industrialized societies. Social life is not always and everywhere either secular or sacred. Julian Pitt-Rivers (1986:126) expresses this misgiving when he writes, 'l'existence d'une fonction utilitaire n'enlève rien à la valeur symbolique d'un act, et vice versa'. There are others who do not wish to draw a sharp distinction between the everyday world and the world of ritual: Roberto Da Matta, for example, (1977:256–9) argues that both are built up from more or less arbitrary things and conventions. There is no essential or qualitative shift between the categories and relations of the everyday world and those used in rites. Rites must not be taken as events which are essentially different in form, quality, and substance from those which constitute and inform the so-called routine of daily life. The study of ritual is not a search for the essential qualities of a peculiar and qualitatively different event; it is a way of examining how trivial elements of the social world can be elevated and transformed into symbols, categories, mechanisms, which, in certain contexts, allow the generation of a special or extraordinary event. Rites manage to place aspects of the social world in 'close-up'. By way of example, Da Matta points out that a finger is only a finger joined to a hand, and the hand to an arm, and the arm to a body. But at the moment when a ring is placed on the finger, marking the matrimonial status of the person concerned, the finger changes in its significance. The finger, normally seen as an element which is an integral part of a biological and individual universe, becomes a symbol of a set of social relations. Rites, in other words, are an aspect of social ties, which explains the use made of ordinary articles in rites, such as fingers, rings, or even towels (Joy Hendry in this volume), brooms (Ian Reader in this volume), and foodstuffs (Jane Cobbi in this volume).

Barbara Myerhoff (1977:200), too, argues that rites are not simply either sacred or secular. Rather, some are closer to the sacred, associated with supernatural or spiritual beings, while others are closer to the mundane world, concerned with propriety and relations between people. William Partridge (1977:61–2) feels that the orthodox convention in anthropology which reserves the term ritual for magical and religious behaviour is hard to maintain because a 'two-part universe' in which everything is either sacred or profane is difficult to justify ethnographically. It makes more sense to consider ritual as a mechanism or kind of behaviour which operates in all spheres of social life. Secular rituals are the same kind of phenomena as sacred rituals, the main difference being the assertion of participants in the latter that supernatural forces are brought to bear. Thus, although some scholars maintain that the notion cannot be given up, others contend that an all-embracing sacred–profane division is untenable: 'any theory which uses terms such as "sacred" and "profane", terms which cannot be given extracultural referent, cannot form the basis of a general theory of [rites] or of anything else' (Bloch 1992:28).

The debate affects the theorem of the secularization of industrialized societies. In Japanese cities comprehensive ancestor worship was seen to be in decline in the 1960s and 1970s in favour of the tendency to show affection for recently deceased kinsmen only, in the form of simplified memorialism (Smith 1974:223). At the same time it was noted that '[m]ore Japanese participate in the rites marking memorial observances for the spirits of the dead than in all other rites combined' (Smith 1974:vii). In Japanese mortuary rites new practices clearly make up for the loss of earlier customs, as Nakamaki shows for businesses and Buddhist establishments (in this volume).[6] Near cities, 'spirit parks' (*rei-en*) are laid out where families buy a memorial plot to venerate their deceased on ritual occasions.

It is remarkable how urban intellectuals, in the East as well as in the West, seem to believe that true religion is chiefly to be found in the traditional practices of the countryside and that it changes or disappears under the influence of civilization – literacy, urban life, the state – and as a result of industrialization. One meets this assumption in the work of the Shintō scholar Hirata Atsutane (1776–1843), one of the forerunners of modern Japanese folklore studies, who lived in the Edo period (Blacker 1963, 1967; Miyata 1991:36–7). It can also be found in the works of modern scholars. Possibly under the influence of modernization theories, students of Japan have until recently held that archaic mysticism and shamanic practices were fast disappearing as a result of the onslaught of civilization, urbanization, and industrialization. But in the past thirty or forty years a number of basic reorientations have taken place in the study of Japanese religion. One is that the assumption has been abandoned that progress in science and technology in Japan automatically carries with it a corresponding decline in the belief in magic. It is clear that, if anything, there has been a steep increase in these beliefs (Blacker 1990). Today, diviners – whether operating on the sidewalk or in an office – and shamanistic healers – often the centre of a religious group – can be found in significant numbers in every city in Japan.[7]

To understand industrialized societies one must see beyond the apparent secularization. Along with loss and discontinuity, newly constituted religious practices can be found in abundance in Japan, Taiwan and Korea. Religious rites in Japanese factories or memorial services held by Japanese enterprises (Nakamaki in this volume) are but two among a large number of telling examples. Mary Picone responded to 'success story literature' such as Vogel's (1979) *Japan as Number One*, by saying:

This school maintains that Japan's economic progress has been achieved by the members of an irreversibly secular society, working in sinister harmony at the refinement and mass-production of western technological gadgets . . . . I have attempted to examine the possibility of the coexistence of technological expertise on the one hand, and of the new forms of traditional religious ideas on the other. The most important of such ideas are karmic causality, the veneration of one's ancestors and faith-healing. In the case of Japan, it would seem that not only is such coexistence possible, but that industrialisation has served to create a vast public hungry for instantaneous remedies of all ills.

(Picone 1984:3)

This argument does not deny that there has been an erosion of pre-industrial religious practices, but neither does it ignore the fact that traditional religious ideas reappear in new forms. Industrialization affects religious practices in so many ways. Fleur Wöss (1992:80) points out that 1,500 years of Buddhism did not lead many Japanese to take up the practice of cremation, but that in the course of Japan's industrialization the cremation rate went up from about 25 per cent in 1896 to over 90 per cent in the 1980s. The cremation rate now is practically 100 per cent in large cities in Japan and growing in the countryside (Jane Bachnik in this volume).

Religious institutions all over Japan have benefited from the effects of industry on transportation. A railway line built in western Japan in 1915 by the Kintetsu company brought the shrines and temples in the Ikoma mountains near the city of Ōsaka within easy reach of the urbanites. The religious institutions there, both long established and more recent, have profited immensely from the much improved accessibility afforded by the railway. The Nankai railway linking Ōsaka and Mount Kōya, which plays such an important role in the company memorial services surveyed by Nakamaki (in this volume), is one more example. The study by Sylvie Guichard-Anguis (in this volume) of the shrine of Ebisu at Nishinomiya, also in western Japan, industrialized and urbanized, shows that its prosperity is closely linked to industrialization. In 1874 the national railway company linked Ōsaka to Kōbe by rail and opened a station at Nishinomiya. In 1905 the Hanshin private line duplicated the Ōsaka–Kōbe link. In 1920 a third private line, the Hankyū, made the same link but alongside the mountains. In 1964 the town was crossed by the Meishin motorway, matched in 1970 by the new Hanshin motorway. The three large train stations of Hanshin, Hankyū and the old national railways are between 350 metres and 1,300 metres away. The Hanshin motorway passes less than 50 metres to the south of the temple. This close proximity to transport systems is one of the main reasons for the temple's attraction in the eyes of its visitors.

The secularization of industrialized societies is a myth. Findings refute the theorem that industrialization annihilates religious practices. Moreover, social life is not simply either secular or sacred at any one time or place. Rites are not so different from other social practices. The similarities between ceremonies and rites of all kinds need to be acknowledged.

## CEREMONIES AND RITES

Every student should scrutinize received wisdom. Since Edmund Leach (1961) published his thoughts on anthropology more than thirty years ago, the activity has been known as 'rethinking', or even 'reinventing' (Hymes 1969). It also occupies minds in Japanese studies (see Boscaro, Gatti and Raveri 1990). Some anthropologists are experimenting with new ways to present the data they collect in Japan (see Ben-Ari 1990). They try to overcome limitations of the received forms of ethnography.[8] Kohl (1993) distinguishes four genres in the experimental ethnographies: (1) confessional literature (*'Das Tagebuch tritt an die Stelle des Forschungsberichts'*, 1993:124); (2) ethnographic biographies (life histories of informants); (3) dialogue-ethnographies (exchanges between informants and ethnographer); and (4) multivocal ethnographies. Earlier examples of these experiments can be found. Others place the revision of received explanatory paradigms on their research agendas (see Aoki 1990). It has been argued, for example, that 'contextual models' need to replace 'egocentric models' if one is truly to grasp Japanese society (Hamaguchi 1985). Again, it has been contended that 'conflict models' must augment or displace 'consensus models' if one is to see social realities clearly in Japan (Mouer and Sugimoto 1986). Or, alternatively, it is said that contemporary Japan should be understood in the light of its own recent past. An example of this view is to regard the feudal domains of the Tokugawa period as the models of the modern Japanese business corporations, more so than contemporary Western commercial enterprises, as is done by Nakamaki (1992).

The changes that have taken place in Japanese religious practices in the course of the transformation from a predominantly agrarian to a highly industrialized society have received much scholarly attention. The irreversible loss of pre-industrial religious practices in the wake of Japan's growing industrialization and urbanization has been deeply mourned (Blacker 1975:315–16; Tison 1988:96). Although generally put in abstract terms, the forces of annihilation have not all been faceless. The eclipse of local festivals and life-cycle ceremonies during Japan's century of industrialization and metropolization has been largely due to efforts by government officials to curtail the expenditure involved (Smith 1978:1–3; Linhart 1984:213). The irony which this at times entails is vividly depicted in a vignette recorded by the ethnologist Yamamoto Yoshiko at the end of her book on a traditional Namahage[9] festival in north-east Japan:

> Still, among the young men in the hamlet there is a tendency to conserve the festival as a traditional custom. A high school teacher I met who prohibited his students from joining the festival because it involved drinking stated that there were quite a few students who showed an interest in joining the festival as a significant experience of their youth, something they would always remember. The same teacher, who is a local folklorist, showed his own interest in the festival by tape recording its varied sounds.
>
> (Yamamoto 1978:127)

Tourist bureaus began to advertise the festival, TV stations to broadcast the celebration, souvenirs connected with the observance began to be sold to visitors to the area, and semi-professional part-time Namahage were being hired by hotels to entertain guests all year round (Yamamoto 1978:125–6). Villagers pay little attention to these contrivances and continue to hold their own celebration at the proper time. In this Yamamoto perceives a basic difference between rites and spectacles:

> The Namahage observance is basically a drama for insiders only; it is a series of intimate scenes in which actors and audience participate. It is not a production that easily lends itself to the entertainment of a passive audience of strangers.
>
> (Yamamoto 1978:126)

D.P. Martinez (1990) made a similar discovery in the village of Kuzaki on Shima Peninsula in Mie prefecture, where a thrice-yearly sacred ritual is the exclusive concern of the community, not open to participation by outsiders or tourists. Documentary recording on film is permitted, but when this happens changes occur. Outsiders such as a Shintō priest and a film director now direct the ritual. They make participants wear costumes and behave differently from when the rite is performed by the villagers alone (Martinez 1992).[10]

Anthropologists have made several contributions to the study of rites. Some studies are descriptive and show the seeming variety and complexity of ritual activities; others are analytical and seek to transcend local particulars in order to find general forms and functions, structures and sequences of rites. Still others ask what, as synaesthetic events, rites mean to the actors, helpers, and audiences trying to understand the ludic and mobile surfaces of rites (Shore 1990:226–7). Jacob Raz (1992:228–9) took the latter approach in Japan: 'What we call the "atmosphere" of the *matsuri* [festival] consists of the combination of the feast of senses, the taste of vulgarity and the coupling of the sacred and the profane'.[11] Two notions in particular seem to inform the perception of rites in anthropology today. One view is expressed by Da Matta (1977:264): '[t]o rethink rites . . . we must first de-ritualize'. The other idea is that it is more useful to ask how ritual works than to ask what ritual is (Bell 1992:159, note 190).

Rites are perhaps less complex than is generally assumed, but there are several stumbling blocks to understanding. Received terminology and ways of thinking can be misleading.[12] Alan Campbell asserts that:

> the noun/verb distinction in our habits of thought allows the proliferation of hypostases – things, categories, abstract entities – which we bestow haphazardly on ourselves and others in the form of names and diagnoses (What actually makes a thief a thief and a boxer a boxer is that they *do* something) . . . . [A] statement such as 'The Wayãpí have shamans' is misleading and I suggest that we should try to loosen up our categories of noun, adjective, and verb and learn to place more emphasis on the verb. In other words, there is no such *thing* as a shaman. People shamanize. They use a quality.
>
> (Campbell 1989:2–3; italics in original).[13]

Following a corresponding line of thought, Da Matta says that a profitable approach to rites is to create,

> a grammar or system of combination which would give us a way of entering the 'ritual world' and the central point of such a study would be this grammar, not the substantive categories which have been traditionally used to describe and interpret these events. From this point of view, ritual is something completely compatible with the world of ordinary events, the elements of everyday life being the same as those of the ritual.
>
> (Da Matta 1977:255)

In understanding rites, Da Matta (1977:256) brands as a major obstacle the notion that they constitute a special kind of action or a special kind of event. In reality, anthropologists distinguish a range of ritual types: rites, ceremonies, festivals, celebrations, performances, holidays, and so on (Bell 1992:69–70). They also tend to qualify rites by adjectives – religious, secular, personal, communal, funerary, seasonal, civil, state, interactive, rebellious, defiant – and by nouns – solidarity, affliction, passage, childhood, initiation, marriage, and so forth (Da Matta

1977:256). In sum, there seem to exist as many 'rites' as there are events or domains in the social world which can be perceived, distinguished, and classified. For each established domain, the word 'ritual' can be applied, and a corresponding 'rite' emerge from it. The immense possibilities of defining rites are the result of the fact that social life is a 'rite' or is 'ritualized'. Since the social world is based on conventions and symbols, all social actions are ritual acts or acts arising from a ritualization.

Following this line of thought Catherine Bell (1992:107) also argues that the habit of thinking about ritual as an entity of some sort is wrong. Ritual is not an entity but a practice that exists only in the specific cultural schemes and strategies for ritualization embodied and accepted by persons of specific cultural communities. In the same way as rites are produced, ideas of the sacred and secular are produced:

> From the perspective of ritualization the categories of sacred and profane appear in a different light. Ritualization appreciates how sacred and profane activities are differentiated in the performing of them, and thus how ritualization gives rise to (or creates) the sacred as such by virtue of its sheer differentiation from the profane. Whereas Durkheim defined religion and ritual as that which is addressed to the sacred, the approach presented here is an inverse of his, showing how a particular way of acting draws the type of flexible distinctions that yield notions and categories like 'ritual' or 'religion'. The relative clarity and flexibility of the boundaries, of course, are also a highly strategic matter in a particular cultural community and are best understood in terms of the concrete situation.
>
> (Bell 1992:91)

In the light of these statements one is led to think of rites as a Durkheimian social fact. Language is often given as the choice example of a social fact because it is externally imposed on individuals and presupposes the existence of a group of speakers prior to individual speaking acts (Elias 1991:21). In much the same way rites require a group of people and forms of co-ordinated action, and thus dictate individual ritual actions. Participants in rites can usually say little about the things they do or the paraphernalia they use. They can usually say little about other customs they follow or the phonetic or grammatical structures of the languages they use. Referring to this fact, Robert Smith explains for Japan that:

> A striking aspect of Japanese ritual is, in fact, the frequent encountered inability of participants and observers alike to offer any

exegesis of it whatsoever . . . . Actually this is not surprising. . . .
After all, ritual and ceremonial behaviour share with all behaviour
the characteristic that they are both learned and taught. . . . In Japan
. . . [o]ne learns *how* things are done rather than *why* they are done
the way they are . . . . No rationale can be offered because the young
have learned from their elders in a context in which exegesis plays
little or no part.

(Smith 1978:4–6; italics in original)

Studying a periodic rite in the fishing village of Shingū in Fukuoka
prefecture, Arne Kalland (in this volume) also found that people did not
usually know what something was, what it meant, or why something was
done. He concludes that, 'where individuals know only bits and pieces,
it is the aim of the anthropologist to put these bits and pieces together
in order to present the local reservoir of ritual knowledge'. Jane Bachnik
(in this volume) takes up this point in her concepts of 'pragmatic
meaning'. It is also addressed by D.P. Martinez (in this volume).

A social fact, in other words, is collective and cannot be dissolved
into individual actions. It is usually found, and not only in Japan, that
people do not know and nor do they see any need to question why they
perform rites. Sugishima Takashi (1990:841–53) learned that the
Lionese, a people living on the island of Flores in eastern Indonesia, do
not give any explanation of their agricultural rites beyond the standard
response, 'It is our custom'. Likewise Needham (1983:66–92) found
that his informants treated headhunting as something you simply do and
not question. Where there are specialists there may be a traditional
explanation, but such traditions are themselves part of the ritual. One
cannot explain the enactment or the form of a rite simply with reference
to the opinions of those who participate in it. The characteristic features
of rites and symbolic ideation, for instance the symbolism of sacrifice
in the Eucharist, do not contain in their turn more fundamental
explanations of the rite (Needham 1985).

Ritual is just one aspect of social life, and just one variety of symbolic
action. As for the explanation, Needham feels that one cannot do better
than to make clear descriptions or 'perspicuous representations', to use
Wittgenstein's term. To want to explain a practice, a rite, is a mistake.
One ends up explaining it the way one thinks and sees oneself, as
Campbell (1989), among others, cautions.

Reviewing studies on ritual, Bell says that daily activities involve
conviction and sincerity while ritual occasions demand consent:

These studies give evidence for the ambiguity and instability of
beliefs and symbols as well as the inability of ritual to control by

virtue of any consensus based on shared beliefs. They also suggest that ritualized activities specifically do *not* promote belief or conviction. On the contrary, ritualized practices afford a great diversity of interpretation in exchange for little more than consent to the form of the activities. This minimal consent actually contrasts with the degree of conviction frequently required in more day-to-day activities as, for example, the spontaneous sincerity that must be conveyed in many forms of conversation.

(Bell 1992:186; italics in original)

Ethnographers report that rites can be intelligible across barriers of language, culture, and place. Edmund Leach (1964: 102, 279) wrote of rites in northern Burma that the basic elements of ritual expression were not very numerous, and that rites could be a common 'language', understood across linguistic divides and different ways of life. Others corroborate these assertions. Maurice Bloch (1992) argues that along with variations, rites display a 'minimal structure', 'matrix', or 'core'. David Holmberg's study of the ritual life of the western Tamang in Himalayan Nepal, points to 'elementary structures in ritual life' and the necessity to see not only the separable strands but also to contrast the 'total ritual systems' in Hindu–Buddhist Asia (Holmberg 1989:1, 6). Along these lines, a group of anthropologists and historians found that in late-imperial China death rites as well as marriage rites had a singular structure of their own, uniform across boundaries, local, cultural or linguistic (Watson and Rawski 1990). An elementary structure in these rites was found to be present across regional and ethnic divides, consisting of an orthopraxy that had been disseminated over a long period of time (Watson 1990a:132–3). The 'elementary structure' in the mortuary rites consisted of a basic configuration of nine elements, which had to be adhered to if a funeral rite was to be truly 'Chinese'. At the same time, the burial or other rites of disposal followed local practice or another distinctive protocol (Watson 1990b:12–15). In Japan, elementary similarities are found alongside multiple local variations in ancestor veneration and the cult of the dead (Smith 1974:97, 99; Picone 1984). Clearly, rather than going for ever more refined classifications, one should look for the basic properties of the rites.

Modern anthropologists have been too preoccupied with the attempt to grasp what alien ideas and practices mean to those whose lives are framed by them (Needham 1978:6–7). They have neglected to look for the uses or the causal connections and properties of institutions – ideas and practices like rites or kinship. Needham (1978:16–17) noted that as early as 1917 Lowie argued that, in descent systems, the emphasis should be not on types and systems named after particular tribes, but instead on the principles that articulated the social forms defined by descent. When Needham tried to take this approach in the 1970s he came to an encouragingly simple conclusion: namely, that given two procreative sexes, only six elementary modes of descent were logically possible, and that of these six only four were pragmatically feasible as ways of organizing social life.[14] It is by virtue of these principles that descent systems are alike and comparable, in other words, that the social forms are universally determined by a restricted number of relational factors that express logical constraints and alternatives.

Rites, having a small number of features, are easier grasped as a 'ritual complex'. Shamanism is an example of a nearly universal ritual complex. Another example is not nearly as universal but has nevertheless an impressive historical and territorial span. It is the custom of blood-offering to a thunder deity that is practised in Malaya, Borneo, and the Philippines, 'a form of sacrifice in which some nine or ten discrete features, the presence of none being entailed by any others, cohere remarkably into a ritual complex that is almost identical among culturally very different peoples' (Needham 1978:19).

Rites are social facts of the order of languages and descent systems, and one advances only very little if one proceeds by measuring isolated words, symbols, or acts of behaviour. Behavioural, sound, and symbolic patterns are socially established and carry their message clearly only if they are socially standardized and are part of a composition. Rites constitute a natural resemblance in human societies. They range from elaborate and lengthy events to the micro-rites executed in daily life. Arnold van Gennep remarked that, 'à coté des grands cycles cérémoniels ... il éxiste des rites inhérent à la vie quotidienne' (quoted in Niederer 1986:170). He meant activities such as greetings in public or forms of conduct at railway stations – the forms of behaviour which Goffman (1967) would call 'interaction ritual'. The purpose and meaning and effect of a rite may consist in no more than the performance of the rite itself. Ritual can be self-sufficient, self-sustaining, and self-justifying. 'Considered in its most characteristic feature, it is a kind of activity, like speech or dancing, that man as a "ceremonial animal" happens naturally to perform' (Needham 1985:149–77).

## INDUSTRIALIZED JAPAN

It is still widely believed that anthropologists have no dealings with industrialized societies. They are held to study exotic ways of life in non-industrialized societies, or peoples living on the fringes of industrialized societies, seeking to record what remains of cultures that are on the verge of extinction. But anthropologists have long been studying industrialized societies. It may be telling that in an assessment of the headway made in the study of contemporary urban life, the sociologist Brunt (1989:26) believes that among the various disciplines studying cities, anthropology makes the most useful contributions.

Anthropology first became an academic discipline and a profession about 100 years ago. Taking the 1830s as the beginnings of the modern societies known today (Johnson 1991), industrialization was as basic to the development of modern anthropology as colonization. Moreover, industrialized societies are not only the birthplace of academic and professional anthropology, but also places where fieldwork has been done. Fieldwork began in Japan in the 1920s and 1930s. Japan has been studied by native and foreign scholars from Europe, America, Australia, and Asia. It comes as a surprise, therefore, to find that Japan has generally been ignored in the construction of social theories. There is little or no reference to Japan in textbooks and histories of anthropology. Except for the occasional study, Japan is not used in contrastive research.[15] In the 1970s, two authors interested in Japanese imperialism found that:

> Japan is largely absent from the current debate on imperialism. But it is also largely absent from the classical texts on imperialism, too. In his preface to *Imperialism, The Highest Stage of Capitalism*, Lenin almost apologizes for using Japan as an example on the question of annexation.
>
> (Halliday and McCormack 1973:224)

In classical ethnology, Emile Durkheim was interested in industrial Japan and referred to it while criticizing social types (*espèces sociales*):

> L'etat économique, technologique, etc. présente des phénomènes trop instables et trop complexes pour fournir la base d'une classification. Il est même très possible qu'une même civilisation industrielle, scientifique, artistique puisse se rencontrer dans des sociétés dont la constitution congénitale est très différente. Le Japon pourra nous emprunter nos arts, notre industrie, même notre organization politique; il ne laissera pas d'appartenir à une autre espèce sociale que la France et l'Allemagne. Ajoutons que ces tentatives, quoique conduites par des sociologues de valeur, n'ont donné que des résultats vagues, contestables et de peu d'utilité.'
>
> (Durkheim 1987:88, note 1)

Ethnologists see continuities, transformations, and parallels between rites in pre-industrial and industrial Japan. Tanikawa Ken'ichi (1991) and others see the anti-American protest movements in the 1960s known as 'Ampo' in this light. The Ampo movement and demonstrations have traits in common with protest and eschatological movements in the nineteenth century known as '*ee-ja-nai-ka*', '*okage mairi*', and '*miroku shinkō*' movements. Rites being prominent in society, now as in the past, a group of scholars led by Kurabayashi Shōji (1982) is calling Japan 'a culture of ritual'.

Turning again to industrialized Japan, studies were recently made of rites in commercial wedding halls (Edwards 1989), children's games (Hendry 1990), institutions like temples, schools and youth hostels (Reader in this volume), the exchange of common commodities such as towels between households (Hendry in this volume), or staging public rituals such as imperial funerals (Smith in this volume). The studies enrich the ethnography of ceremonies and rites in Japan and mirror global concerns. Edwards's (1989) portrayal of rituals of gender, person, and society in one of the numerous commercial marriage halls operated by the wedding industry in Japan compares to Elshof's (1991) study of the socialist marriage palaces and their rites in the cities of Moscow, Leningrad, and Kiev in the former Soviet Union. They add to the growing body of literature about commercial, state, and public rituals. Befu has studied the cultural construction of national identity and the use of instruments of national identity such as the national anthem, the national flag, the national emblem, and national monuments and rites in post-war Japan (1992a, 1992b).[16]

It is often said that rites perpetuate 'tradition' but findings modify that theorem. Tradition is a construct. Rites change prior practices or legitimize new ones. Augustin Berque (in this volume) stresses that rites are not predominantly agents of equilibrium, repetition, and reproduction, but agents of change. Robert Smith (in this volume) found that the imperial marriage and funeral rites in the twentieth century are not ancient but new rites. Early in the century, Chamberlain (1912) saw in modern Japanese emperor worship 'the invention of a new religion'. For something to be called a 'tradition' it needs to have been performed 'at least once'. Linhart (in this volume) found that instead of establishing lasting traditions that would preserve and hand on certain forms of the game, excessive ritualization in the form of over-elaborated 'ways' and the establishment of schools spelled the end for most forms of *ken* in the early modern period.

It is said that rites are a force of conservatism or social control in certain societies:

Based on [Mary] Douglas's analysis . . . ritual is an important and effective means of social control in only certain types of societies, namely, closed and hierarchical ones. Such societies must have a marked hierarchical structure of differentiated positions as well as a strong sense of corporate identity, both evidenced in an assumption that interpersonal relations should be subordinated to the ordering of roles or positions. The group is simultaneously both highly differentiated *and* exalted as a corporate unity above the interests of the self.

(Bell 1992:178, italics in original)

Japanese social organization is often described and understood in such terms, but while the studies in this volume partly bear out Douglas's theorem, it is also true of Japan that:

ritual systems do not function to regulate or control the system of social relations, they *are* the system, and an expedient rather than perfectly ordered one at that. In other words, the more or less practical organization of ritual activities neither acts upon nor reflects the social system; rather, these loosely coordinated activities are constantly differentiating and integrating, establishing and subverting the field of social relations. Hence, such expedient systems of ritualized relations are not primarily concerned with 'social integration' alone, in the Durkheimian sense. Insofar as they establish hierarchical social relations, they are also concerned with distinguishing local identities, ordering social differences, and controlling the contention and negotiation involved in the appropriation of symbols.

(Bell 1992:130, italics in original)

Certain aspects of rites have been neglected in many studies, violence first among them. It must be studied in rites like lynchings and the violence perpetrated in the ritual murders committed during 'communal riots' in South Asia (Das 1990) or in South-African township executions.

Maurice Bloch (1992) sees violence as an integral part of transition and other rites. Margaret Lock (1991) found that refusal to attend school takes ritual forms in Japan that entail a noted element of violence to self and others as a reaction to overdemanding rules imposed upon both children and parents. Generally, disembowelment (*hara-kiri*) is among the best-known rites of violence in Japan. Massimo Raveri pleads that other rites of violence should also be studied and from new vantage points: rites in religious and social movements which are fundamentally violent but also creative. Raveri (1990:255), who studied self-mummification in Japan, appreciates ascetics as rare witnesses of perilous experiences that often bring them to the extreme limits of the mind, the body and the language. They are creative and mediate between past and future. 'These humble ascetics are an integral part of the history of a collective passage. They make their appearance at sunset, to announce a dawn which they will never see' (Raveri 1990:260). Schieffelin (1977) describes ritual performances in New Guinea given by visitors in the long houses of their hosts. The performers are made to suffer for the emotions they awake in their audience: the pain of the dancers and the sorrow of the lonely. Among the studies of violent rites is one of three incidents of ritual murder that occurred among Calvinists in The Netherlands this century.

Neglected in the study of rites is the place, the role, and the meaning of food:

> With one or two notable exceptions, anthropologists and raconteurs alike have been content to vaguely sketch the kind of foods presented, failing to detect the semantic significance entailed in the choice of one sort of offering instead of another.
>
> (Thompson in Watson and Rawski 1990:77)

In the anthropology of Japan, work by Matsunaga (1986) and the contribution by Jane Cobbi to this volume are such exceptions.

Gender issues too are often neglected in the study of rites, and the contribution to this volume by Martinez on the role of women in ritual is therefore important and timely. Finally, there is a growing literature on rites in Japanese communities and Japanese religions abroad. It should be compared with studies of ceremonies and rites in Japan, the better to understand the religious practices found in Japan and other societies in the world, whether industrialized or not.

## NOTES

1 I should like to thank Dolores Martinez and David Gellner for reading and improving my text.
2 Except where I follow the usage of other authors, I use 'ceremonies' and 'rites' interchangeably, following the example of Arnold van Gennep, who first entitled his book, 'Les rites de passage: étude systématique des rites de la porte et du seuil, de l'hospitalité, de l'adoption, de la grossesse et de l'accouchement, de la naissance, de l'enfance, de la puberté, de l'initiation, de l'ordination, du couronnement, des fiançailles et du mariage, des funerailles, des saisons, etc.', but then wrote as a correction on his personal copy: 'étude systématique des cérémonies' (Belmont 1986:10).
3 See for instance Bestor (1989) and Robertson (1991) on ritual integration and rivalry in Japanese neighbourhoods; Stefánsson (1991) on Taiwanese funerary accessories; Honda (1993) on memorialism in Korea. Comparative studies like Moon (1992) show parallels and differences.
4 The evil was as much in society. The unavailability of contraceptives led

to the widespread practice of abortions, profiting medical and Buddhist establishments, but paid for by the women and their families.

5 Grimes (1990:142) argues that Victor Turner had similar views.
6 Honda points out that

> These kinds of events [commemorating ancestors] have been carried out widely in Korea for many years, but, in recent years, they have been held more often than before thanks to the rise in the standard of living among the [rural] descendants.
>
> (1993:166)

On the other hand, in the process of urbanization and Westernization, ways of performing *hyō* [Confucian filial piety to ancestors] for distant ancestors are getting simpler and simpler.

(1993:168–9)

7 See the *Shinshūkyō jiten* (Dictionary of new religions) compiled by Inoue Nobutaka, Kōmoto Mitsugi, Tsushima Michito, Nakamaki Hirochika, and Nishiyama Shigeru (1990), Tokyo: Kōbundō. Twenty religious leaders and their followers have been portrayed by the photographer Fujita (1992).
8 Earlier examples of these experiments are found before the 1980s and 1990s.
9 *Namahage* are young men who dress and behave like demons.
10 John MacAloon (1984) has explored the differences for participants and spectators in rites, dramas, festivals, and spectacles.
11 'Japan at play: the ludic and the logic of power' was the theme explored in the sixth Japan Anthropology Workshop (JAWS), convened by Massimo Raveri of the University of Venice in Berlin during the European Association for Japanese Studies (EAJS) conference in September 1991. A volume of papers is being edited.
12 Views taken around the turn of the century by Ludwig Wittgenstein, Rainer Maria Rilke, and Frederik van Eeden, among others, began to influence anthropologists in the 1970s, first amongst them Anton Blok (1975) and Rodney Needham (1975).
13 I thank Ruport Cox for directing my attention to this book.
14 As explained in Needham (1974:47).
15 The classic example in anthropology is *Agricultural Involution* by Clifford Geertz, published in 1966. New is Joy Hendry's, *Wrapping Culture: Politeness, Presentation, and Power in Japan and other Societies*, Oxford: Clarendon Press, 1993.
16 It is tempting to keep adding studies that would bear comparison with material from Japan: Schulte Nordholt's (1991; 1993) studies of the changing relationships between state, locality, and rites in Bali and the perceptions of them; Handelman and Shamgar-Handelman's study of the choice of the national emblem of the state of Israel (in Ohnuki-Tierney 1990), to name just a few.

## BIBLIOGRAPHY

Note: Throughout this volume bibliographic entries appear under family names. Within entries they appear according to convention. Thus, Western names are presented as given name followed by family name; and Japanese names the reverse.

Aoki Tamotsu (1990) *Nihon bunkaron no henyō: sengo nihon no bunka t aidentitii* (Transformations in the 'theories of Japanese culture': post-wa Japanese culture and identity), Tokyo: Chūō Kōronsha.

Befu Harumi (1992a) 'Symbols of nationalism and *nihonjinron*', in R. Goodma and K. Refsing (eds) *Ideology and Practice in Modern Japan*, London an New York: Routledge, pp. 26–46.

—— (1992b) 'Cultural construction and national identity: the Japanese case *Culture and Communication Working Papers* No. 5, Honolulu, Hawai Institute of Culture and Communication, The East–West Center.

Bell, Catherine (1992) *Ritual Theory, Ritual Practice*, Oxford: Oxford Univer sity Press.

Belmont, Nicole (1986) 'La notion du rite de passage', in Pierre Centlivres an Jacques Hainard (eds) *Les rites de passages aujourd'hui: Actes du colloqu de Neuchatel 1981*, Lausanne: Editions l'Age d'Homme, pp. 9–19.

Ben-Ari, Eyal (1990) 'Many voices, patial words: on some conventions an innovations in the ethnographic portrayal of Japan', in Eyal Ben A *Unwrapping Japan*, Manchester: Manchester University Press.

—— Brian Moeran and James Valentine (eds) (1990) *Unwrappin Japan*, Manchester: Manchester University Press.

Bestor, Theodore C. (1989) *Neighborhood Tokyo*, Stanford: Stanford Universit Press.

Blacker, Carmen (1963) 'The divine boy in Japanese Buddhism', *Asia Folklore Studies*, XXII: 77–88.

—— (1967) 'Supernatural abductions in Japanese folklore', *Asian Folklor Studies*, XXVI (2):111–48.

—— (1975) *The Catalpa Bow: A Study of Shamanistic Practices in Japan* London: George Allen & Unwin Ltd.

—— (1990) 'Rethinking the study of religion in Japan', in A. Boscaro F. Gatti and M. Raveri (eds) *Rethinking Japan, Volume II, Social Sciences Ideology and Thought*, Folkestone, Kent: Japan Library, P. Norbury.

Bloch, Maurice (1985) 'Religion and ritual', in Adam Kuper and Jessica Kupe (eds) *The Social Science Encyclopedia*, London: Routledge and Kegan Pau pp. 698–701.

—— (1992) *Prey into Hunter: The Politics of Religious Experience*, Cam bridge: Cambridge University Press. The Lewis Henry Morgan Lecture 1987.

Blok, Anton (1975) *Wittgenstein en Elias: Een Methodische Richtlijn Voor d Antropologie*, Assen: Van Gorcum.

Boissevain, Jeremy (ed.) (1992) *Revitalizing European Rituals*, London Routledge.

Boscaro, A., F. Gatti and M. Raveri (eds) (1990) *Rethinking Japan, Volume II Social Sciences, Ideology and Thought*, Folkestone, Kent: Japan Library P. Norbury.

Broekhuijse, Johan Theodorus (1967) *De Wiligman-Dani: Een Cultureel anthropologische Studie over Religie en Oorlogvoering in de Baliem-vallei* Tilburg: H. Gianotten. Doctoral dissertation, University of Utrecht.

Brunt, Lodewijk (1989) *De Magie van de Stad*, Meppel: Boom. Inaugura Lecture, University of Amsterdam.

Campbell, Alan Tormaid (1989) *To square with Genesis: Causal Statement and Shamanic Ideas in Wayāpí*, Edinburgh: Edinburgh University Press.

Chamberlain, Basil H. (1912) *The Invention of a New Religion*, London Watts & Co.

Da Matta, Roberto (1977) 'Constraint and license: a preliminary study of two Brazilian national rituals', in Sally F. Moore and Barbara G. Myerhoff (eds) *Secular Ritual*, Assen/Amsterdam: Van Gorcum, pp. 244–64.

Das, Veena (ed.) (1990) *Mirrors of Violence: Communities, Riots and Survivors in South Asia*, Delhi: Oxford University Press.

Durkheim, Emile (1987) *Les règles de la méthode sociologique*, 23rd edition, Paris: Presses Universitaires de France.

Du Toit, Brian M. (1977) 'Ethnicity and patterning in South African drug use', in Brian M. du Toit (ed.) *Drugs, Rituals and Altered States of Consciousness*, Rotterdam: A.A. Balkema, pp. 75–99.

Edwards, Walter (1989) *Modern Japan Through Its Weddings: Gender, Person, and Society in Ritual Portrayal*, Stanford: Stanford University Press.

Elias, Norbert (1991) *The Symbol Theory*, edited with an introduction by Richard Kilminster, London: Sage.

Elshof, Frank (1991) 'Het socialistisch huwelijksritueel. Het ritueel van de macht', *Skript* 13 (3): 157–66.

Fujita Shōichi (1992) *Reinō no higi* (Esoteric rites of spirit control), Tokyo: Fuyōsha.

Geertz, Clifford (1966) *Agricultural Involution: The Processes of Ecological Change in Indonesia*, Berkeley: University of California Press.

—— (1988) *Works and Lives: The Anthropologist as Author*, Stanford: Stanford University Press.

Gluckman, Mary and Max Gluckman (1977) 'On drama, and games and athletic contests', in Sally F. Moore and Barbara G. Myerhoff (eds), *Secular Ritual*, Assen/Amsterdam: Van Gorcum, pp. 227–43.

Goffman, E. (1967) *Interaction Ritual: Essays on Face-to-Face Behaviour*, New York: Doubleday.

Goodman, Roger and Kirsten Refsing (eds) (1992) *Ideology and Practice in Modern Japan*, London and New York: Routledge.

Grimes, Ronald L. (1990) 'Victor Turner's definition, theory, and sense of ritual' in Kathleen M. Ashley, (ed.), *Victor Turner and the Construction of Cultural Criticism: Between Literature and Anthropology*, Bloomington: Indiana University Press, pp. 141–77.

Halliday, Jon and Gavan McCormack (1973) *Japanese Imperialism Today: 'Co-Prosperity in Greater East Asia'*, New York and London: Monthly Review Press.

Hamaguchi Eshun (1985) 'A contextual model of the Japanese: toward a methodological innovation in Japan studies', *Journal of Japanese Studies* 11 (2): pp. 289–321.

Hendry, Joy (1990) 'Children's contests in Japan', in Andrew Duff-Cooper (ed.) *Contests*, Edinburgh: Edinburgh University Press, pp. 81–93.

—— (1993) *Wrapping Culture: Politeness, Presentation, and Power in Japan and other Societies*, Oxford: Clarendon Press.

Holmberg, David H. (1989) *Order in Paradox: Myth, Ritual, and Exchange among Nepal's Tamang*, Ithaca and London: Cornell University Press.

Honda Hiroshi (1993) 'Haka wo baikai to shita sosen no "tsuibo": Kankoku nanseibu ichi nōson ni okeru san-il no jitsurei kara' (Commemorating ancestors: remaking graves in a mountain village in south-west Korea), *Minzokugaku Kenkyū* (The Japanese Journal of Ethnology) 58(2): 142–69.

Howe, James (1981) 'Fox hunting as ritual', *American Ethnologist* 8(2): 278–300.

20   *Ceremony and Ritual in Japan*

Hymes, Dell (ed.) (1969) *Reinventing Anthropology*, New York: Pantheon.
Ileto, Reynaldo Clemeña (1989) [1979] *Pasyon and Revolution: Popular Movements in the Philippines, 1840–1910*, Quezon City, Metro. Manila: Ateneo de Manila University Press.
Johnson, Paul (1991) *The Birth of the Modern World Society 1815–1830*, New York: HarperCollins.
Kohl, Karl-Heinz (1993) *Ethnologie – die Wissenschaft vom Kulturell Fremden: Eine Einfürung*, München: C.H. Beck.
Kurabayashi Shōji (1982) *Girei bunka jozetsu* (Introduction to the culture of ritual), Tokyo: Daigaku Kyōikusha.
LaFleur, W.R. (1992) *Liquid Life: Abortion and Buddhism in Japan*, Princeton, N.J.: Princeton University Press.
Leach, E.R. (1961) [1954] *Rethinking Anthropology*, London: Athlone Press.
—— (1964) [1954] *Political Systems of Highland Burma: A Study of Kachin Social Structure*, London: G. Bell & Sons, Ltd.
—— (1966) 'Ritualization in man', *Philosophical Transactions of the Royal Society of London*, Series B, 251(722):403–8.
Lewis, David (1986) 'Religious rites in a Japanese Factory' *Japanese Journal of Religious Studies*, 13 (4): 261–75.
Lewis, Gilbert (1980) *Day of Shining Red: An Essay on Understanding Ritual*, Cambridge: Cambridge University Press.
Linhart, Sepp (1984) 'Some observations on the development of the "typical" Japanese attitudes towards working hours and leisure', in Gordon Daniels (ed.) *Europe Interprets Japan*, Tenterden, Kent, England: Paul Norbury Publications, pp. 207–14; 269–70.
Lock, Margaret (1991) 'Flawed jewels and national dis/order: narratives on adolescent dissent in Japan', *The Journal of Psychohistory* 18(4): 507–31.
MacAloon, John (ed.) (1984) *Rite, Drama, Festival, Spectacle: Rehearsals Toward a Theory of Culture Performance*, Philadelphia: Institute for the Study of Human Issues.
Martinez, D.P. (1990) 'Tourism and the Ama', in Eyal Ben-Ari, Brian Moeran and James Valentine (eds) *Unwrapping Japan*, Manchester: Manchester University Press, pp. 97–116.
—— (1992) 'NHK comes to Kuzaki: Ideology, mythology and documentary film-making', in Roger Goodman and Kirsten Refsing (eds) *Ideology and Practice in Modern Japan*, London: Routledge, pp. 153–70.
Matsunaga Kazuto (1986) 'The importance of the left hand in two types of ritual activity in a Japanese village', in J. Hendry and J. Webber (eds) 'Interpreting Japanese Society: Anthropological Approaches', Oxford: *Journal of the Anthropological Society of Oxford, Occasional Papers* no. 5:147–56.
Miyata Noboru (1991) *Nihon no minzokugaku* (Folklore studies in Japan), second edition, Tokyo: Kōdansha.
Moon, Okpyo (1992) 'Confucianism and gender segregation in Japan and Korea', in Roger Goodman and Kirsten Refsing (eds) *Ideology and Practice in Modern Japan*, London and New York: Routledge, pp. 196–209.
Mouer, Ross and Sugimoto Yoshio (1986) *Images of Japanese Society: A Study in the Structure of Social Reality*, London: Kegan Paul International.
Myerhoff, Barbara G. (1977) 'We don't wrap herring in a printed page: fusion, fictions and continuity in secular ritual', in Sally F. Moore and Barbara G. Myerhoff (eds) *Secular Ritual*, Assen/Amsterdam: Van Gorcum, pp. 199–224.

Nakamaki Hirochika (1992) *Mukashi daimyō ima kaisha* (Formerly feudal lords, presently corporations), Tokyo: Tankōsha.

Namihira Emiko (1991) 'Shisha no kotoba. Shisha ni tsuite no katari' (Words of the dead. Tales about the dead), in Namihira Emiko (ed.) *Densetsu ga Umareru Toki* (When a legend is born), Tokyo: Fukutake Shoten, pp. 217–41.

Needham, Rodney (1974) *Remarks and Inventions: Skeptical essays about Kinship*, London: Tavistock Publications.

—— (1975) 'Polythetic classification: Convergence and consequences', *Man*, 10(3): 349–69.

—— (1978) *Primordial Characters*, Charlottesville: The University Press of Virginia.

—— (1983) [1976] 'Skulls and causality', reprinted in Rodney Needham (ed.) *Against the Tranquillity of Axioms*, Berkeley: University of California Press.

—— (1985) 'Remarks on Wittgenstein and ritual' in *Exemplars: A Collection of Works by Rodney Needham*, Berkeley: University of California Press.

Niederer, Arnold (1986) 'Elements de ritualité dans la vie quotidienne', in Pierre Centlivres et Jacques Hainard (eds) *Les rites de passages aujourd'hui: Actes du colloque de Neuchatel 1981*, Lausanne: Editions l'Age d'Homme, 170–8.

Ohnuki-Tierney, Emiko (ed.) (1990) *Culture Through Time: Anthropological Approaches*, Stanford: Stanford University Press.

Partridge, William L. (1977) 'Transformation and redundancy in ritual: A case from Colombia', in Brian M. du Toit (ed.) *Drugs, Rituals and altered States of Consciousness*, Rotterdam: A.A. Balkema, pp. 59–73.

Picone, Mary J. (1984) 'Rites and symbols of death in Japan', Unpublished D.Phil. thesis, University of Oxford.

Pitt-Rivers, Julian (1986) 'Un rite de passage de la societé modern: le voyage aerien', in Pierre Centlivres et Jacques Hainard (eds) *Les rites de passages aujourd'hui: Actes du colloque de Neuchatel 1981*, Lausanne: Editions l'Age d'Homme, pp. 115–30.

Raveri, Massimo (1990) 'In search of a new interpretation of ascetic experiences', in A. Boscaro, F. Gatti and M. Raveri (eds) *Rethinking Japan, Volume II, Social Sciences, Ideology and Thought*, Folkestone, Kent: Japan Library, P. Norbury.

Raz, Jacob (1992) 'Self-presentation and performance in the *yakuza* way of life: Fieldwork with a Japanese underworld group', in Roger Goodman and Kirsten Refsing (eds) *Ideology and Practice in Modern Japan*, London: Routledge, pp. 210–34.

Robertson, Jennifer (1991) *Native and Newcomer: Making and Remaking a Japanese City*, Berkeley: University of California Press.

Schieffelin, Edward L. (1977) [1976] *The Sorrow of the Lonely and the Burning of the Dancers*, St. Lucia: University of Queensland Press.

Schulte Nordholt, Henk (1991) *State, Village, and Ritual in Bali: A Historical Perspective*, Amsterdam: Comparative Asian Studies (CAS) Vol. 7.

—— (1993) 'Leadership and the limits of political control: A Balinese "Response" to Clifford Geertz', *Social Anthropology*, 1(3): 291–307.

Shore, Bradd (1990) 'Ritual frames of mind', *Reviews in Anthropology*, 15(4): 225–37.

Smith, Robert J. (1974) *Ancestor Worship in Contemporary Japan*, Stanford: Stanford University Press.

—— (1978) 'Foreword: the eclipse of the communal ritual in Japan', in Yamamoto Yoshiko, *The Namahage: A Festival in the Northeast of Japan*, Philadelphia: Institute for the Study of Human Issues, pp. 1–8.

Stefánsson, Halldór (1991) 'The art of moving house to heaven and absolving spirits from defilement: on Taiwanese forms of funerary accessories', reprinted from the *Bulletin of the Cultural and Natural Sciences in Ōsaka Gakuin University*, (23–4): 91–114.

Sugishima Takashi (1990) 'Rio zoku ni okeru nōkōgirei no kijutsu to kaishaku', (Description and interpretation of the Lionese agricultural rituals), *Kokuritsu Minzokugaku Hakubutsukan Kenkyū hōkoku* (Bulletin of the National Museum of Ethnology), 15(3): 573–846.

Tanigawa Ken'ichi (1991) [1969] 'Matsuri to shite no "Ampo"' ('Ampo' as a festival), *Tanigawa Ken'ichi chosakushū* (collected works), Tokyo: San Ichi Shobō. Vol. 7:322–35.

Tison, Nathalie (1988) 'Osorezan, pèlerinage et tourisme', unpublished thesis, Paris: Institut National des Langues et Civilisations Orientales.

Watson, James L. (1990à) 'Funeral specialitists in Cantonese society: pollution, performance and social hierarchy', in Watson and Rawski (eds) *Death Ritual in Late Imperial and Modern China*, Berkeley: University of California Press.

—— (1990b) 'The structure of Chinese funerary rites: elementary forms, ritual sequence, and primacy of performance', in Watson and Rawski (eds) *Death Ritual in Late Imperial and Modern China*, Berkeley: University of California Press.

—— and Evelyn S. Rawski (eds) (1990) [1988] *Death Ritual in Late Imperial and Modern China*, Berkeley: University of California Press.

Wöss, Fleur (1992) 'When blossoms fall: Japanese attitudes towards death and the otherworld: opinion polls 1953–87', in R. Goodman and K. Refsing (eds), *Ideology and Practice in Modern Japan*: pp. 72–100.

Yamamoto Yoshiko (1978) *The Namahage: A Festival in the Northeast of Japan*, Philadelphia: Institute for the Study of Human Issues.

# Part I
# The question of tradition

# 1 Wedding and funeral ritual

## Analysing a moving target

*Robert J. Smith*

I am by no means the first, and surely will not be the last to try to make some sense of the Japanese scene as it flashes by. Perhaps it would be more fitting to say as it *appears* to be flashing by the necessarily fixed vantage point on which any observer must stand. In that effort, I find myself in numerous, if not always the best of company. Among the more illustrious of that number is Arnold Toynbee who, it has been pointed out (Gibney 1985:107), in *The Study of History* noted that Japan was a classic instance of cultural conflict between two contending factions which he identified as the Herodians and Zealots. It is highly likely that Toynbee assumed initially that one of them was destined to win out in the end, the other to be vanquished. The Herodians, named after Herod Agrippa, who ruled Galilee, pursued a policy of assimilating foreign culture as thoroughly as possible. The Zealots, who take their name from the Maccabees and the early Jewish zealots, championed tradi-tional culture. In the course of his analysis of the Japanese case, it appears that Toynbee had second thoughts about the aptness of his scheme for Japan, for he concludes that the Meiji Restoration repre-sented a pursuit of Zealot ends by Herodian means. Marius Jansen (1970:111) was making what I take to be the same point when he wrote of the policies pursued by the Meiji oligarchs: 'Seeking revolution, they preached restoration'. And only thirty years after that revolutionary restoration, Basil Hall Chamberlain (1898:2, 3, 8) commented on one of its salient outcomes:

> Whatever you do, don't expatiate, in the presence of Japanese of the new school, on those old, quaint, and beautiful things Japanese which arouse your most genuine admiration. . . . [For] all this is [today regarded as] merely a backwater. Speaking generally, the educated Japanese have done with their past. They want to be somebody else than what they have been and still partly are. . . . [Yet] it is

abundantly clear to those who have dived beneath the surface of the modern Japanese upheaval that more of the past has been retained than has been let go.

The impatient reader of this kind of thing is bound to protest and ask, 'Well, which is it?' And so we may recommend that the question be directed to the editors of a volume that has attracted a great deal of attention in the past few years, for there appears to be the beginnings of an answer in Hobsbawm's comment towards the end of *The Invention of Tradition* (1983:266):

> A 'modernization' which maintained the old ordering of social subordination (possibly with some well-judged invention of tradition) was not theoretically inconceivable, but apart from Japan, it is difficult to think of an example of practical success.

Indeed it is difficult to think of another example, and so we must regret that there is no answer to our question, for not a single contributor to the book makes so much as a passing reference to Japan. But we are used to such snubs from our Eurocentric colleagues and until they give up marginalizing the rest of the world there is nothing for it but to get on with the job of analysing that singular society ourselves.

Although it leaves much to be desired I now realize, I was much taken with a distinction drawn by Hobsbawm between custom (which he defines as 'mere usages') and tradition, which combines ritual and symbol. Imagine my astonishment when I came across the following passage in Maxine Hong Kingston's *Tripmaster Monkey: His Fake Book* (1989:195). Wittman Ah Sing, the Chinese-American anti-hero of this curious work, takes his new wife to meet his family. When he discovers that his grandmother's room is empty, he suspects that his mother has put her in an old folks' home without letting him know. As Wittman Ah Sing and his Caucasian bride set out to look for the old lady, he says:

> 'See how neglectful of her family my mother is? I wouldn't put it past her to give Grandma the old heave-ho.'
> 'You have the same custom as the Eskimo?' asked Taña.
> 'I don't know. How many times does something have to be done for it to be a tradition? There has to be ceremony. You can't just toss a grandmother on an iceberg and run.'

He might have added another question or two. How *long* does it take for something to become a tradition? Must customs or traditions necessarily reflect established cultural predispositions and constructs? Is it possible simply to make them up out of whole cloth?

My topic is Japanese weddings and funerals. Rather it is, on the one hand, the style of weddings in which most people are married these days – the typical and without a doubt what will come to be commonly viewed as the traditional wedding ceremony. On the other hand, and in sharp contrast, I propose to consider only one kind of funeral – the kind represented by that of the Shōwa Emperor. The contemporary ordinary wedding and the recent extraordinary imperial funeral reveal something of the nature of Japanese culture, why I have called it a moving target, and what forces appear to cause it never to reach stasis even while giving every appearance of being highly conservative in character.

Let me hasten to add that I do not think Japan is at all unique in this respect, but it does seem to me a particularly striking instance of that seemingly boundless capacity for invention and malleability which can easily be represented as cultural conservatism. In stressing the flexibility of culture, I follow Edmund Leach (1989:138, 141):

> Ever since the days of Herodotus . . . ethnographers have written as if customs were normally static. When change occurs it has to be explained as if it were an anomaly. But historical records everywhere suggest that what would need to be explained is an ethnography that did not change. Why should anthropologists take it for granted that history never repeats itself but persuade themselves that cultures never do anything else? The answer is that it is often convenient so to believe. Malinowski believed that the Trobriand *kula*, as he observed it, had been working like that for hundreds of years. He mentions this belief only in a footnote. The evidence is that it had in fact been in existence for less than 50 years and was changing rapidly all the time.

Would it have made any difference had Malinowski realized that the *kula* trade had been in existence for only fifty years – or ten – or five hundred? I rather doubt that functionalism would have assumed a different form, but knowing how deep or shallow the history of this particular cultural practice might well have had a profound impact on the anthropological study of system change.

And so we come to my metaphor of the moving target. As I have argued elsewhere, we begin with the realization that we have lost our anchor in time (Smith 1989a: 718). Conventional wisdom notwithstanding, culture has never depended on genuine antiquity to lay legitimate claim to authenticity. I would argue that the proper study of culture *requires* us to slip our moorings in history and accept that all points once thought fixed in fact are in constant motion. Sally Falk Moore (1978:6) has put it with characteristic eloquence in a discussion of law as process, in which she takes the view that existing social and symbolic orders are being made and reiterated continuously. They are made, unmade, remade, and transformed endlessly, and even when they are only 'maintaining and reproducing themselves, staying as they are, [that too] should be seen as a process'. It is that process that I wish to consider in the Japanese context.

Were you to ask a young Japanese to describe a typical wedding, I have no doubt that you would be given an account of one version or another of a ceremony of no great antiquity. Indeed, its major components assumed their present relationship only a generation or two ago. This in no way means that the ceremony is somehow 'less Japanese', for it has no real parallel in any other society. Does it, then, mean that because it is a recent invention it is not traditional? It is not old, but it is rife with ritual and symbol, some appropriated from the Japanese past, some from the pasts of other peoples, and some inventions as new as yesterday. We know how all this came about, for the history of wedding ceremonies is well documented (Edwards 1989; Ema 1971; Emori 1986). A salient theme of most of these surveys of changes since the 1870s is how the old commoner classes attempted to emulate the customs of the warrior class. There can be no doubt that this was the case in many matters of etiquette and ceremony.

It is clear, however, that the Japanese wedding ceremony of today owes less to the traditions of the old warrior class than to a far more august inspiration – the wedding of the Crown Prince (later the Taishō Emperor) in 1900, which was the first to be held at a Shintō shrine. When I asked them, virtually none of my Japanese acquaintances turned out to know this, nor is there any reason why they should. It came as a surprise, of course, because today by far the majority of weddings have two major components. One is a 'religious' ceremony specifically Shintō in character; the other the highly secular reception that follows it. It is fair to say that the contemporary ritual has only the shallowest of roots in this century, for when weddings by custom were held in the home, the only specifically religious observance in the domestic rites was the presentation of the bride (or in-marrying groom) to the ancestors of the household. The memorial tablets were displayed in a Buddhist altar (*butsudan*) or on an ancestor-shelf (*senzodana*) and no priest's services were required. The marriage being a domestic matter, those who officiated at the ceremony were members of the household.

By now, however, it has become the almost universal practice to hold weddings in a commercial wedding hall, hotel, or Shintō shrine. The first act in the ritual drama is a very contemporary Shintō ceremony (Edwards 1989:15–19). As an illustration, we may take the establishment described by Edwards, which has a standard shrine-room in which a Shintō priest officiates. He is trained and certified by a shrine, but need not necessarily be of a priestly family.[1] He is assisted by two 'shrine-maidens' (*maiko*), wedding-hall office workers who receive no training other than that given them by the management of the firm. Most of the rites performed by these people in this shrine-room are indeed drawn directly from Japan's past, but the ways they are combined and the manner in which they are meshed with new elements are quite striking. An example or two will suffice. It is the groom alone who reads the wedding vows, which have no precedent in the past. For her part, the bride is required only to acquiesce to them silently, surely a tribute to the persistence of strong cultural predispositions concerning gender-linked propriety. Today the occasion is likely to close with a double-ring ceremony; the rings are brought to the couple by one of the aforementioned shrine-maidens clad in full Shintō regalia. Nowadays the typical wedding party moves on through the photographer's studio into the banquet hall. There, inventiveness has made of the secular half of the ceremony what has been aptly termed a production of which the couple are the stars.

Yet for all the *mélange* of elements, there can be little doubt that the rituals performed at weddings and funerals today contain many of the core symbols – and are designed to embody some of the most deeply held convictions – of the members of any society. It is a commonplace among us, as among those who know little else about the country, to say that Japan is unusual in that things so basic – so fundamental – appear to change with such ease and without causing much concern among the populace. I suggest we set aside the question as to whether they really do change more rapidly in Japan than elsewhere, and note only that it is not foreigners alone who think so. When Edwards (1989:145) mentioned to a Japanese sociologist that he proposed to study weddings by working in an urban wedding hall, the sociologist advised him to find instead a remote village where, he suggested, it was just possible that they still held *real* wedding ceremonies.

Such advice is unambiguous; if you want to find the real Japan, you must look to the past or in places where remnants of the past may yet survive. What you see all around you, in this view, is dismissed either as less Japanese or more Western than it once was, or – harshest judgment of all – spurious. But it seems to me obvious that the observer is too easily distracted by what appear to be glaring inconsistencies. Is it that the Japanese are particularly prone to them, or that they leap more readily to the eye in Japan than elsewhere? I confess that it is hard to ignore such apparent anomalies as the double-ring ceremony presided over by the Shintō shrine-maiden, the young Buddhist nun with her hula hoop, or (swallowing hard) the *Nichigeki* chorus line in spangled tights kicking its way through a routine before the great image of *Dainichi nyorai* at Nara's Tōdaiji – in celebration of the 1200th anniversary of the construction of the temple!

But all this is mere fluff, borne past our fixed vantage point on winds so powerful and currents so deep that we find it difficult to find a means to focus on them. The wedding ceremony, carefully observed, remains as it always has been a great deal more than the mere product of commercial invention and capitalizing on a desire for novelty. It is true that it no longer centres on the household, nor is it any longer held in the home, near the hearth and in the presence of the ancestors.[2] The ceremony has instead come to centre on the couple who, as is repeatedly affirmed during the rites, are destined to found a family, become parents, and thus take their place as fully fledged members of society. All this is expressed in the Shintō idiom and elaborated by entrepreneurs who have devised ingenious ways to make their services ever more costly. But imbedded in it, as in all other superseded forms of the Japanese wedding of the recent past, are principles and cultural values that represent a remarkably consistent and essentially conservative view of what marriage entails. Some of what it entails is affirmation of gender inequality; almost total interdependence of husband and wife; and a host of indicators – symbolic, structural, rhetorical – that deny autonomy to the individual and stress the ultimately social nature of the person (Edwards 1989:143).

Hobsbawm observed that Japan's modernization may represent a uniquely successful blend of what he called old orderings and judicious invention of tradition. The death of the Shōwa Emperor provides an opportunity to explore some consequences of that blend for the study of contemporary Japanese society and culture. As we all know, that event precipitated heated debate over plans for the first imperial funeral to be held in sixty-two years. The central issues, both constitutional and political, were two in number. The first was the central one: Should it be what generally was termed a 'traditional Shinto funeral' in accordance with what are assumed to be the ancient practices of the imperial family? The second followed directly on the first: Whatever the decision on the style of funeral, who was to pay for it – the government or the family?

After considerable and often heated debate, the government cut the Gordian knot by announcing that it had devised a plan that would conform to the requirements of immemorial tradition, preserve the constitution, *and* honour the late emperor. Thus, some segments of the day-long rite were designated as private, conducted by and for members of the family, and some were to be considered public – defined as the state funeral. As a consequence, the Japan Communist Party boycotted the entire affair; the Japan Socialist Party boycotted the rites designated as private; the Liberal Democrats attended them all. Despite all the politics and posturing, the day ended with the entombment of the emperor at night, as has often been the ancient custom, near the mausoleums of his parents at Hachiōji.

During the interval between the emperor's final long hospitalization and the government's announcement of the plans for the funeral, I found it remarkable that none of the parties to the debate had much to say about imperial funerals of Japan's recent past.[3] There had been three: those of the Kōmei Emperor in 1867, Meiji in 1912, and Taishō in 1926. The last of these is the first that I think may be called an official 'Shintō' imperial funeral, for it took place soon after the Imperial Mortuary Rites Law (*kōshitsu sōgi rei*) had been promulgated with the explicit aim of reviving the ancient rites of a pre-Buddhist past. It is worth noting that it thus transpired that the first member of the imperial family to be married in the newly created Shintō wedding ceremony became the first emperor to be interred in the newly created rite, and that near the new capital of Tokyo rather than Kyoto, where his father is buried.[4] I heard little discussion of any of this by my Japanese friends and acquaintances, nor did I see much reference to the issues of cremation versus interment or the style of the imperial tombs at Hachiōji and the one being constructed for the Shōwa Emperor – all of which are in a style revived for the Kōmei Emperor's tomb only a little over a century ago. Wittman Ah Sing asked how many times does something have to be done for it to be a tradition. The answer appears to be – at least once, possibly twice.

I have dealt elsewhere with the general issue of the policy of the separation of Buddhism and Shintō (*shinbutsu bunri*) as it affected the imperial household (Smith 1974:26–33; 1989b). Clearing Buddhist objects from shrines and palaces; converting the imperial ancestors into *kami*; cataloguing the tombs of past emperors, even the mythological ones; establishing Shintō rites where it suited their purpose – all these and many other steps could be taken by the government with relative ease compared to the problem posed by the imperial obsequies. That problem, put as simply as possible, is that at the most fundamental level, a Shintō funeral is a contradiction in terms. Shintō abhors pollution in any form – that being virtually its only tenet. Along with blood and excreta, the corpse is held to be the most ritually polluting object in nature. The point was not lost on the Shintō revivalists of the early Meiji period, who were faced with the question of how the newly Shintōized imperial household was to deal with death and its attendant pollution.

They found a partial answer in the not too distant past. During the period of government-supported Buddhist dominance, even the priests who served shrines had been given Buddhist funerals. Over the years, however, many Shintō priestly families and some high-ranking warriors had petitioned for the right to choose their own ritual. So it came about that by the early nineteenth century, many such households observed what they regarded as purely Shintō rites, shorn of the trappings of the alien religion. But their mortuary rites were almost pure invention in every particular, modelled closely on their Buddhist prototype. The numerology is different, but the patterns are quite similar (Macé 1989:35). Thus, from the 1870s on, the funerals of members of the imperial family were conducted in a remarkable syncretic fusion of diverse practices that were called Shintō. The 1895 funeral of Prince Arisugawa, described as 'pure Shintō' by the Baroness Sannomiya, for example, is a blend of ancient court practice that had been revived after a lapse of centuries, substantial Buddhist elements, and what was known of European royal usage of the late nineteenth century. Nonetheless, interment took place in the (Buddhist) *Gokoku-ji*, grave site of princes of the blood.

Turning now to the funeral of the Shōwa Emperor, let me point out one outstanding feature of the rites conducted at the *Shinjuku-gyoen* that has not been much commented on. In the cortège and at the altar before the coffin were several officiants, dressed in Shintō priestly robes of surprisingly sombre hue. The chief ritualist, similarly clad, presided over the placement of the offerings, read a brief eulogy in archaic Japanese, and assisted members of the family as they passed through the torii to pay their last respects. What is noteworthy is that so great is the Shintō abhorrence of the pollution of death that not one of these men was a priest; all were surrogates, albeit of an interesting sort. The rites at the altar before the coffin were conducted by palace chamberlains (*jijū*) and the coffin was borne by members of the Imperial Guard. Watching the proceedings on television, it occurred to me that the last rites for the Japanese emperor are conducted almost exclusively by those who served him directly in life. Viewed in that light, the proceedings are entirely consistent with a wide range of ritual occasions in Japan that involve kin, but dispense with the services of religious specialists, just as weddings once did.

In summary, then, much of the pomp and paraphernalia of Shōwa's funeral does come directly from the earliest periods of Japanese court ritual, well attested in archival sources. Most had not been used for centuries before the Shintōization of the court in the late nineteenth and early twentieth centuries, and of course many of them are of Chinese origin. Other elements of the imperial funeral, like those of the popular wedding ceremony, are quite new and some are outright borrowings from other societies made in recent decades.

And so I come to the metaphor of the moving target. How can we possibly think about Japanese culture as anything but a process? Given what we know about them, shall we dismiss ordinary weddings and extraordinary funerals as spurious because they are not old or because their content is not completely indigenous? Surely not. As I have already noted, neither occurs in any other society, so without doubt they are Japanese, and therefore they must be understood to embody and reflect particular Japanese cultural constructs and predispositions.

But those of us long engaged in the study of Japan can almost hear the objections now. 'Real' weddings, some city folk and many folk-lorists tell us, are to be found in the remote countryside, if at all. Perhaps it is so, but forty years ago the Shikoku villagers among whom I lived assured me that the country weddings to which they invited me were very different from the ceremonies of pre-war days. John and Ella Embree were told the same thing by the Kyūshū villagers they knew in the mid-1930s. It is entirely likely that similar claims stretch back as far in time as we might be able to push research into the question.[5] The documentation on funerals reveals that they, too, have a chequered history. Like weddings, they exhibit no marked tendency to stasis of form, but it is clear that powerful cultural understandings still profoundly affect substance.

These two instances of fluidity suggest that we must avoid the trap of thinking of 'a culture' as an immutable set of practices, beliefs and meanings. In an earlier anthropological discourse, it was common to speak of 'Zande culture', 'Iroquois culture', and even 'Chinese culture', in the comfortable assumption that they were relatively self-contained entities that might occasionally 'come into contact' with others. It was also generally assumed, as Leach has reminded us, that they had persisted over long periods of time, for the most part changing only in response to the incursions of the West in one guise or another.

I have always had difficulty in seeing how the student of Japanese society and culture could ever have adopted that point of view. In the late 1950s I was invited by a colleague, devoted to teaching Americans about the traditional culture of Japan, to lecture on Japanese music to his class in the arts. I selected several discs from my collection of pre-war records and after necessarily brief introductory remarks started off with what he and the class incorrectly assumed to be an ancient piece. In fact, it was a thoroughly hybrid performance of *Kimi ga yo* on *gagaku* instruments that merely sounded as though it must be old.[6] I proceeded through a reasonably standard unilinear review of Japanese musical forms and ended with a spirited late-1930s rendition of *Ōsaka bugi-ugi*. I thought it obviously Japanese, too; my host never invited me back.

Which leads me to my final point. Like Chamberlain, we all know that the culture of contemporary Japan in some ways is like that of a century ago, but clearly different in others. Whether the elements of the culture of the Japanese today are, or in 1890 were, newly acquired items, traditions of long standing, or hybrids of highly diverse origins is of considerable interest, but of little moment to my larger purpose. In recent years it has become a tradition in Japan to schedule performances of Beethoven's Ninth Symphony to usher in the New Year. For contemporary Japanese, it is as much a part of routine seasonal observances as are glutinous rice cakes (*kagami mochi*), Buddhist temple bells pealing 108 times to ring out the old year (*joya no kane*), and all the rest. 'But Beethoven's Ninth is not JAPANESE!' my students protest. Quite right, but then neither were glutinous rice cakes or Buddhist temple bells, once upon a time. They are not Japanese in exactly the same sense that those seemingly permanent fixtures of the American Christmas – Christmas trees, Dickens's *A Christmas Carol*, and the *Nutcracker* – are not American.

I do not mean to argue that there are *no* continuities, for it is clear that there is a feature of the moving target I have chosen to call Japanese culture that commands our attention. At any given moment, it represents the current state of assumptions, attitudes, meanings and ideas (including ideology in the non-pejorative sense) of the members of that society. What each generation thinks of as its culture is made up in important ways of what it has been taught and learned. For all the slippage and fluidity, then, there necessarily will be overlap and continuity at some basic levels. That continuity gives the lie to those who charge that the Japanese are abandoning their culture. What Japanese culture are they abandoning? The one in place at the end of the Heian period? The culture of the warrior-class hegemons of the various shogunates? The culture of the 1920s or 1930s or of wartime Japan? They are *not* abandoning their culture; they could not do so if they wished. They *are* constantly remaking and redefining it, and not only responding to the ideologies being imposed upon them, as Hobsbawm would have it.

I have known actors of the *nō* theatre, dedicated to the perfection of their art who, off-stage, delight in pipe and tweeds, pizza and jazz. Who is to say that the combination of interests is specious or that one of its terms is more genuine, the other spuriously not Japanese? In his great book *Houses and People of Japan* Bruno Taut (1958) saw the issue very clearly. There you will find the Bauhaus sensibility applied to Japanese use of materials, definition of interior space, and all those aspects of Japanese architecture that so bedazzled the Europeans in the inter-war period. But there is also a marvellous chapter on kitsch, for Taut saw that the sophistication of the Katsura *rikyū* and the ornamental excesses of country inns were equally expressions of Japanese taste.

Is Japanese culture today more or less authentic than it was at some time in the past? I remind you of the admonition by Chamberlain with which I opened, for it forces us to remember that for each successive senior generation in all societies, the pace at which the target moves will seem to accelerate, and its very shape to change as it passes out of our control and into the hands of younger members of society. They may or may not be sensitive to the character of the changes they will surely work upon it, but it is unlikely that they will be much concerned with the problem of authenticity until they begin to notice that their definition of Japanese culture is being challenged in turn.

## NOTES

1 As it happens, I know one such wedding-hall priest. After he retired, his wife found his unrelieved presence in the house too much to bear, so persuaded him to take a training course at the local shrine. He rather enjoys the work, has little idle time on his hands, and makes a nice income to supplement his retirement pay. His only previous close association with Shintō ritual before his retirement had been in the course of discharging his duties as mayor of a small town.

2 In 1975, however, I was told by a resident of a rural community in Kagawa prefecture that if the groom is the eldest son, the bride is brought from the wedding hall in the nearby town to pay her respects to the ancestors of his house. It is the only break in the otherwise carefully crafted programme of events scheduled by wedding-hall management.

3 Among the many publications dealing with the complexities of that history which appeared after the funeral was held are Macé 1989; Mayer 1989; and Smith 1989b.

4 But, be it remarked, he was not the first member of the imperial family whose obsequies were specifically not Buddhist. See the account of the funeral of Prince Arisugawa by the Baroness Sannomiya (1896). The British wife of the Vice-Grand-Master of Ceremonies of the time, she remarks in passing that the anti-Chinese feeling in Japan at the time would have made it entirely inappropriate to observe what she calls Buddhist rites!

5 In the early fourteenth century, Yoshida Kenkō lamented the recent disappearance in the capital of the custom of paying respects to the souls of the deceased, who were thought to return to their homes on the night of the last day of the year. He was cheered, however, upon learning that the

rites were still performed elsewhere in the country (Keene 1967:20–1). On the other hand, in modern Japan, rather than fading away, some religous customs and practices of long standing are becoming increasingly popular (Nakamaki 1984:87–8).

6 *Kimi ga yo* is widely regarded as the Japanese national anthem, although it has no official status. On the record in question, this late nineteenth-century composition is played on instruments whose prototypes were incorporated into the imperial court's ceremonial music (*gagaku*) more than a millennium ago.

## REFERENCES

Chamberlain, B. H. (1898) *Things Japanese, Being Notes on Various Subjects Connected with Japan for the Use of Travellers and Others*, third edition, revised, London.

Crowley, J. B. (ed.) (1970) *Modern East Asia: Essays in Interpretation*, New York: Harcourt, Brace and World.

Edwards, W. (1989) *Modern Japan Through Its Weddings: Gender, Person, and Society in Ritual Portrayal*, Stanford: Stanford University Press.

Ema T. (1971) *Kekkon no rekishi* (A history of marriage), Tokyo: Yūzankaku.

Emori I. (1986) *Nihon no kon'in: sono rekishi to minzoku* (The history and folklore of Japanese marriage), Tokyo: Kōbundō.

Gibney, F. B. (1985) 'Meiji: a cultural revolution', in Nagai M. and M. Urrutia (eds) *Meiji Ishin: Restoration and Revolution*, Tokyo: United Nations University.

Hobsbawm, E. (1983) 'Mass-producing traditions: Europe, 1870–1914', in E. Hobsbawm and T. Ranger (eds) *The Invention of Tradition*, Cambridge: Cambridge University Press.

—— and T. Ranger (eds) (1983) *The Invention of Tradition*, Cambridge: Cambridge University Press.

Jansen, M. B. (1970) 'The Meiji state: 1868–1912', in J. B. Crowley (ed.) *Modern East Asia: Essays in Interpretation*, New York: Harcourt, Brace and World.

Keene, D. (1967) *Essays in Idleness: The Tsurezuregusa of Kenkō*, New York: Columbia University Press.

Kingston, M. H. (1989) *Tripmaster Monkey, His Fake Book*, New York: Knopf.

Leach, E. (1989) 'Writing anthropology', *American Ethnologist* 16:137–41.

Macé, F. (1989) 'The funerals of the Japanese emperors', *Bulletin of the Nanzan Institute for Religious Studies* 13:26–37. (Translated from an article – title not given – which appeared in *Cah. d'Extrème-Asie* 4 (1988):157–65.)

Mayer, A. C. (1989) 'The funeral of the emperor of Japan', *Anthropology Today* 5:3–6.

Moore, S. F. (1978) *Law as Process: An Anthropological Approach*, London: Routledge & Kegan Paul.

Nagai M. and M. Urrutia (eds) (1985) *Meiji Ishin: Restoration and Revolution*, Tokyo: United Nations University.

Nakamaki H. (1984) 'The structure and transformation of religion', in Umesao, T., H. Befu, and J. Kreiner (eds) *Japanese Civilization in the Modern World: Life and Society* (Senri Ethnol. Stud. 16).

Sannomiya, [Baroness] A. Y. (1896) 'A Shintō funeral', *The Nineteenth Century* 40:974–81.

Smith, R. J. (1974) *Ancestor Worship in Contemporary Japan*, Stanford: Stanford University Press.

—— (1989a) 'Something old, something new: tradition and culture in the study of Japan', *Journal of Asian Studies* 48:715–23.

—— (1989b) 'Japanese culture reconsidered', lecture delivered at the 18th Annual Meeting of the International Society for the Comparative Study of Civilization in Berkeley, California.

Taut, B. (1958) *Houses and People of Japan*, second edition, Tokyo: Sanseidō.

Umesao, T., H. Befu, and J. Kreiner (eds) (1984) *Japanese Civilization in the Modern World: Life and Society* (Senri Ethnol. Stud. 16).

# 2 Rituality in the *ken* game

*Sepp Linhart*

## WHAT IS *KEN*?

*Ken* is a game which enjoyed great popularity in Japan at least from the beginning of the eighteenth century until the 1950s, after which its popularity rapidly declined.[1] Nowadays *ken* is mainly preserved in the form of *jan-ken* (paper, scissors, stone), a game played all over the world, which is generally used in Japan as a means to arrive at decisions similar to tossing up a coin in the West as well as a children's game in combination with other games. *Jan-ken* belongs to the basic vocabulary of Japanese children which according to Sanseidō's *Yōji no kokugo e-jiten* (Ōkubo 1971:3: 16) should already be mastered at the age of two.

In some remote districts of Japan, *ken* is also preserved in special forms such as the *hashi*- or chopstick-*ken* of Tosa (Katsurai 1959:12–21; Hashitsume 1968; Katsurai 1976) or the *Kuma-ken* in Kuma county, Kumamoto prefecture, where Embree did his famous study of *Suye-mura*, in which he of course mentions the villagers' liking of this game on the occasion of drinking parties (Embree 1939:102; Ushijima 1973:206–7, 1987:426; Hirayama 1976).

In this essay I intend to deal only with historic forms of *ken*. In order to deal with the ritual elements I will also have to outline briefly the history and development of *ken* in Japan. My hypothesis is that many Japanese forms of games and amusements tend to become 'ways' (*michi, dō*), when some overeager proponents try to raise the status of their beloved activity, giving them a (pseudo-) philosophical base and a (pseudo-) religious aura. These *dō* are highly ritualized actions, and the extent of rituality in these *dō* increases with their general acceptance as *dō*. *Ken* might be called a typical example: it developed a certain ritual and also aimed at becoming one of the ways, but for various reasons it never quite succeeded, which in the long run has meant the complete disappearance of *ken* as an activity for grown-ups.

In this short essay I shall first present an overview of the main forms of *ken*, after which I would like to describe the ritual aspects of this game, and finally I would like to speculate on the reasons why *ken* did not last as a way.

## THE MAIN FORMS OF *KEN*

There were two main forms of *ken*, into which all the many variations of this interesting game can be classified. The older form is called *hon-ken* or 'original *ken*'. Since it is said that it reached Japan from China via Nagasaki, it is also called *Nagasaki-* or *Kiyō-ken*.[2] Another name is *kazu-ken* or '*ken* of numbers', because the players have to shout numbers. Two players sit opposite each other and indicate numbers from zero to five with the fingers of their right hands. At the same time they have to shout the likely sum of the addition of the numbers shown with the fingers. The numbers announced can therefore range from zero to ten. The player who has guessed the result correctly wins.

The loser has to drink a cup of sake, which is a very important rule of this game. *Ken-zake* was a widely used expression during the Edo period, and it also made the theme of a highly praised woodblock print by Ikeda Eisen in 1823 (*Edo geijutsu* 1988:7). If both players shout the same number, or if both players shout the wrong number, it is a draw, which is called *aiko*.

From *ken* teaching books and other instructions of the *ken* game, the earliest of which date back to 1743 (*Yoshiwara saiken kayou kami* 1743), we know the different representations of numbers by fingers (Figure 2.1). It is also important to note that the numbers had to be called in a language which pretended to be Chinese. Instead of shouting '*ichi, ni, san*' or '*hitotsu, futatsu, mittsu*' the players had to learn a special way of counting numbers. The most common ran as follows: '*ikkō, ryan, sanna, sū, gō, roma, che, pama, kwai, tōrai*' (from 1 to 10, as well as *mute* for 0). In my opinion this way of counting in and of itself is already a ritual; if ritual is defined as everything which is not particularly functional for a certain action, but at the same time is considered as absolutely necessary for the performance of this action. In *hon-ken* every player had first of all to give proof of his professionalism by mastering the real way of counting used in this game.

The other main form of *ken* is called *sansukumi-ken* or '*ken* of the three which cower one before the other', the best known form of which is of course the already mentioned *jan-ken*. Every figure has one opponent over which it wins and one to which it loses. With two players and three figures there are nine possible results only, of which three are

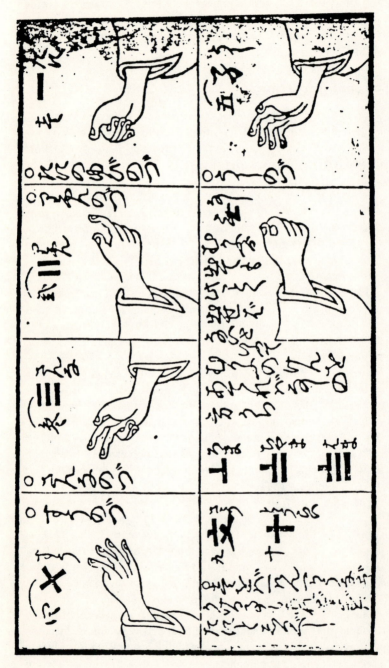

*Figure 2.1* The representation of numbers with the fingers according to the *Yoshiwara saiken kayou kami* (1743) Tokyo Metropolitan Central Library.

draws when both players choose the same figures. This is of course a much more simple game than the *ken* with numbers, but at the same time the idea that one element is stronger than another one, but weaker than the third one makes it quite interesting.

The oldest form of *sansukumi-ken* in Japan seems to be *mushi-ken* or '*ken* of small animals', which can be found already on picture scrolls of the Heian and Kamakura periods (Shibuzawa 1966:228–9; 1968:20–1). In this form the thumb represents the frog which wins over the slug which is represented with the little finger. The slug triumphs over the snake which is shown by the forefinger and which again wins over the frog (Figure 2.2).

The combination of these three animals is also a common theme in Japanese art and can be found as *netsuke* carving or in various pictorial forms. In Western understanding it seems to be unlikely that the snake cowers before the slug, but in Japan it is said that no snake creeps over the trace which a slug has left behind. It seems that the Japanese, when importing this game from China, mistook the Chinese character of the poisonous centipede (*mukade*), for that of the harmless slug (*namekuji*).[3] According to Chinese zoological tradition the centipede climbs on the head of the snake and eats its brain.

While *mushi-ken* did survive for a long period as a children's game there were other forms of *sansukumi-ken* which were mainly played by grown-ups. The most important of these was *kitsune-ken*, also called *shōya-ken* or *Tōhachi-ken*. While the first two names are taken from two figures which are represented in the game, the fox and the village headman, the third name's origin is not clear. The most widely used explanation is that one day a guest in Yoshiwara heard the voice of a wandering salesman for medicine called Tōhachi, who praised his pills by calling '*Tōhachi, gomon, kimyō*' (Tōhachi's pills for only five *mon*, but with a strange effect!). He thought it would be a good idea to use these words as an introductory shout in the *kitsune-ken* instead of only counting: 'One, two, three!' Not only was his idea fully accepted, the game even changed its name into *Tōhachi-ken* sometime before the Meiji Restoration. In this particular *ken*, in which the fox wins over the village headman, who again is superior to the hunter or gun, which can kill the fox, the figures are no longer expressed only with one hand, but both hands are used to express one figure (Figure 2.3).

Again there are numerous representations of *kitsune-ken* on woodblock prints from the time of Harunobu who made a nice drawing of *ken*-playing courtesans in his *Yoshiwara bijin awase* from 1765 (Watanabe and Mogami 1975:113–14). Similar themes were drawn by Kitagawa Utamaro, Kubo Shunman, Utagawa Kuninaga, Utagawa Toyokuni II,

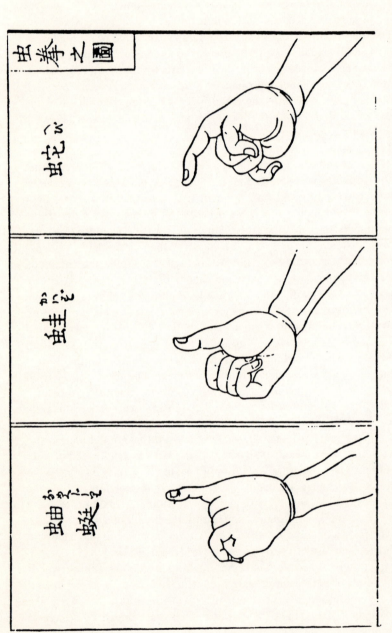

*Figure* 2.2 Representation of snake (*hebi*), frog (*kawazu*) and slug (*namekuji*) in the *mushi-ken* according to the *Kensarae sumai zue* (1809). Research Institute for Humanistic Studies, Kyoto University.

and Kikugawa Eizan among others. *Kitsune-ken* can also be found as a motif of *netsuke* (Joly 1967:147; Coullery and Newstead 1977:234–5); furthermore there exist some old photographs from the Meiji period (Brownell 1903:81). It was of course used as a motif in the children's game called *menko*, from the Meiji period until recently, as well as in *sugoroku* (Takahashi 1980:14–15). At the end of the Edo and at the beginning of the Meiji period it was also made the object of many comic pictures (*giga*) by Kuniyoshi, Toyokuni III and their pupils.

An even more dramatic form of a *sansukumi-ken* game is the *tora-* or tiger-*ken*. There the three figures to be performed by the players are a tiger, Watōnai – the famous half-Chinese, half-Japanese pirate of the Ming period, who is internationally better known under the name of Coxinga – and Watōnai's Japanese mother. The tiger loses against Watōnai, but Watōnai according to Confucian tradition has to obey his mother. His mother as a weak old woman of course loses against the tiger. Watōnai's victory over the tiger is a well-known scene from one of Chikamatsu's most famous plays *Kokusenya gassen*, first given in Ōsaka in 1715. In this game the players do not only use both hands, they act with their whole body. In order to make the game possible, they have to enter the room from different doors at the same moment, or they have to hide behind a screen from which they appear at the same moment after the other participants in the party have finished singing a ballad about Watōnai (Figure 2.4). *Tora-ken* is even today remembered by elderly *geisha* in the Gion district of Kyoto.

There exist besides a large number of other *sansukumi-ken* games, but only a few of them really became popular. One which apparently did at the end of the eighteenth century was the *Daibutsu-ken*, which was also played with two hands. In this *ken* the big wooden statue of Buddha loses to the carpenter who made it, but wins over the pilgrim, who again, as a holy man, wins over the carpenter (Yamato 1931:612). Between 1847 and the early Meiji years a great number of similar *sansukumi-ken* groupings were created. This can be seen from a variety of interesting *ken* woodblock prints of that time, as I mentioned already. In a version from the Second World War children played *ken* consisting of the three figures of destroyer warship, which won over the bomber, while the bomber won over the bomb which it dropped, and the bomb won over the warship (Miyao 1979:205).

Perhaps the fact should be mentioned that *ken* was so popular during the Edo period that many games in which two parties competed for a victory were called *ken*, even if they had no relation to one of the two real forms of *ken*. A good example of this third group of *ken* games is the well-known game in which a wooden ball with a hole through its

*Figure 2.3 Shōya-ken* (more commonly called *kitsune-ken* or *tōhachi-ken*) according to the *Kensarae sumai zue* (1809). Research Institute for Humanistic Studies, Kyoto University.

*Note*: The three men take the postures of gun (*teppō*), village headman (*shōya*) and fox (*kitsune*) (from right to left)

*Figure 2.4 Tora-ken* according to the *Kensarae sumai zue* (1809). Research Institute for Humanistic Studies, Kyoto University.
*Note*: The man standing next to the screen is in the posture of Watōnai; the man to the left of the screen is in the posture of the tiger

centre and tied to a wooden pole by a rope has to be flung into the air and be caught by that pole (Figure 2.5). This is called *sukuitama-ken* (catch the ball-*ken*) or *kendama* (*ken*-ball) (Nakada 1970:303–14).

Another interesting game is the *mōshin-ken* or *tōshin-ken*, described in a text of 1792. These terms mean foreigners' *ken*: two people sit opposite each other and say silly words which have no meaning, accompanied by many gestures; in this way imitating foreign speakers. The one who does so more convincingly has won (Hyōsanjin 1974:168–9, 173).

In the remainder of this chapter I shall leave aside these many forms of *ken* and concentrate only on *hon-ken* and *Tōhachi-ken*. Let me now turn to the ritual aspects of *ken*.

## MATERIAL ASPECTS OF RITUALITY IN *KEN*

Similar to many other competitions or contests, be they games or sports, *ken*, from at least the first half of the eighteenth century, also was called *sumō* after the famous wrestling competition. But it did not only borrow the term *sumō* to become *ken-zumō*, it also transferred the various material attributes of the *sumō* contest to the *ken* contest. The earliest reference, usually cited as a proof for this, is in Santō Kyōden's *Zuihitsu, kinsei kiseki kō* (Reflections on Miracles from Recent Times, 1804), in which he writes:

> In the Kyōhō period the people who indulged in sake drinking used to play *ken-zumō*, and it was terribly popular. It is said that Tamagiku was especially skilful. This Tamagiku from the Odawara House of the New Yoshiwara introduced the decoration for the hand as we know it today, which fits the hand perfectly. From black velvet she had made something like a cover for the back of the hand, and with a golden thread she embroidered the emblem on it which is shown here. This is the hand-cover which is used when playing *ken-zumō*.
>
> (Santō 1928:784)

In Japanese this hand-cover modelled after the decorative apron used at *sumō* contests (where it is called *keshō mawashi*), was called *ken-kin* or *ken-mawashi* (Figure 2.6).

Kitamura Nobuyo in his encyclopedia *Kiyū shōran* (Smiling contemplations on happy playing, 1830–50) heavily criticizes Santō Kyōden, saying,

> even though he has written so, *ken* was not performed in that way in that early period, because the Yoshiwara guide book *Tora no fumi*

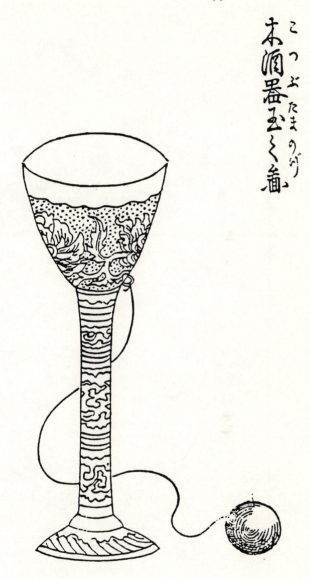

こつぶたまのけん

本洒器玉く亩

*Figure 2.5  Sukuitama-ken* or *kendama*, here called *kobbutama*, according to the *Kensarae sumai zue* (1809). Research Institute for Humanistic Studies, Kyoto University.

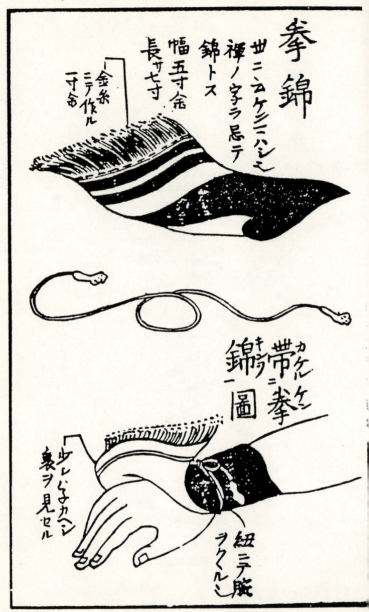

*Figure 2.6* The *ken-kin* or *ken-mawashi* according to the *Fūgetsu gaiden* (1771). National Diet Library, Tokyo.

from Enkyō 2 (1745) which contains a detailed description of *ken* does not mention it. Therefore it has to be from a later period.

(Kitamura 1929:428)

It has to be said, though, that Kitamura Nobuyo seems to have not known all the many guides to the Yoshiwara – there were at least 202 *saiken* published during the Edo period – because in another guidebook, *Yoshiwara saiken kayou kami* from Kanpo 3 (1743), we find pictures of courtesans from the Eastern League (*higashi no kata*) playing against those from the Western League (*nishi no kata*), and as can be seen clearly in this illustration by Nishimura Shigemasa all the female players have *ken-mawashi* attached to their wrists (Figure 2.7).

The hand-cover continued to remain an important ritual accessory, and good players tried to have it made from the finest materials available, as we can see from a short notice in *Yūbin hōchi* newspaper of 28 October 1875, about Kakusai, a *Tōhachi-ken* player from the Shibatō-ren, who had his *ken-mawashi* made from gold braid for which he paid seven yen (Shinbun shūsei Meiji hennen-shi hensan-kai 1936:2: 421). This was roughly the same amount of money which you had to pay in this year for one *koku* of rice (6.9 yen), which is said to be enough for one person to live on for a year!

Let us turn again to the 1743 illustration. The picture covers two adjacent pages and divides the players, as already mentioned, into those of the Eastern and those of the Western League, consisting of twenty-six and twenty-three players respectively. The players' names and the houses to which they belong are listed on two pages before and after the illustration. This organization, of course, was also taken from *sumō*, where it was introduced during the Genroku period, only fifty years earlier. Both leagues were led by *tayu*, courtesans of the highest rank, which is also true for the referee, who in this picture is a *tayu* by the name of Hanamurasaki (Flower Purple). Just as the referee in *sumō* she holds a referee's fan (*uchiwa*) in her hands. This fan is also represented in the next picture which furthermore shows a branch with plum blossoms, three sake cups and a *haiku* poem (Figure 2.8):

| | |
|---|---|
| *Tōrai ya* | It arrived! |
| *kesa wa ureshiki* | What a pleasant morning |
| *ume no sake* | with plum liquor! |

*Tōrai* is also the *ken* number for ten, so that the sake mentioned in this poem is at once understood to be *ken-zake*. It should also be added that the plum blossom with its five leaves is used as a symbol of the *ken* game, because the hand has five fingers.

*Figure 2.7* Komurasaki from the Eastern League is fighting against Usukumo from the Western League with Hanamurasaki acting as referee in an illustration from the *Yoshiwara saiken kayou kami* (1743) by Nishimura Shigemasa. Tokyo Metropolitan Central Library.

The fan (*uchiwa*) as the symbol of the important function of the referee is not the only utensil taken from *sumō*. Almost everything is copied meticulously, as already can be seen in the 1771 instruction book *Fūgetsu gaiden* (Unorthodox Tradition of Nature): the fan, the wooden clappers (*hyōshigi*), the hand-cover, the wooden buckets with washing water (*chōzu oke*), the seats for the players (*koshikake, aibiki*), the religious ornaments for the ring, the bow for the bow-twirling ceremony to announce the end of the tournament (Figure 2.9); and of course the ring itself (Figures 2.10 and 2.11) (Kikusha 1771).

Other utensils of the elegant *ken* player were *kengi*, woodsticks which were made from fine foreign wood and which were carried in a small brocade case. Ten in number, these chopsticks were used to determine the relative strength of two players. These *kengi* can be seen in the 1830 instruction book *Ken hitori keiko* (Sanō and Ikken) as well as in Matsuura Seisan's most interesting collection of essays *Kashi yawa* (Matsuura 1911:9). It is said that the name of the famous *gesaku* writer

Jippensha Ikku is derived from such a contest, meaning 'Ten times played, one victory, nine losses!' (*jippen ja ikku*) (Watanabe and Mogami 1975:99).

For training purposes players were advised to use a device consisting of five sticks which was thought to substitute for a living opponent (Yoshinami and Gojaku 1809).

One last material ritual aspect which already crosses into the spiritual ritual aspects of *ken* has to be mentioned here, namely the *banzuke* (ranking lists of players), a common trait of many arts, sports, and entertainments. In these *banzuke* the ranks were of course again modelled after *sumō*. The earliest designation of a famous *ken* player as *ōzeki*, the highest rank in *sumō* then, I found in the 1771 *Fūgetsu gaiden* (Kikusha 1771). The *Kensarae sumai zue*, an instruction book of 1809, contains lists of fifteen groups of *ken* players in Ōsaka, ordered by rank. There is always one *ōzeki*, one *sekiwake*, and one *komusubi*, as in the three ranks of *sumō*, while the list of players from Nagasaki

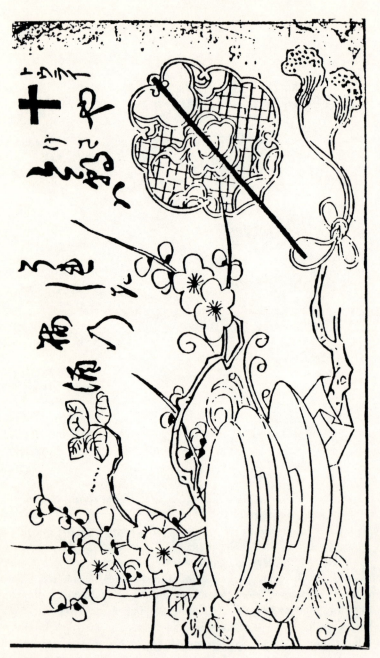

*Figure 2.8* An illustrated *ken* poem from the *Yoshiwara saiken kayou kami* (1743). Tokyo Metropolitan Central Library.

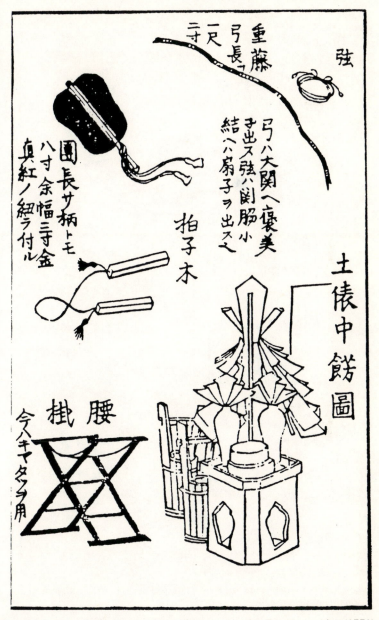

*Figure 2.9* Utensils for *ken-sumō* as illustrated in the *Fūgetsu gaiden* (1771).
National Diet Library, Tokyo.
*Note*: In the upper row we see the bow and the string as well as the referee's fan; in the
middle there are wooden clappers; and in the lower row the wooden buckets, religious
ornaments and the seats for the players

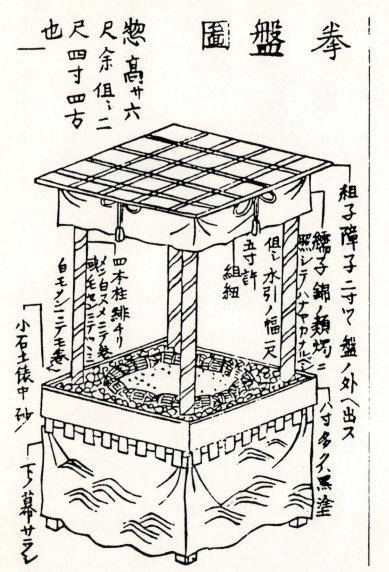

*Figure 2.10*  The ring used in *ken-sumō* according to the *Fūgetsu gaiden* (1771). National Diet Library, Tokyo.

in the same book is already in the later style of a real *banzuke* with players divided into those of the Eastern and Western Leagues. The Nagasaki list from 1809 contains the names of 126 famous *ken* players, which might serve as an indication of the popularity of *ken* at that time.

There were two different kinds of *banzuke*: those for the internal use of the group to which a player belonged, and others for a region or a city, as the one given in Figure 2.12 for Ōsaka. The first ones, 'small lists' or 'fan lists' (*kobanzuke* or *uchiwabanzuke*), were decided upon by the head of a specific group, while the 'big lists' (*ōbanzuke*) were made by consultation (*hanashiai*) of the different group leaders as well as through tournaments. In the twentieth century people who twice were *ōzeki* became *yokozuna* and, afterwards, referees. Finally, after having served as referee for some time, they were promoted to the rank of *toshiyori*, and as such their names were also inscribed on the *banzuke*.

Players who were not yet promoted to the *maegashira* rank were also divided according to strength into *tamari* (those waiting), *jō no kuchi* (those entering), *jō nidan* (second class), and *jō sandan* (third class). At the end of the list we find the names of influential people from the *ken* world, such as former champions and heads of different groups. In the centre of the *banzuke* the names of the organizers and sponsors, of inspectors and advisers are given (Kubota 1941:119–21).

According to a newspaper announcement in the *Tōkyō Yorozu Chōhō* of 6 January 1907, after the Meiji Restoration, no general *banzuke* for Tokyo had been made since the Restoration, and thus on that date a great *ken* meeting was scheduled in order to create a new list. The referee was the female owner of the restaurant Suekichi in Ushigome, who in earlier times (under the name Imaharu) was a well-known player. The head of the beriberi hospital, Tōda, became a honorary member under the name Azumanobori Ōasahi (Shinbun Shūsei Meiji hennen-shi hensan-kai 1936:13:195–6).

## SPIRITUAL ASPECTS OF RITUALITY IN *KEN*

As already mentioned above, in the eighteenth century *ken* players began to form groups, mostly on a regional basis. When *ken* gradually moved away from the amusement quarters, with which it was associated for a long time, these groups developed into *iemoto* groups like those of the tea ceremony or flower arrangement schools. Matsuura Seisan, the author of the interesting *Kashi yawa*, mentions that within the precincts of the Mimeguri shrine in Edo there can be found a memorial stone for a famous *ken* player with the name Sha Ō (his real name was Nozaki Seizō), who is said to have had more than 500 pupils. On the

*Figure 2.11* A *ken-sumō* scene as given in the *Fūgetsu gaiden* (1771). National Diet Library, Tokyo.

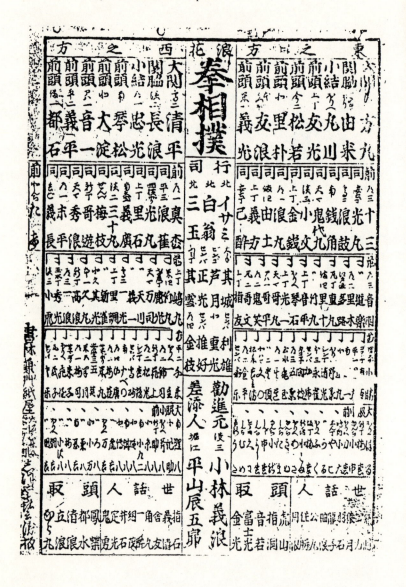

*Figure 2.12* A *ken-sumō banzuke* from Ōsaka

*Note*: No date given, but since Yoshinami, the author of the 1809 instruction book
*Kensarae sumai zue* is given as promoter (*kanshinmoto*), it is probably from the first half
of the nineteenth century (author's collection)

stone there are inscribed the names of 108 of them (Matsuura 1911:8–9). But Matsuura does not mention, whether Sha Ō founded a school of *ken* or not.

In the foreword to the *Ken hitori keiko* there is a short notice which can be interpreted that at this time, around 1830, there already existed different schools with differing interpretations of the proper way to play. Everything we report 'is in the style of the Sansui-group and not bad *ken* as is practised by the Mitōshi, the Shiraori and other groups', it says (Sanō and Ikken 1830). To outsiders, 160 years later, such remarks sound rather funny, but for the players of that time differing interpretations of the right way to play could serve as a legitimation for founding a new school.

It has to be mentioned here, that in the Bakumatsu period the main stream of *ken* changed from *hon-ken* to *Tōhachi-ken*, which seems to have attracted more people. So everything which we know about *ken-iemoto* is related to *Tōhachi-ken*. The first *iemoto* is said to have been Harunoie Sōgan, who made this game popular among the *hatamoto* in Edo. Around 1850 several other schools appeared, such as the Azuma, Hide, Asahi, Azumanobori, Kozakura and Musashino Schools. The Ryuō-School was founded by a *samurai* of the Tayasu house, Kaneko Zōjirō, whose name as a player was Kigan, which, at the time of the Restoration, he changed to Kiō, when, as a retainer of the *bakufu*, Kakinuma Chōhō, became his successor. Kakinuma changed his name as player from Zengyō to Kigan II and transferred his former name Zengyō to a flower arrangement and tea ceremony master by the name of Seibyōan Sōgetsu, who thus became Zengyō II. Seibyōan later selected Hamamura (Tanimura) Tetsutarō to follow him as Zengyō III. On 28 October 1906, Tanimura invited the Asahi, Futaba, Azuma and Kozakura Schools on the occasion of this name-transferring ceremony to a great *Tōhachi-ken* tournament at a restaurant in Kagurazaka (Komiya 1955:448–9; Shinbun shūsei Meiji hennen-shi hensan-kai 1936:13:160).

In 1941 Kubota, himself an *iemoto* of the Tōkensha School by the name of Tendō, wrote that there once existed more than thirty *iemoto*, but that around 1940 because some groups had ceased their activities while other groups had merged, only a few *iemoto* were left (Kubota 1941:115).

The relations between the *iemoto* and the members were of a strictly hierarchical nature. A person excluded from one group would never be accepted again by any other group. A *ken* player's name could only be earned through an *iemoto*. The first name given is formed by combining the player's personal name with the group's name. Players who gained a certain strength were given a new name by their master in a special ceremony. Since the masters usually included part of their own name, people with some knowledge of the *ken* world knew at once to which group a certain person belonged (Kubota 1941:115–16).

Besides *iemoto* organizations and *banzuke* rankings which as described above contained also certain spiritual ritualistic aspects (the official acceptance into a school, the name transferring ceremony, the *banzuke* tournament, the discussions about the new *banzuke* by the *iemoto*, the promulgation of a new *banzuke*, the form in which it is written), there existed many more elements in *ken* which can be interpreted as spiritual rituals. Let us return to the instruction book of 1809 again. It starts with the proper introductory speech for a *ken* contest which has to be given by the referee. This begins with thanks to all the people attending, players as well as fans, after which the referee gives a short outline of the history of this game from the times of the wise kings in China. From China where it served as a means to make drinking parties more interesting, it spread to Nagasaki at the time when the amusement quarters of Maruyama were opened there in the middle of the seventeenth century. At this time a group of Chinese once held a party in Maruyama to which they invited several courtesans. They put up a precious wine glass and the eight delicacies, accompanied by Chinese songs and music. After some time they divided themselves in two groups and began to play *ken* in the proper manner by the light of fireworks. Those who had lost took two or three sips from the precious glass of red wine and retreated. It is difficult to put it into words how well they behaved. This is the beginning of what we call today *Nagasaki-ken*. They tried to select the best five players, and for those they had prepared in advance five tiger skins, five leopard skins, five red woollen cloths, five woollen cloths, five beautiful maidens and other things as prices. The five maidens were positioned besides the players so that Yin and Yang were in harmony. After this historical introduction the referee explains various aspects of the ring and says that each direction has its own colour and its own element. Finally he has to apologize for speaking so long, when all the people are already waiting for the contestants to enter the ring.

After this lengthy speech the referee has to turn to the ring, on the right and left side of which there are papers showing the names of the players. He should first call the *degake* and then the *yorikata*. When both combatants kneel before the ring, the *degake* has to introduce himself first and then the *yorikata*, after which the fight begins (Yoshinami and Gojaku 1809).

The same instruction book contains also a Chinese text from 1619 which is said to be a secret doctrine that can only be understood if studied together with a teacher; as well as a short text about the 'Five

States of the Heart' (*ken no gogyōshin*), – *kaku, chi, gu, shō, u* – which are also the denominations for the five tones in Chinese and Japanese music. If the heart is in the state of *gu*, the middle, the player has the best chances of winning. After this there follows a note about ridding oneself of sense of self when playing *ken* (Yoshinami and Gojaku 1809), which is reminiscent of *zen* in the art of archery as described by Herrigel (1956).

All these attempts to give some philosphical foundation to *ken* lead to the assumption that a number of *ken* zealots wanted to change it into a way (*dō, michi*) in order to receive for their favourite activity greater acceptance and a higher reputation, as the many other *dō* in existence in Japan already had. According to their wishes *ken* was no longer to be only a funny game to liven up sake-drinking parties as it clearly had been in the eighteenth century.

## OVER-RITUALIZATION: THE END OF *KEN*

The already mentioned Kubota in 1941 in his book *Kenzen goraku Tōhachi kendō* (The way of *Tōhachi-ken* – a healthy entertainment) also stresses the fact that there are very strict rules in *Tōhachi-ken*. The *iemoto* would never allow their members to participate in sake-drinking parties and play *ken* there. The better a player was the more restraint he had to show. Therefore common people had little idea of how *ken* was properly played, and they had to play it according to their own wrong ideas.

> *Ken* of the *geishas* which can be observed when drinking sake is not the real *ken* (*seiken*), but at the best gesticulation. Since style and ceremonials are only passed on from mere hearsay there exists a great variety, and seen from the standpoint of *ken* playing groups it is all completely ridiculous. Real *ken* is never performed with *shamisen* or any other kind of music.
>
> (Kubota 1941:116–17)

According to Kubota's book, by 1941 *ken* had become a rather difficult, complicated matter. The original three patterns of *kitsune*, *teppō* and *shōya* had changed to twenty-four variations of these patterns, which had to be performed at the beginning and at the end of the contest by both players in a certain prescribed form. As Kubota explains these ritual movements were performed as a means to show the spectators the beauty of the movement of the hands. It is evident that this kind of *ken* was no longer a simple form of enjoyment, but had become a complicated procedure in which only experts competed with each other. They had to wear the ceremonial dress in the ring, and their hands wore the hand-covers bearing their individual emblems. With all that amount of accumulated ritual it has to be asked why *Tōhachi kendō* has virtually ceased to exist after the Second World War as did *hon-ken* at the end of the Edo period.

The answer can only be hypothetical, but I think that there are various reasons. First of all it has to be remembered that *ken* had always been an element of the amusement quarters' culture, as I would like to call it. Its early descriptions are in guidebooks to the amusement quarters, and even short leaflets about the correct behaviour in the *yūkaku* such as one from the 1780s, the *Kaihō eidai yūri zassho*, contain the words to be used in this game. *Ken* could never quite shake off this widely known association with the amusement quarters, as can be seen from Kubota's denounciation of *ken* as played by *geisha*. The *Tōhachi kendō* people tried to cut the links of *ken* to the world of amusement similar as they tried to eliminate the most important rule of *ken* introduced from China, namely that the loser has to drink a cup of sake.

Furthermore, *ken* had become a game played by children, as it is today. Already from the *bakumatsu* period we have statements that children prefered to play *ken* more than other games. Under such circumstances it seems clear that it was very difficult for *ken* to gain recognition as a way such as *chadō* (tea ceremony) or *kōdō* (the way of scent), both former entertainments which became ways, but which were never incorporated into the world of children's play.

*Ken* players always used to stress that *ken* needed nothing to be performed. It therefore can be played everywhere and any time, if two people meet who know the rules. But I think that such a pure game does not really fit into our commercialized world and tends to be quickly forgotten when material affluence is everywhere.

Another reason for the disappearance of *ken* might lie in the fact that the rules had become too complicated, without offering much to the players. The main attraction lies in the beauty of the movement of the hands, but it seems that this was not enough when compared to the art of Japanese dance or Chinese shadow boxing to which it finally showed a little resemblance. Of course, *ken* is great fun with all its imitations of *sumō*, but many people probably think that this aspect is ridiculous, especially if it is overstressed.

One of the greatest deficiencies of *ken* is probably that its spiritual foundation to become a way was rather weak. There never was a great personality who wrote something like a 'holy book of *ken*'. Kubota tried to do so in 1941, but at that time it was obviously already too late.

Given all these reasons I am of the opinion that the enormous amount of rituality in *ken* actually brought about its final decline, since it pretended to be more than it was, when it was introduced to Japan – a fun game for drinking parties. It is no wonder, then, that it is today mainly preserved in those parts of society where it was developed and where for centuries it played an important role: in the world of *geisha* entertainment.

## NOTES

The author wishes to thank the following for permission to reproduce artwork used in this chapter: Tokyo Metropolitan Central Library; Research Institute for Humanistic Studies, Kyoto University; The National Diet Library, Tokyo.

1 Good overviews of *ken* are given in chronological order of publication in: Joden 1893; Sakai 1933:822–43; Nakada 1970:369–95; Watanabe and Mogami 1975; Masuda 1989:370–5, 676–84.

2 Kiyō is the name of Nagasaki used by Japanese Sinologists during the Edo period.

3 Personal communication from Professor Yamada Keiji of the Jinbun kagaku kenkyūsho of Kyoto University, July 1988.

## BIBLIOGRAPHY

Brownell, Clarence Ludlow (1903) *The Heart of Japan: Glimpses of Life and Nature far from the Travellers' Track in the Land of the Rising Sun*, London: Methuen.

Coullery, Marie-Thérèse and Martin S. Newstead (1977) *The Baur Collection Geneva: Netsuke (selected pieces)*, Geneva: Collections Baur.

*Edo geijutsu* (1988) *Shinshū ukiyoe hanga mokuroku*, vol. 27, Tokyo: Hara Shobō.

Embree, John F. (1939) *Suye mura: A Japanese Village*, Chicago: The University of Chicago Press.

Hashitsume Kenjirō (1968) 'Hashi-ken', *Tosa shidan* (15 March): 27–8.

Herrigel, Eugen (1956) *Zen in der Kunst des Bogenschieβens*, München-Planegg: O.W. Barth.

Hirayama Kenjirō (1976) 'Kuma-ken', in Ushijima Morimitsu (ed.) *Kumamoto no minzoku: Kumamoto no fūdō to kokoro 12*, Kumamoto: Kumamoto Nichinichi Shinbunsha, pp. 204–5.

Hyōsanjin (1974) [1793] 'Ehon zoku otona no asobi', in Matsuda Osamu, Moriya Katsuhisa and Yoshida Mitsukuni (eds) *Nihon shōmin bunka shiryō shūsei 9: Asobi*, Tokyo: Sanichi Shobō, pp. 158–74. (Modern reprint of the Kansei 5 (1793) edition.)

Joden Kyoshi (1893) 'Ken no koto', *Fūzoku gahō* 51:25–7; 52:26–7; 53:23–5; 55:25–6; 57:21–2; 58:25–8; 60:22–3; 62:25–7.

Joly, Henry L. (1967) [1908] *Legend in Japanese art: A Description of Historical Episodes, Legendary Characters, Folk-lore Myths, Religious Symbolism Illustrated in the Arts of Old Japan*, Rutland and Tokyo: Tuttle.

'Kaihō eidai yūri zassho' (1981) Mizuno Minoru *et al.*(eds) *Sharebon taisei 11*,

Tokyo: Chūō Kōronsha, p. 398. (Modern reprint of the late-18th-century edition.)

Katsurai Kazuo (1959) *Oranku hanashi – Tosa fūbutsu kō*, Kōchi: Kōchi Shinbunsha

—— (1976) 'Hashi-ken', in Kōchi Shinbunsha (ed.): *Kōchi hyakka jiten*, Kōchi: Kōchi Shinbunsha, p. 707.

Kikusha Namitaka (1771) *Fūgetsu gaiden*. 2 volumes. (Original in Kokuritsu Kokkai Toshokan, Tokyo).

Kitamura Nobuyo (1929) *Kiyū shōran* Tokyo: Nihon Zuihitsu Taisei Kankōkai. (Modern reprint of the original, written between Tenpō 1 (1830) and Kaei 3, (1850), edited by Nihon zuihitsu taisei kankōkai as special volume B of the second series of *Nihon zuihitsu taisei*)

Komiya Takanori (ed.) (1955) *Meiji bunka-shi 10: Shūmi goraku hen*, Tokyo: Yōyōsha.

Kubota Magoichi (1941) *Kenzen goraku tōhachi kendō*, Tokyo: Seishin Kagaku Shuppansha.

Masuda Yasuhiro (ed.) (1989) *Asobi no daijiten*, 2 vols, Tokyo: Tokyo Shoseki.

Matsuura Seisan (1911) *Kashi yawa zokuhen 2*, Tokyo: Kokusho Kankōkai. (Modern reprint of the original probably written after 1830.)

Miyao Shigeo (1979) 'Ken', in Nihon fūzoku-shi gakkai (ed.), *Nihon fūzoku-shi jiten*, Tokyo: Kōbundō, pp. 204–5.

Nakada Kōhei (1970) *Nihon no jidō yūgi*, Tokyo: Shakai Shisōsha.

Ōkubo Ai (ed.) (1971) *Yōji no kokugo e-jiten*, 6 vols, Tokyo: Sanseidō.

Sakai Yasushi (1933) *Nihon yūgi-shi*, Tokyo: Kensetsusha.

Sanō Renren and Ikken Yōshū (Bunsei 13/1830) *Ken hitori keiko*, Author's collection.

Santō Kyōden (1928) [1804] 'Kinsei kiseki kō', in Nihon zuihitsu taisei kankōkai (ed.), *Nihon zuihitsu taisei*, Second series, vol. 3., Tokyo: Nihon Zuihitsu Taisei Kankōkai, pp. 671–796. (Modern reprint of the Bunka 1 (1804) edition.)

Shibuzawa Keizō (ed.) (1966–8) *Emakimono ni yoru Nihon jōmin seikatsu ebiki*, 5 vols, Tokyo: Kadokawa Shoten.

Shinbun shūsei Meiji hennen-shi hensan-kai (ed.) (1936) *Shinbun shūsei Meiji hennen-shi*, 15 vols, Tokyo: Rinsensha.

Takahashi Junji (ed.) (1980) *Nihon e-sugoroku shūsei*, Tokyo: Kashiwa Shobō.

Ushijima Morimitsu (1973) *Nihon no minzoku: Kumamoto*, Tokyo: Daiichi Hōki Shuppan.

—— (1987) *Zusetsu Nihon minzoku-shi: Kumamoto*, Tokyo: Iwasaki Bijutsusha.

Watanabe Shinichirō and Ryotarō Mogami (1975) 'Ken', *Kokubungaku. Kaishaku to kanshō* 519: 95–114.

Yamato Hachimitsu (1931) [1794] 'Ikkō futsū kawari sen', in Takagi Kōji *et al.* (eds) *Sharebon taikei* 6, Tokyo: Rokugōkan, pp. 597–618. (Modern reprint of the Kansei 6 (1794) edition.)

Yoshinami and Gojaku (Bunka 6/1809) *Kensarae sumai zue*, 2 vols. (Original in the library of the Jinbun kagaku kenkyūsho of Kyoto University).

*Yoshiwara saiken kayou kami* (Kanpo 3/1743). (Original in Tokyo Toritsu Chūō Toshokan.)

# 3 The parish of a famous shrine

## The influence of rites and ceremonials on urban life.
## The sanctuary of Ebisu in Nishinomiya.[1]

*Sylvie Guichard-Anguis*[2]

## INTRODUCTION

This study represents part of a broader concern with the relationships between Japanese towns and their past. It is also an opportunity to clarify the relationships between the forms and modes of urban life on the one hand and religious worship on the other. We have chosen a shrine (*jinja*) linked to the Shintō religion in an endeavour to understand what a parish could signify in the Japanese urban context.

The shrine of Ebisu at Nishinomiya,[3] in the Kansai region, one of the most highly developed and industrialized places on earth, ranks as one of the most important and prosperous in Japan. Of ancient foundation, its history allows us to appreciate the ways in which religion has influenced urban history. The uninterrupted popularity of Ebisu worship throughout the centuries enables us better to perceive how it and the society to which it is linked have developed.

We have decided to approach the subject by analysing the rites and ceremonies which have their origin in the shrine. The relations the sanctuary maintains with the urban network surrounding it, particularly through the festivals (*matsuri*), will guide us throughout this work. By 'rite' we mean the definition given by the Le Robert dictionary (1985): all the ceremonies of worship in use in a religious community; and the traditional organization of those ceremonies.

We shall firstly give a brief overview of the place occupied by the shrine in the town throughout the centuries. Then we shall successively consider the development of worship and that of the shrine, still from the historical point of view. Lastly the role of the shrine in the contemporary town will enable us to point out some of the essential characteristics of Japanese society. In conclusion, we shall try to locate this fieldwork in a wider context.

# FROM STAGING-POST TO CENTRE FOR EDUCATION, CULTURE AND RESIDENCE

Nishinomiya, situated on the north shore of the Bay of Ōsaka, in the western part of the district of Hyōgo, had 424,280 inhabitants in 1988. The history of Nishinomiya dates back to antiquity, since the town appears as a place-name in the *Manyōshū*. During its history Nishinomiya has combined several functions. The first role of a *monzen machi* (shrine town) gave it its name. It originated from the two shrines Hirota *jinja* and Nishinomiya *jinja*, around which the urban area progressively developed. The second function as a *shukuba machi* (staging-post) is linked with its position at the intersection of two main traffic routes. The third function as a *minato-machi* (port) and ware-housing town made it so prosperous that it attracted the attention of the Shogun authority of Edo which placed Nishinomiya under its direct control in 1787.

In 1874 the national railway company linked Ōsaka to Kōbe by rail. A station was opened at Nishinomiya. In 1905 the Hanshin private line duplicated the Ōsaka–Kōbe link. In 1920 a third private line, the Hankyū, made the same link but alongside the mountains. Nishinomiya lost its role as a staging-post and became progressively integrated into the urban region of Kansai.

Making the most of its position and its site, the town progressively developed into a large residential area between Kōbe and Ōsaka. Divided roughly into two parts between a coastal plain to the south and part of the Rokko mountain chain to the north, its slopes were ideal for suburban development.

Nishinomiya suffered severely from bombing in the Second World War, like the whole of the Kōbe-Ōsaka region, when about 80 per cent of the houses were destroyed. In 1964 the town was crossed by the Meishin motorway, matched in 1970 by the new Hanshin motorway. Nishinomiya found itself cut into longitudinal strips by the railways and motorways which form barriers to internal communications.

In 1963 the town declared itself a 'Town of Education, Culture and Residence'. The new *shin sōgō keikaku* development plan of 1977 emphasized the priority to be given to education, culture and residence. Green areas are protected in the form of a network of protected zones (*fūchi chiku*). Because of the presence of woods, most of the shrines and temples come into that category. *Hirota san chiku*, the green area of the Hirota shrine, covers about fourteen acres. The landscape of the wood of Ebisu *jinja* is protected by the district known as *keikan jurin hogo chiku*. The wood has also been designated by the district of Hyōgo as a natural monument (*tennen kinen butsu*) since 1961. Since then it has been an island of greenery in the middle of the built-up area.

## EBISU *JINJA*, AN ISLAND OF GREENERY

The wood of the Nishinomiya *jinja shasō* shrine which consists mainly of evergreens covers about 10 acres in the heart of the town. It is particularly well served by the various methods of transport as the prospectus distributed by the sanctuary proudly points out. The three large railway stations of Hanshin, Hankyū and the old national railways are between 350 metres and 1,300 metres away. The Hanshin motorway passes less than 50 metres to the south of the temple. The shrine's land seems to be locked between these various routes.

This proximity to transport systems is one of the main reasons for its attraction in the eyes of Japanese visitors, as is proved by the crowds progressing from the Hanshin station, which is the closest to the sanctuary, around New Year's Day or about the 10 January. We must remember that Japanese society honours above all the practical aspect of things (*benri*).

The great main gate (*omote ō mon*) dates back to the Azuchi-Momoyama era (1573–1603). With its four-pillar style (*yotsu hashira*), it is designated as an important cultural asset (*jūyō bunka zai*) by the Ministry of Culture. The wall with its covering of plaster (*neribei*) which must also date back to Momoyama times forms the boundary to the south and east. Stretching for 247 metres, it is one of the most important walls of this type in Japan.

Most of the buildings inside were destroyed during the bombing of 1945. The interior *honden* sanctuary and the *haiden* prayer room were rebuilt in 1961. The first, in the *sanren kasuga* style, was designated a national treasure. A *kaikan* communal house in the 'traditional Japanese style' (*wafu kenchiku*) has 2,000 square metres of reception area and a meeting room designed for weddings which can hold up to 250 guests. In a Rokueidō villa, the former residence of Iwakura Tomomi (1825–83) in Tokyo, the *zashiki* rooms are used for meetings of people practising the traditional arts.

## THE PAST AND PRESENT OF A SHRINE TOWN: EBISU, EBISU SABURŌ AND EBISU-KŌ

Before approaching the history of the shrine, we shall give a few brief explanations of the origins of the cult and its subsequent development. From reading the many works on the subject of Ebisu (see the bibliography at the end of chapter), it must be acknowledged that this collection of beliefs has not yet yielded all its secrets. There are numerous hypotheses. We shall not embark on a controversial discussion here as this is not the main objective of this work.

The historical dictionary of the Franco-Japanese House will be our chief guide in this summary. The information the shrine itself provides on these matters will help us complete a rather sketchy picture. We shall confine ourselves to the three great origins of the cult on which the opinions of specialists seem to agree.

Ebisu is nowadays a god associated with fishermen, business and happiness (*fuku*). He is usually represented catching a sea bream (*tai*). The origin of the word itself is still the subject of much debate among specialists. The hypothesis most often adopted to the name is that of a being alien to Japanese civilization, coming from overseas and bringing happiness. *Emishi* is another way of pronouncing the same character.

There is a tradition which identifies Ebisu as Hiruko, the first child of Izanagi and Izanami, the couple credited with the formation of the Japanese archipelago. His parents apparently abandoned him on a boat because he could not stand up by the age of three.

Another tradition identifies him as the deity of Izumo Ōkuninushi no mikoto. Saburō, which means the third son is, according to another tradition, identified as Izumo Ōkuninushi no mikoto or his third son, who is described as devoting himself to fishing off cape Miho at Izumo.

At the end of the Heian era (794–1185), Ebisu became the protector of fishermen as the deity who could bring good luck from across the sea. He was considered to be the protector of sea voyagers and shell-gatherers. The worship of Ebisu and Saburō appears in the Middle Ages in the ports of the Inland Sea such as those of Hyōgo, Sakai and Hakata. After the thirteenth or fourteenth century with the development of trade, the worship of Ebisu was further enriched. He also became the protector of markets and a deity capable of offering wealth and prosperity to traders.

Already in the twelfth century Ebisu's name appeared in various shrines, for example the Tōdaiji Hachiman at Nara, a proof of his popularity. The celebrations of Shintō ceremonies devoted to Ebisu multiplied in the great *taisha* sanctuaries. Itsukushima on the Island of Miyajima and Tsuruoka Hachimangū at Kamakura are among them.

The two big markets (*tōzaiichi*) to the east and west of the ancient capital of Heiankyō (the future Kyoto) would have had an image of Ebisu. He then acted as the god who protected exchange activities in the climate of insecurity caused by the fall of the Tairas. Products originating from the sea and from unknown lands were offered on the markets. Therein, perhaps, resides one of the explanations for the development of the cult. It was moreover in that region of the Kinki district that the influences from the north and the south of the country came to merge.

In the middle of the Kamakura era (1192–1333) a subordinate shrine (*massha*) appeared on the coast to the west of the Hirota sanctuary. It became usual to call it the (Ebisu) shrine to the west of the great shrine '*Nishi no miya*'. At that time Ebisu and Saburō had either distinct or joint shrines. In any case, their names came to be spoken one after the other. Then gradually Saburō's name disappeared and only that of Ebisu remained.

Another confusion arose from the association of the Ebisu-Saburō pair at Daikokuten which has their statue in the refectories of the monasteries and the kitchens, as the deity who dispenses food. The Japanese pronunciation of their name may also have helped to identify them as Ōkuninushi no mikoto. During the Muromachi era (1392–1490) the Ebisu–Saburō pair became very popular with the development of trade and during the Edo era (1600–1868) with that of the merchant class. Associated with wealth, Ebisu and Daikoku were to become part of the seven popular divinities of happiness (*shichi fukujin*).

Ebisu kō has two meanings. One concerns the meetings of merchants and craftsmen concerned with the same product. They not only facilitated the celebration of worship but also provided an opportunity for making fruitful contacts. They were called Ebisu kō of such and such a product. As a rule they corresponded to *nakama* commercial organizations, which sometimes included a right of *kabu* participation. These *kabu nakama* developed in particular after the Genroku era (1688–1703).

The other meaning of Ebisu kō is linked to the great festivals of the worship of the god. They take place on 10 January (Tōka Ebisu) and 20 October. They figure among the major events of the annual calendar of the *nenjū gyōji* (annual festivals).

## Ebisu *jinja*, the '*nishi no miya*'

Four deities are worshipped in the main *sōhonsha* shrine: Nishinomiya no Okami, Amaterasu no Okami, Susanō Okami and Ōkuninushi no Okami. Tiles discovered in the course of excavations, dating back to the second half of the Heian era, show how old the shrine is. According to the annals of names of divinities mentioned in *Engishiki* (957), a certain Ōkuninushi *jinja* was in Settsu (one of the five provinces of Kinai) which could well be this same shrine. A document states that the Emperor Sutoku attended a poetry meeting (*uta awase*) there in 1128. As the religion spread to other shrines during the Middle Ages, the *sōhonsha* of the deity Ebisu became an expression which spread throughout society.

During the civil wars or the numerous natural disasters which marked the Muromachi and Sengoku eras (1490–1600), belief in a god who could give protection against all forms of human tragedy grew continually stronger. The construction of a great *honden*, the constitution of a wide *keidai* enclosure, the numerous references to the sanctuary in the Nō plays or the comic *kyōgen* entertainments show the ever-increasing popularity of the sanctuary. In 1309 a document bears witness to the existence nearby of a market of which only the placename Ichiniwa chō survives, attributed to a group of houses (*machi*).

Following several fires which destroyed the sanctuary, Tokugawa Ietsuna (1641–1680) had it rebuilt in the *sanren kasuga* style in 1663. In order to find new financial resources the sanctuary obtained the right to sell *fuda* amulets bearing the image of Ebisu. This image quickly spread throughout Japan.

In 1617 Nishinomiya was included in the fiefdom of the town under the *jōkamachi* castle of Amagasaki whose income came to 40,000 *koku* of rice (a *koku* is about 317 pints). The shrine received from the different lords who succeeded one another at the head of the fiefdom an annual income of thirty *koku*.

A map from 1686 shows the two shrines of Hirota and Ebisu. The different components of the landscape presented by the sanctuary were already present by the end of the seventeenth century. The boundary wall, the great red door, the *honden* and the pool in the middle of the enclosure are shown on it. The only great difference lies in the proximity of the sea just to the south of Ebisu *jinja*.

The present shrine is not very different from the one Tokugawa Ietsuna had built. Destroyed during the Second World War, its main buildings have been reconstructed in identical style. Only Rokueidō and some contemporary buildings like the offices of the shrine and the *kaikan* communal house have introduced a few slight alterations in the modern era. Kiosks offering food make it possible to extend one's visit inside the enclosure or to come and relax while the children play.

## FROM TŌKA EBISU TO THE ROLE OF A CULTURAL AND LEISURE CENTRE

### Community and Shintō ceremonies

We shall not dwell on the Shintō ceremonies which take place in all sanctuaries. Some of them are connected with various rites of passage.

Their presence is an almost permanent feature of the shrine. The first visit to the shrine of the new-born (*hatsu mairi*), the ritual visits at the ages of 3, 5 and 7 years (*shichi-go-san*), the assumption of adulthood at the age of 20 (*seijin shiki*), weddings, and so on, are among the most typical.

The statistics supplied by the shrine office give the following breakdown of the different kinds of prayers offered in 1985. The second figure represents the most important month of the year. The figures are given in descending order of magnitude.

- *Shichi-go-san*: 3,229 (3,202 in November)
- *Hatsu mairi*: 1,968 (254 in November)
- Professional success: 1,882 (1,584 in January)
- Miscellaneous: 466 (286 in January)
- Road safety: 238 (31 in December)
- Fishing: 213 (114 in January)
- Business travel: 195 (23 in March and April)
- Domestic safety: 99 (16 in January and June)
- Protection against evil spirits: 54 (28 in February) (undoubtedly connected with New Year (*setsubun*))
- Prompt recovery: 30 (6 in April)
- Safety at sea: 6 (6 in January)

These prayers come to an annual total of 8,380, of which 2,099 were in January and 3,630 in November.

These figures show the close relationship maintained by the residents of Nishinomiya with their titular divinity. A comparison of these figures and the figures of other shrines in towns of similar size and function would be most informative. The importance of the months of January and November reflects the special features of the cult as does the pride of place given in contemporary Japanese society to shrine visits at the start of the year and *shichi-go-san*.

The relationship with the maritime world is falling off considerably. This phenomenon is scarcely surprising considering the position of Nishinomiya in the middle of one of the most highly developed and industrialized parts of the earth. The shrine is now several kilometres from an artificial coast which continues to expand with the extension of the landfill (*umetate*) into the sea.

The remaining ceremonies punctuate the year and are usually based on the agricultural calendar. Unsurprisingly, the spring with its sowing and the autumn with its harvests are the two high points. These festivals (*matsuri*) are held in honour of the titular divinity (*ujigami*). They are the occasion for the meeting of all the members of the parish (*ujiko*).

They vary from one shrine to another according to the nature of the divinity and its history.

The following are the main festivals in the Ebisu *jinja* calendar:

- *Tōka Ebisu*, on 9, 10 and 11 January.
- *Kinen-sai*, 22 February.
- *Kōshasai daidaikagura sai*, from 1 to 6 May.
- *Okosha matsuri* or *shinkoshiki* or again *yukata matsuri*, 14 June.
- *Natsu matsuri*, summer festival, 20 July.
- *Reisai* or *shinkoshiki*, 22 September.
- *Seimon matsuri*, 20 November.
- *Niihame sai*, 23 November.

We shall confine ourselves to the most important which contribute to the originality of the sanctuary of Nishinomiya.


## *Tōka Ebisu*

Until the middle of the Meiji era (1868–1912) *igomori* continued to be observed. The great gate (*mon*) was closed at midnight on 9th January until the morning of the 10th. No one left home, in order to observe silence. During the three days which constitute *Tōka Ebisu*, the religious rites (*kamigoto*) consist essentially of the sale of good-luck charms (*engimono*) and in prayers addressed to the divinity by the *kannushi* priest. In this they differ from the other great shrine of Kansai, Imamiya *jinja* where theatrical performances are presented. On 10 January the priest informs the deities that all has gone well. More and more people attend the shrine until 10 January. The edition of the daily newspaper *Asahi* for that date gives the following figures for visits on that day in 1990, concerning the three great Ebisu shrines in Kansai:

- 2,250,000 people for Imamiya *jinja* in Ōsaka;
- 200,000 people for Nishinomiya *jinja*;
- 34,000 people for Horikawa Ebisu in Kyoto.

Ebisu *jinja* thus occupies second place in the Kansai region.

The generosity of visitors takes all forms. Sums of money (*saisen*) are thrown into boxes installed throughout the year to receive them, or coins are pressed into an enormous fresh tuna fish supplied for the purpose. The sanctuary's office gave us the following figures for the first ten days of January:

- 17,500,000 yen in 1983;
- 18,587,900 yen in 1988.

Moreover, the sale of good-luck charms considerably increases the sanctuary's resources. Branches of a sort of lucky bamboo called *fukusasa* and rakes made of bamboo (*fukumi*) decorated with a clay figure of Ebisu are bought by visitors to take home for the coming year.

It must be noted that a large proportion of the shrine's financial resources are derived from this festival. In 1990 about 350 open-air stalls were set up along the path called Ebisu suji. The already quoted edition of *Asahi* specifies that the price of amulets bought was on average about 1,000 yen. Professional success and domestic safety were the most sought-after objectives.

## Reisai matsuri

A document states that *reisai matsuri*, the second most important festival, dates back at least to the end of the twelfth century (1180). The same document notes that it takes place on 22 August. Subsequently, only the Shintō rites survived, and they took place every autumn until 1954.

The procession of portable shrines (*mikoshi*) was then re-established, an important phenomenon in post-war Japan when municipalities sought to give themselves a new identity. At the end of the festival, children chosen by the associations of *chōnaikai* districts from among the children's associations dependent on them (membership is fixed after the age of six) process around the shrine. A woman organizer told us that their participation helps to bring them happiness (*shiawase*). When the children are gathered in the courtyard of the sanctuary, a sheet of paper describing the costumes and the way to wear them is handed to each mother. The mothers dress their children in a garment old-fashioned in style but made entirely of synthetic materials. The procession parades slowly round a group of houses. Many of the children are not used to walking barefoot. The mothers stay beside them throughout the parade. When it ends the children separate without any other kind of ceremony.

The next day the streets of the district chosen for the procession (*ujiko machi*) are decorated by members of the same association with strips of white paper and sacred cords. Its residents must benefit in turn from the blessings of the divinity carried through the streets. The entirely motorized procession presents a quite remarkable amalgam of people dressed in ancient style on the backs of lorries, and even a few priests travelling in convertible sports cars. Even characters from strip cartoons are to be found among the participants.

The block of Yasui was chosen in 1989 and the ceremony took place in the Shukugawa tennis club. The contemporary forms borrowed by this rite, whether for the children's procession, the procession of vehicles or the choice of place for the main ceremony are strongly reminiscent of the Japan of the great urban festivals mounted for semi-touristic purposes.

There is a clear lack of interest on the part of the majority of the inhabitants. Formalism predominates. The people involved in the festival seem to be a few devoted members of the *chōnaikai*, especially the elderly. Only two or three people per district association are allowed to take part in the procession. Few residents recognize one another in this demonstration which is intended to strengthen the links of this community – if indeed it can still be considered to be a community in that sense.

### Seimon barai

The practice of *seimon barai* gave rise to *seimon matsuri*. On a given day the traders sell their goods at lower prices than usual. This is their way of thanking the deity for all the benefits accumulated throughout the year. They try to rid themselves of the *seimon* obligation they have undertaken and failed to respect.

The Ebisu-kō to which not only the merchants but also the fishermen belong meet particularly around Kyoto. Bamboo rakes (*kumade*) often appear on the Shintō altar of the restaurants of the town during the last days of the year.

### From sanctuary to house for all (*kōminkaikan*)

Whereas many ceremonies draw their origin from the presence of the *honden*, others depend on ancillary buildings and assume entirely different forms.

In the communal Nishinomiya *jinja kaikan* house, all services related to wedding receptions are offered: clothes hire, choice of presents, catering, video recordings, and so on. The publicity leaflets distributed by the shrine stress the importance of the green setting within the enclosure of the temple. Its spiritual value is very obviously matched by a not inconsiderable commercial value in the town centre.

Throughout the year, numerous demonstrations enliven the buildings of lesser importance: a *sumō* wrestling tournament for children, a chrysanthemum exhibition in the autumn, and so on.

The Rokueidō pavilion is the setting for poetic meetings or *chakai* tea ceremonies. The biggest meeting of the year probably takes place on 19 April, the birthday of the present *iemoto* grand master, Sen Sosetsu of the Urasenke School. On that occasion he prepares tea for the divinity *(kencha)*. On that day 800 tickets to attend are sold, showing the meeting's importance.

The Fukujukai Tea Society attached to the sanctuary has about 600 members and 35 organizers, all of them professors of tea in the Hanshin and Kōbe region, and members of Tankokai, the tea society of the Urasenke school. These professors take it in turns to be responsible for organizing the meeting. Over 250 guests take part in the monthly meetings which are held on the third Sunday of each month and which comprise a single *seki* setting at which the light *usucha* tea is served.

For the first tea ceremony of the year *(hatsu gama)*, over 400 guests take part in the meeting during which tea is served at three different settings, one of which is invariably for the strong tea *(koicha)*.

## CONCLUSION

This description of the rites and ceremonies which take place at Ebisu *jinja* emphasizes the complexity of the relationships maintained between the shrine and the urban society which surrounds it. Its local role as the titular *ujigami* deity seems to have become considerably weakened, as is shown by the sparse enthusiasm found when the big annual ceremonies are being organized. It no longer helps to promote the integration of the community.

Yet the continued importance of regional attendance on the occasion of Tōka Ebisu, combined with its excellent transport links, shows the indisputable vitality of the cult, demonstrated by its remarkable capacity to adapt. It reflects the pragmatism of a society which is today directed towards the search for individual success and the happiness of the family unit, in one of the world's most prosperous regions.

The heart of a shrine town, Ebisu *jinja* now acts as a green leisure area in the middle of a modern town. The rites and ceremonies which take place there have lost much of their religious and spiritual significance and have attached themselves to the world of culture and leisure. One might ask whether this recent development is the result of the special nature of a cult which, throughout its history, has shown a remarkable ability to adapt.

The contribution of this field study still seems rather isolated in France, considering the slight development of the discussion of the rites and ceremonies. The work needs to be placed into a wider context.

Within this wider context, the individualistic nature of the modern cult of Ebisu does not seem isolated. Umesao *et al.* (1990) stress this new phenomenon in an article which relates religion to modernization. In it they affirm that the emphasis is now placed on the divinities who give personal protection and on a cult which can respond to the needs of each person. Moreover, in the same work Befu (1990) emphasizes that religions such as Judaism or Shintōism, based on membership of an ethnic group, depend for their survival precisely on the survival of that population. From this point of view, the progressive internationalization of Japanese society should be contributing to the decline of the cult.

So how should our direct participation as foreigners in some of these ceremonies be interpreted? Two of our children, members of *kodomokai*, were selected for the procession by the organizers of our *chōnaikai*. Was this as *ujiko*, thus informing us of our temporary integration? Or was giving a few young foreigners the opportunity to take part in an event containing certain touristic elements enough to justify their presence as non-believers? We think that the development of cults, and particularly of the rites and ceremonies attached to them, not to mention so-called traditional practices, in relation to the internationalization of Japanese society, is highly instructive as regards the mechanisms which really motivate them.

Does the participation of foreigners in the *matsuri* only correspond to the necessity of making up for the disaffection of part of Japanese society? Are we not witnessing here a more complex phenomenon involving the integration of a fraction of inhabitants sometimes very sensitive to the special nature of some of these celebrations, in spite of being foreign? The development of the *matsuri* itself described by Miyake (1989) would mean today abandoning any sense of contrition, retaining only its festive aspect and emphasizing the sense of merry-making. So the direct participation of foreigners in the *matsuri* would become increasingly easy in that their religious character has henceforward become very blurred. The conjunction of these two types of development ensures the continuation of the *matsuri*. The wish to propagate certain traditional practices abroad is similar. The need to recruit new adherents in order to compensate for a certain nascent disaffection on the part of the Japanese population goes hand in hand with the affirmation of a new spirit. The insistence with which the Urasenke School appeals to the idea of *heiwa*, peace among men around a bowl of tea, is a move in the same direction.

## NOTES

1 The author lived in Nishinomiya from 1981 to 1985, so most of the fieldwork was conducted during that period. As regards data, this was given

as the most recent by the shrine, and therefore belongs to a later period, between 1985 and 1989.
2 This chapter was translated by Langue & Parole, London.
3 At the Ebisu shrine we made full use of the co-operation of some of the residents of Nishinomiya and the most valuable help given by the sanctuary's priests.

## BIBLIOGRAPHY

Befu Harumi (1990) 'Concluding remarks: religion in Japanese civilisation' in Umesao T., H. Hardacre and Nakamaki H. (eds) *Japanese Civilisation in the Modern World, VI Religion*, Senri Ethnological Studies 29, Ōsaka: National Museum of Ethnology.
Kita S. (1976) *Fukujin* (The divinities of happiness), Tokyo: Hōbunsha.
Kurabayashi M. (1983) *Nihon matsuri nenjū gyōji jiten* (Dictionary of festivals throughout the year), Tokyo: Ōfūsha.
Franco-Japanese House, section 4 (1978) *Historical Dictionary of Japan*, Tokyo: Kinokuniya.
Miyake Hitoshi (1989) *Shūkyo minzokugaku* (Anthropology of religions), Tokyo: Tokyo Daigaku Shuppankai.
Miyamoto K. (1987) *Fukushin shinkō* (Belief in the seven divinities of happiness), Tokyo: Yūsankaku.
Miyata N. (1982) *Toshi minzokuron no kadai* (Themes of urban anthropology), Tokyo: Miraisha.
—— (1986) *Gendai Minzokuron no kadai* (Themes of contemporary anthropology), Tokyo: Miraisha.
Naganuma K. (1922) *Fukujin kenkyū – Ebisu to Daikoku* (Research on the seven divinities of happiness – Ebisu and Daikoku), Tokyo: Hinoema.
Nanno T. and Horiuchi, K. (1988) *Furusato no omoide, 323: Nishinomiya* (Souvenir of our city), Tokyo: Kokusho Kankōkai.
Nishinomiya jinja shamusho (1985) *Nishinomiya jinja no rekishi* (History of the sanctuary of Nishinomiya), Nishinomiya: Nishinomiya Jinja Shamusho.
Umesao T., H. Hardacre and Nakamaki H. (eds) (1990) *Japanese Civilisation in the Modern World, VI Religion*, Senri Ethnological Studies 29, Ōsaka: National Museum of Ethnology.

# Part II

# Rituals for the dead

# 4 On structural duality in Japanese conceptions of death

## Collective forms of death rituals in Morimachi[1]

*Halldór Stefánsson*

## INTRODUCTION

Much has been written on the subject of Japanese funeral customs and ancestor worship as these are taken to have occurred in the past, and much has been written on modern practices as well.[2] A striking aspect thereof is the extent to which Buddhism has come to be associated with rites of death from the time it began to spread through all classes of the Japanese population in the late Heian period (794–1185). In fact, Japanese scholars often express the view that Buddhism only became Japanese by 'invading' an area that was taboo in the native culture. Through its capacity to deal with the pollution of death, previously so strictly avoided, it became *sōshiki bukkyō*, or Funeral Buddhism (Sasaki 1989:59; Haga 1987: 55–86).

There have, however, been authors who have chosen in their writings to minimize Buddhist influence in the total history of Japanese death rituals. In playing down 'the Buddhist factor' they prefer to stress the fundamentally indigenous roots of funerary and ancestor rites within the structural building blocks (*ie-dōzoku-kokutai*) of society, these being anchored on conceptions emanating from Japanese folk religion (Yanagita 1929:497–520; 1931:520–49; 1978:233; Takeda 1957, 1976). Finally, there have been scholars who have focused on the structural aspects of Japanese rites of death (Ooms 1976; Tsuboi 1979). These authors have shown how Japanese death rituals, when viewed as a system, form a sort of inverted mirror image to the Japanese rites of passage performed during the life-span of individuals.

The modern standardized version of Japanese death rituals is officially initiated with the funeral proper, and then extended through a series of household rites which, through the passage of time, 'transform' the dead into the indistinct category of revered ancestor.

In this chapter I argue that Japanese death rituals contain yet another dimension, a collective one. I am concerned with a number of rites which have in common the participation of representatives from an entire hamlet. Moreover, rather than idealizing the dead in worship, as it is the case in the household rites, they seem bent on neutralizing, or evicting them periodically. They permit a form of resistance to the accumulated, otherwise disastrous, influence of death through seasonal ritual actions.

The following is a study of some of the instances of collective rites of death which I came across during my fieldwork in five local communities in Morimachi, Shizuoka prefecture. On the surface these rites may seem to be quite disparate and heterogeneous, but I will argue that when viewed collectively they manifest some interesting similarities. We will see, first of all, how all of these serve the social function of emphasizing – through a repeated, active participation – that there are important moments where the interests of the community must take precedence over the more restricted ones of individual households. As for the symbolic dimension of the rites discussed, I will demonstrate how some of these seem to be geared to incorporating individual spirits, or groups of spirits into the cultural category of 'community dead'. In the conclusion an attempt is made to place the collected data within the context of anthropological theory.

## EIGHT EXAMPLES OF RITES EXPRESSING COLLECTIVE CONCERN FOR THE SPIRITS OF THE DEAD IN MORIMACHI

### 1 First-*bon nenbutsu*

In the hamlet Otomaru, a collective sutra performance (*nenbutsu*) takes place at the festival of the dead (*bon*). Then all the adults, with the significant exception of the Buddhist priest, gather in the courtyard in front of the households which have recently had a death in the family – normally one, two, or three a year (see also Smith 1974:103–9). They move between the houses in a procession which according to a predetermined order starts at the top of the village and ends at the bottom, chanting a *nenbutsu* song in each place. The song consists of the simple recital of all the names of thirteen important Buddhist divinities.[3] According to the tradition, each of these is held to preside over one of the thirteen major occasions of death rituals succeeding the funeral, from the first rite on the seventh day after death (*shōnanoka*) until the last memorial rites, 33 years after (*sanjūsankaiki*).

## 2 *Nenbutsu-kō: goeika*[4]

In contrast to the small isolated hamlet of Otomaru, which is in the mountainous north-east, in the rice-growing agricultural communities of Morimachi, on the south-western lowland, the custom of a communal chanting of *nenbutsu* songs at first-*bon* celebrations is unknown. There are no existing records suggesting that they ever existed in the past. However, if there was no common chanting of *nenbutsu* in the south it does not necessarily mean that *nenbutsu* chanting as such was totally absent. Here it just took another and much more specialized form. Old women joined a local association called the '*nenbutsu-kō*' for the chanting of Buddhist sutras, the so-called *wasan*. These were types of simplified and popularized versions of different sutras which had long enjoyed widespread popularity. The members of the *nenbutsu-kō* learned how to master a certain repertoire of sutras. From this they could chose and select according to the sex and age of the deceased when they chanted together at funerals and first-*bon* celebrations.

The original *nenbutsu-kō* have completely disappeared from Morimachi. They have been replaced, or rather supplanted by a new and more formal kind of *nenbutsu* association. Practically all the local temples in Morimachi belong to the Sōtō sect of Japanese Buddhism, which is one of the two major sects of Japanese Zen Buddhism. About thirty years ago the Sōtō sect started organizing their own *nenbutsu* school (the *baika-ryū*) and its local groups (the *baika-kō*). The people of Morimachi commonly refer to these groups as *goeika*, *eisanka*, or even just as *gowasan*, after the chants they intonate.

In the villages which I studied in the south of Morimachi the *goeika* serves as an 'old women's club', since it is considered most appropriate for women to become members after they have turned 60 years old and are entitled for the first time in their married life to some hours of leisure, having been succeeded for most of the household duties by a daughter-in-law.[5] On average, a *goeika* group has between five and fifteen members (about one member from every ten households). They meet twice a month in the local community hall for practice. The date is not fixed, but is decided among the members during the slack moments of agricultural life. When they meet, normally they get together in the morning and continue their *goeika* reunions until around four in the afternoon. The admitted purpose of these meetings is, in addition to the official purpose of practising their religiously inspired songs, to have a merry party – eating, drinking tea, and gossiping. Several of these old ladies told me that these were their principal moments of recreation.

But the *goeika* group naturally also plays a more 'serious' role within the hamlet. There are two sorts of occasions on which they make their public appearances. First, there are the seasonal events: the four major temple rites, the *segaki* (see below) at the time of *bon*, and the autumnal equinox, when they assemble, often in an outer pavilion of the local temple, in order to chant the sutras on behalf of the whole community.[6] Then there are some special appearances, when the *goeika* are called in to chant their songs at peoples' homes as a part of the major death rites of the families. At the time of memorial rites or funerals they are not frequent visitors, while it is quite common to rely on their services for the celebrations of first *bon*. Around *bon* time they are therefore busy visiting the families of their hamlet who have requested their presence in order to give weight to their feelings of concern for the well-being of their 'newly dead'. In some instances, the activities of a given *goeika* group extends beyond the village boundaries: they can be called to chant their sutras in neighbouring villages, which results in a certain criss-crossing of the old-women's-groups of the region.

When performing in their own hamlet they, like everybody else, are subject to elaborate rules of general reciprocity, but at the same time, as specially called-in 'helpers' they should be rewarded. The apparently conflicting situation which arises from the twofold identity of the *goeika* when they make their appearances in people's homes is resolved by employing the symbolic language of gift-giving, but reversing the direction in the rule of unequal exchange that normally applies for the occasions of condolence. When they go visiting for funerals, or first-*bon* celebration, they, like everybody else, bring an envelope containing around 3,000 yen. The family on the receiving end reciprocates when the chanting is over with an envelope with 10,000 yen (*kifu*). The *goeika* then use the money they collect in this way either for covering the cost of their monthly reunions, or they may wish to contribute it to their local temple.

Unlike the old *nenbutsu-kō* with its selection of sutras which expressed various traditional concerns of Japanese culture (female origins of pollution, relative prestige and social importance of age groups, etc.), the sutras used by the *baika-kō* in Morimachi are few in number and more or less uniform for every occasion of death. Both the words, which are inspired by the recital of Buddhist sutras, and the rhythms, which are based on two of the traditional metres in Japanese poetry, are of the utmost simplicity.

### 3 *Dainenbutsu*: The Great *Nenbutsu* of Enshū, Morimachi

In 1572 an important battle took place between Takeda Shingen invading from the east, and the as yet immature Tokugawa Ieyasu, who was defending his home province at a location called Mikatagahara, on the northern outskirts of Hamamatsu in Enshū, now within the prefecture of Shizuoka. It turned into one of those murderous clashes between the armies of retainers of power-hungry warlords which from time to time seriously disturbed the lives of the population at that time. The Tokugawa army, well acquainted with the local conditions, had prepared a trap for the invading easterners by covering a natural crevice, Saikagake, with an enormous blanket, thus providing the battlefield with an artificial bridge, a *nu-no-hashi*. Tokugawa's army, as a part of its strategy, gave in to pressure, retreated suddenly, by-passing the *nu-no-hashi*. They were immediately pursued by Takeda's men, who took the bridge and crowds of them fell into the crevice and lost their lives in a massacre. Yet, in the end it was Takeda Shingen who was victorious, and Tokugawa narrowly escaped being killed in that battle. In the years after the cruel death of the masses of young men in the prime of their lives, the region was visited by a series of natural disasters: epidemics and a mysterious multi-plication of grasshoppers which repeatedly ruined the harvest and left the peasants starving. Soon a rumour spread about cries and screaming voices being heard near that ill-fated crevice (Kōno 1981:86–103).

Learning about the despair and growing unrest among the local population, Tokugawa Ieyasu called in Sōen, a famous priest from Mikawa, to make use of his religious charisma in order to restore order to the farmer's universe. He organized a grand scale *nenbutsu*, a *Dainenbutsu*, to be held at that most ill-fated place of the battle, for the repose of the restless spirits. These rites were then repeated every year by the local population, and are said to have given rise to a particular *Dainenbutsu* tradition which soon became popular in the region. It became an annual event organized by the young men in each local community, first, as stated above, exclusively for the war-dead at Mikatagahara, but then little by little also for warding off and pacifying all the sundry 'evil effects of death' that threatened the collectivity as a whole. These local performances took place each year at the time of the *bon* festival.

In many places in Enshū, to the north and north-east of Hamamatsu, in Hama-kita, in Tenryū, in Toyōka, in Imai, in Fukuroi, and in Morimachi, people in each hamlet seem to have established their own *Dainenbutsu* teams with the best of their young men filling the ranks. After nightfall, they passed in a procession, dressed as wandering monks wearing straw sandals and wide-brimmed, braided straw hats. A couple of lantern-bearers and flag-bearers led the way between those of the houses in the community that were celebrating a first *bon*. There they were greeted by the head of the household who led them into the courtyard, where they performed their dancing and chanting to the accompaniment of flutes, drums and the resounding of huge gongs. The words of the chants of the *Dainenbutsu* chorus were quite simple. For the most part they were borrowed from the *wasan*, the Buddhist chants mentioned above. The lines chosen differed according to the dead's relationship to the person hosting the *Dainenbutsu*, i.e., whether it was his grandparent, parent, child, unmarried sibling, servant, etc.

All the neighbours would gather round, making the spectacle a public event which focused on the dead spirit and his family. This event purified or pacified whatever disturbances might have been introduced into the community by a death occurring in a particular household. After their performance the *Dainenbutsu* team as well as the assembled neighbours received food and great quantities of drink, making it a really festive occasion. Then the *Dainenbutsu* team would continue on to the next household, where another first-*bon* family was waiting. The party would thus continue until the early morning hours.

The *Dainenbutsu* teams travelled on foot, in a procession which grew ever larger as it approached its destination. Its passings through the local community were considered to be one of the major recreational occasions of the year, awaited by everybody, young and old. The young, hungering for diversion, accompanied the *Dainenbutsu* team beyond the boundaries of its home hamlet when it was called in to pay a visit to a first-*bon* family in a neighbouring community. Often they would come across another team travelling on the narrow road on its way to a destination in the opposite direction. The meeting of two teams in the dark of the night, in the open, set the stage for intimate encounters with neighbours which took the form of ritualized confrontations. Insults and verbal abuse are often said to have degenerated into fierce fighting, resulting in serious accidents and even deaths. In fact, to many these seasonal events were known as *kenka-nenbutsu* (*kenka* means 'fight', 'quarrel', or 'dispute').

There was also a less openly confrontational side to the adventure. According to verbal accounts from the beginning of the century, this was still considered to be a privileged occasion for licentious behaviour, drinking, flirting. For young boys and girls this was said to be one of the best chances of the year for showing oneself, proving one's worth and acknowledging that of the others. It was a long-awaited prime time of the year for finding a partner in romance. There are records that show how the Tokugawa regime, once when it was firmly established and set on the absolute priority of order in society, decided to ban the *Dainenbutsu*, because of the boisterous, often quite violent incidents that repeatedly happened.

Whether *Dainenbutsu* continued to be organized, perhaps in a subdued form, after the feudal authorities outlawed it, is possible, but it disappeared from the written records. It was not until the Tokugawas had fallen from power (1867) that the official ban was rescinded.

Unfortunately, reliable historical records relating the circumstances of its revival are also lacking – until 1930. Then, all the different teams of *Dainenbutsu* which had re-emerged within the region formed an association among themselves to protect and strengthen the tradition, setting up their headquarters near the historical Saikagake in Hamamatsu. *Dainenbutsu* teams were registered, and a certain recognition of their respective spheres of influence and co-ordination of all their activities was planned. Since then, the total number of teams has been more or less stable, fluctuating between 70 and 80 in number, and cooperation between them has been smooth and peaceful. They hold a yearly general meeting in the month of June, with the participation of two representative members from each team.

In 1972, the city authorities in Hamamatsu decided to declare the *Dainenbutsu* an important cultural asset of the region, and to support its preservation. Ten years later, in 1982, a centre with an exhibition hall was opened close to the last stretch of the fatal gap of Saikagake that is still left open in the cityscape of Hamamatsu.

The *Dainenbutsu* appears to be a particular local development within the general *nenbutsu* tradition that had already implanted itself widely in the country since the Heian period. It permitted the application of the magical powers of Buddhism for pacifying the spirits of the dead through their salvation, *jōbutsu*, first and foremost for the purpose of improving people's lot on this side of the Great Divide. But this had also been the *raison d' être* and primary purpose of the pre-existing folk-religious custom of a seasonal *mushi-okuri* (see p. 94), with its concern for the collective purification of lingering effects associated with death.

All the teams which are actually active throughout Enshū are busy practising for about two weeks every year at the beginning of July before they are invited by those households in their respective areas of operation who are celebrating the first-*bon* for a dead relative, and wish to add a more public, spectacular and festive aura to the occasion. This contrasts with the original situation, when the *Dainenbutsu* was hamlet-based and automatically and indiscriminately visited all the families who had suffered death during the preceding year. Then each death, excluding those of infants and younger children who had not yet acquired any form of social status, called for a distinctive, public classification of the spirit into the social hierarchy of the other world. These distinctions were signalled by the *Dainenbutsu* chorus through its repertory of chants.

The *Dainenbutsu* are now hired performers called in from the outside primarily to add prestige to the family reputation. It is now principally 'used' by bereft families for celebrating socially prescribed ideals in death: the transformation of parents and grandparents into benevolent ancestors. The original attribute of driving spirits away, containing them, keeping them from turning into baleful ghosts with the show of Buddhist magic and physical vitality of the living are associations which today appear for the most part to be absent from people's minds.

The southern part of Morimachi, while it does not even have a single team of its own, still belongs geographically and culturally to the area of the *Dainenbutsu* tradition (Enshū). *Dainenbutsu* groups are called in from the neighbouring Hamma-Kita, and Toyōka to perform before the sumptuously decorated altars set up in the first-*bon* households.

The *Dainenbutsu*, having lost its basis within the hamlets, now operates on a much larger, and rather more businesslike scale, for a considerable fee. Officially, the cost of calling in the *Dainenbutsu* is around 100,000 yen. When a team has to travel long distances, transporting people and lots of baggage, the total expenses for the families with everything included can rise to around 300,000 yen. In this somewhat commercialized form that the resurrection of *Dainenbutsu* took in the mid-1920s, it has become an economic question of who can afford to have it visiting their homes. The demand for their services has then increased remarkably following the relative economic prosperity of the modern Japan, which has inflated middle-class identification out of all hitherto known proportions, even in the most isolated of mountain villages. Now, most families feel they should show that they, like everybody else, can afford the fullest honours for their dead.

The arrival of the *Dainenbutsu* still is a rare happening during *bon*, and attracts people in the hamlets, young and old. It turns their minds for a while away from their television sets and makes them gather in front of the first-*bon* altars in the courtyards of the hosting families, which then momentarily become the absolute centre of hamlet attention. Their middle-class status is affirmed and enhanced with this sort of conspicuous consumption since only the poorest families in the villages can neither afford to call in the *Dainenbutsu*, nor to rent the more magnificent first-*bon* decorations. Furthermore, in Morimachi, first *bon* among the better-off families have developed into sumptuous feasts of which the *Dainenbutsu* is but one aspect, albeit the most spectacular one. It is a demonstration of 'success in death', concluding the long process of funerary rites as practised by those who can afford it for establishing the socially good reputation of their 'honourable dead'.

## 4 *Kodomo-nenbutsu*

In the preceding passages we saw how the *Dainenbutsu* tradition which grew out of local communities tended towards a ritualized form of rivalry between neighbouring villages. Subsequently, the feudal authorities established law and order as the principal values in society. Consequently the carnival-like and violent exuberance that often accompanied the *Dainenbutsu* spectacles – ironically first introduced into the region to quell a growing unrest among the farming population – could no longer be tolerated, and it became the object of strict suppression. When it was finally lifted things were not the same in rural Japan, and the *Dainenbutsu* has never regained its former place in hamlet life. During the era of industrialization, cities started draining the countryside of the more mobile and turbulent parts of its population who might otherwise have resuscitated the *Dainenbutsu* as an outlet for their energies. But as we saw, the revival of this local tradition was accomplished through other means: namely, cultural revivalism and commercialization.

A miniaturized replica of the *Dainenbutsu* came into being in many hamlet communities in the Enshū region, and these were called *kodomo-nenbutsu*, or *kodomo-ren* (children's *nenbutsu*, or the children's team). Instead of adults, people started organizing groups of children for going around at the time of the *bon* festival. Neither historical records nor living memory can determine whether the *kodomo-nenbutsu* existed already in feudal times, perhaps as a popular way of disguising the *Dainenbutsu*, for defying the authorities, concealing it behind a more innocent and childlike appearance; or whether it started after the ban had been lifted as a hamlet substitute for 'the real thing'. Alternatively, the *kodomo-nenbutsu* might even have developed late in the Meiji era in response to the growing commercialization of the *Dainenbutsu* which in the pre-war period, as well as in the immediate post-war period, represented a luxury that none but the better-off families could permit themselves. Taking a somewhat unimaginative view of history, informants concluded that the *kodomo-nenbutsu* must have existed as a part of the local *bon* rituals from an early time or at least as long the oldest among them could remember. Between the two world wars, however, the *kodomo-nenbutsu*, like its adult counterpart, were interrupted everywhere. The former were then revived in many villages in the early 1950s, and enthusiastically carried out until the present time by successive groups of boys from third graders in primary school up to second graders in middle school.

An average *kodomo-nenbutsu* group consists of no less than ten to fifteen young boys, taught and trained by representatives from the *seinenkai*, the young-men's association of the hamlet, who often happen to be their fathers. After a period of occasional practices, back from the beginning of the month of *bon*, the groups start circulating in the afternoon and continue until late in the night of the 13, 14 and 15 August. First, they do the round of all the houses in the hamlet, and then they make a special visit to all the first-*bon* families in the vicinity, who often live well beyond the confines of the hamlet community to which the group belongs. The same 'first-*bon*' family can therefore be visited several times over these days by different groups, whether or not its own hamlet can pride itself of having one of its own. The sight and sound of these processions crisscrossing the area is therefore one of the things that gives colour to the *bon* festival in the countryside of southern Morimachi.

At the head of the procession goes the team leader, the oldest boy carrying a *jizō kasaboko*, a red, decorative parasol. Behind him then march a dozen or so younger boys, each carrying a paper lantern, and clad in white, which follows Chinese fashion in being the colour used for mourning, while their heads and faces are hidden from view under widebrimmed straw hats. At the end comes a wheeled cart pulled by one of the four or five adults, responsible for looking after the *kodomo-ren*. The boys take turns in sitting on the cart beating the big drum attached to the top of it. When they arrive at their destination, at the decorated home of a family celebrating its first *bon*, they line up in the courtyard, facing the special altar set up for the newly-dead on the inside and chant their songs. That part, strongly inspired by the Buddhist tradition of *nenbutsu* chanting, is similar to the adult *Dainenbutsu* performances, while the drum dances that are particularly a great pride of these latter are absent.

Formerly, the songs used by the *kodomo-ren* were five in number: first and foremost there was the '*Somosomo Enshū*' recalling the historical happenings that gave rise to the *Dainenbutsu*. Then, if the dead was the former male head of the household they chanted '*Oyawasan*'; this was replaced with '*Tsumawasan*' if it was the former mistress who was having her first *bon*. If, on the other hand the household was celebrating the first *bon* following the death of a child of the family, they sang a song entitled '*Hammachidori*'; finally, there was a song to be chanted by the local temple, the '*Terawasan*' for the repose of all the dead of the hamlet who were not particularly 'attended to' by any of the families in the hamlet. Today, the repertory has been reduced to only three: *Somosomo*, *Oyawasan*, and *Terawasan*.

The older among my informants claimed that in their childhood the participation in the *kodomo-ren* demanded much more endurance on the part of the children than now, and consequently that it used to be much richer in adventure. Since there was no electricity and the roads within the community were poorly developed the *kodomo-ren* had to thread its way through narrow paths between the rice fields and often got lost in the night, even though adults from the young-men's association were there to look after the children and lead the way. As with the earlier *Dainenbutsu*, after sunset during the days of *bon*, many young men and women used to follow 'their' group around, the occasion being a form of seasonal socializing across village boundaries. The drinking of sake and the presence of young women also stimulated the desire for showing off. Since there were several *kodomo-ren* belonging to the same vicinity, these different groups would meet on the way to the different localities, and these anticipated encounters permitted largely ritualized forms of competitions, conflict, and fights, but also for romantic dalliance between the sexes.

The older among my informants seemed to agree that before the war there was no attempt made to imprint on the children-participants in the *kodomo-nenbutsu* any special religious understanding of the words of the different songs, nor the general purpose in carrying out the *kodomo-nenbutsu*. It was just one of those things that children at a certain age should do, and do properly, for the honour of their elders, and of the whole hamlet community. It was therefore considered to be of primary importance to memorize the words of the songs, learn how to deliver them at the top of one's voice, and how to beat a powerful rhythm on the drums. Whatever the possible religious sentiments that may have been enjoyed on the receiving end, (in the first-*bon* families), the *kodomo-ren* as a minor institution within the hamlet communities served among other roles that of a prolonged rite of passage from childhood into youth. One of the things that went into the training of these children in one of the villages studied, was a lone run in the dark of the night from the community hall to a location in the collective graveyard on a wooded hill a little outside the hamlet. The child had to bring back a handful of ashes from a ditch used for cremations which was inside the graveyard. Only those who had the courage to accomplish this were eligible for the team that year.

## 5 *Mushi-okuri*

Before the introduction and massive use of insecticides in modern times, the threat of damage done to crops by insects constituted one of the principal, if not the major source of anxiety among the agricultural population of Japan. Occasionally, imbalances in the ecological system gave rise to an explosive increase in the different species of locusts which descended on the rice fields as if from nowhere and which would totally ruin the harvest. These tended to be associated in folk belief all over Japan with the evil workings of an 'unnatural' death occurring within the community. To counter this most dreaded of collective disasters, a variety of rituals commonly designated as *mushi-okuri* or 'the sending off of the insects' are to this day organized in local communities all over Japan. With the participation of all the households in the hamlet, gigantic dolls are made out of rice straw. These are then burned while chanting *nenbutsu* songs. In other places, farmers also make boats from straw, provide them with offerings of pounded rice-cakes, and send them floating on a river or out on the waves at the seashore. Either way, these are symbolic gestures aiming at ridding the community of the danger from 'bad deaths' that accumulates in its midst throughout the year.

In Morimachi informants also brought up the subject of *mushi-okuri*. I was told that in the eastern, and somewhat isolated Amagata, until about twenty years ago farmers used to get together for a *mushi-okuri* around the midsummer *bon* festival. Dressed in white, carrying gongs and drums, and chanting refrains from *nenbutsu* songs, they circled all the major rice fields belonging to their hamlet in a procession. In the end, they proceeded to a point held to separate the community from their immediate neighbours, beyond which the nuisance was then symbolically expelled. In Otomaru I have observed the most simple form of *mushi-okuri* which was still being practised. Around the time of *bon* a representative member from each family takes two logs of firewood to a gathering.[7] One is brought to a designated place by the local Buddhist temple, and the other by the Shintō shrine. After sunset, these are then burned while chanting a *nenbutsu* song. These mid-summer bonfires are called *mushi-okuri*.

## 6  *Segaki: tera-segaki/uchi-segaki*

*Tera-segaki* is a name for a ritual that takes place in the local temple in each hamlet around the time of the *bon* festival. It is organized for the other-worldly benefits of all their dead. The Buddhist priests in the vicinity collaborate amongst themselves (normally in groups of three) for the organization of this major rite of the religious calendar. The date for holding the *tera-segaki* in Morimachi falls on any of the three days of *bon*.

The old men of the hamlet elected to the temple committee set up a high altar on several levels just inside the main entrance to the temple, facing the enshrined Buddhist divinity. On it are placed a number of memorial tablets: those of the Buddhist priests who have served in the past and died in the temple; tablets for the war-dead, the war heroes; tablets for those who have died without progeny; tablets for those who died young; for those who died in accidents; for the *mizuko*, i.e., aborted or miscarried foetuses; and finally all the temporary tablets for all those who have died during the year in the hamlet. All around these tablets, placed on the middle of the altar, facing the Buddha, are arranged offerings in great quantities, mainly agricultural products from the region: sacks of rice, vegetables, fruits. At the end of *tera-segaki*, the food offerings are left as a donation to the temple. Two small containers, one with water and the other with incense powder, are also placed next to an incense burner before the memorial tablets.

In principle, there should be at least one representative member from each family in the hamlet in attendance. The actual participation varies greatly from one hamlet to another, but everywhere it is the occasion of the year when the greatest numbers of people from the hamlet appear at the temple. The families which have had a death in the family during the year are everywhere expected to attend to the event, all their adult members dressed in black. Participation on this occasion is of a major importance to the temple priest, since each household should make a contribution to the temple, the amount of which differs according to each household's status within the hamlet.

All those who are gathered are seated on straw mats inside the temple, between the *honzon* and the special *segaki* altar. The temple priest dressed in his colourful ceremonial gowns is seated in front of the Buddha, facing the tablets on the temporary altar. Assisted by his colleagues from the neighbouring hamlets he chants several sutras. When the priests have finished their merit-making religious services, all those present finish by lining up, passing one after the other in front of the altar making offerings of incense and water before the memorial tablets.

The other form of *segaki* that takes place in Morimachi around *bon*, is the *uchi-segaki*. For the most part it is in fact a household ritual, a supplement to the *tera-segaki*. It ends the funerary process with one last rite offered to the dead in his home by the temple priest on behalf of those of the families wanting to emphasize the importance of the occasion at the time of *bon*. A significant part of it, though, takes place in public, just outside the courtyard of the family house, clearly emphasizing the passage of the dead from the family domain to the other world. *Taitaki* is a name of this concluding part of the *uchi-segaki*. It is the only aspect of the ceremony that marks it off from the *tera-segaki*. In both instances, the priest chants sutras before memorial tablets arranged specially for the occasion. In the case of the *uchi-segaki* these tablets are naturally confined to the 'family dead' which should benefit particularly from the occasion, gaining in spiritual merits in the other world. After the chanting of the sutras, the priest, and then all present make an offering of water and incense to the dead spirits. Then, all present go outside for the *taitaki*. Before the entrance, a construction made of three tall branches of bamboo, knit together in order to make a stand for the small altar-shelf of braided straw has been set up (always prepared by the women of the family). On this sacred shelf they place the temporary tablet for the recently deceased family member, along with some offerings of cooked rice and vegetables, incense and water in tiny containers and an incense pot. In front of this altar 108 pieces of pine are arranged on the ground with regular intervals of about 10cm. These are then burnt while the priest chants a sutra facing the altar. The 108 pieces of wood represent the 108 *bonnō*, human passions, earthly desires, or the different attachments that so far have been obstacles for the salvation of the dead and delayed his passage into the other world. When the priest has finished chanting the sutra before the altar and the 108 *bonnō* have been destroyed on the ground the male members of the family remove the altar and also burn it. Burning branches of fresh bamboo tend to crack loudly. These noises are taken as signs of gratitude from the other world, showing the dead's gratefulness for having been so piously attended to by his descendants.

## 7 *Bon odori* in Kusagaya

In every hamlet of Morimachi people organize outdoor dancing at the time of the *bon* festival, called *bon odori*. The dancing starts after sunset, and lasts for about two hours. Though these dances are quite simple in nature it is commonly held that they should be taught and prepared beforehand so that everybody can join in without feeling the slightest need for embarrassment when the time comes.

In one of the hamlets where I did fieldwork in 1989, Kusagaya in Sonoda, close to the geographical centre of Morimachi, the ten members nominated for the local committee, *chōnaikai*, and represent-atives from the local women's association, *fujinkai*, decided to invite a knowledgeable teacher from a neighbouring community for the demon-strations of the *bon-odori* dances. Then the women's association in the hamlet was put in charge of organizing the subsequent public practises of the dances. The visiting teacher demonstrated a repertoire of fifteen different forms of dances, from which seven were selected to be taught and danced that year.[8]

At the opening of the modern era in Japan, the dances were still performed in many places to the musical accompaniment of drums, gongs, and flutes, and often to the chanting of religiously inspired songs. At present, the musical accompaniment that goes with *bon odori* is entirely secularized. In the summer of 1989, *bon odori* took place after sunset on the second day of *bon*. The younger among the men in the hamlet took turns in beating a big drum placed on a wooden scaffold towering in the middle. The drum-beat followed the rhythm of popular songs played over loudspeakers. Seven songs were played in succession, one after the other, and each time the pattern of dancing changed slightly according to the seven chosen forms of dancing, the *kata*.[9] When they had finished one round of all the songs they returned to the beginning again, three times over. The songs used in the modern period are mainly popular folk ballads which are familiar to all the participants. Highly sentimental local songs praising the natural and social beauty of the hometown are also commonly used. Lately, title-songs from TV programmes for children ('Bungakyakka', 'Doraemon', 'Panman', etc.) have started appearing, enriching and rejuvenating the repertoire.

Whatever *bon odori* may have represented in the past, today it is just one of these seasonal events for socializing, like the local hamlet festival and the autumnal sports meeting. It is one of those privileged occasions for demonstrating in an idealized form the collective nature of existence in the hamlet. It should give expression of the joyful (*akarui*), the wholehearted (*isshokenmei*), and the earnest (*majime*), spirit which unites its members. On these privileged occasions the hegemony of the group tolerates no signs of resistance, masking the fact that the participation in these events is of limited interest to some individuals, or even to whole sections of the local population. At the time of *bon odori* this was revealed to me in what at first struck me as a curiously reserved enthusiasm for *bon odori* among many of the younger housewives I questioned. Yet, they were the ones supposed to be its organizers!

From the women's point of view the problem involved in the timing of the *bon odori* is a thorny one. They may enjoy participating in the preparations and the practices that take place at the beginning of the month of August. The actual dancing on the *bon* festival is another matter. While it should ideally be an expression of hamlet harmony, in fact many of the younger women would much prefer to be absent from it. The *bon* festival is traditionally the time, when women who have married into the community are permitted, if not expected, to return to visit their parents' families. If they are also expected to show up for the hamlet *bon odori*, they are obliged to cut short their *sato-gaeri*. This might possibly explain the striking lack of expression on the faces of many of the kimono-clad, younger housewives moving somewhat ghost-like around the drum tower.

In Morimachi people undoubtedly view these dances simply as a form of entertainment without any religious significance whatsoever. When asked about its general connection to the *bon* festival of the dead, they explained that since so many people return to their hometown over the days of *bon* it is a good time for a gathering of all, young and old, for a recreative round of collective dancing. Japanese folklorists seem to suggest on the other hand, that *bon odori* has an ancient history within Japanese folk traditions, in which it has been, and still is in some places, associated not only with the most evident desire for midsummer socializing, but also with the more abstract purpose of pacifying the spirits of the dead who were seen as crowding the world of the living at that time of year, through the collective demonstration of vitality and joyous harmony (Hagiwara and Sudō 1985:30).

## 8 The Gion festival at Yamana *jinja*

We have seen how a particular form of communal effort at purification from the evils of death in Morimachi, the *mushi-okuri*, has all but disappeared from the local culture. If ever there was a time when it was a common practice, it has now fallen into oblivion almost everywhere, leaving but a passing trace here and there, on written records or in old people's memories. Yet, the legend about the historical conditions which gave birth to the *Dainenbutsu* strikingly reflects a similar underlying mentality and view of the relationship between the world of the living and the world of the dead. The Gion festival on 16 and 17 July at Yamana shrine in Iida on the south-eastern side of Morimachi can be seen as at least partially giving expression to similar views of the world.[10] The Gion in the name of the festival is borrowed from one of the most famous of the innumerable festivals in Japan, the Kyoto Gion festival. Its origins go back to around the middle of the Heian period (794–1185) when the official worship of revengeful ghosts appears to have become one of the most important factors of religious life in the empire. The intrigues and power struggles between factions and clans bent on gaining the upper hand in imperial politics often claimed many victims. Some of the most famous personalities, courtiers and imperial ministers at the time, were driven into fatal exile, or assassinated in their homes (Borgen 1986:270–89). Anger at being submitted to such a disgraceful death, combined with the extraordinary power that these dignitaries formerly held, was believed to turn them into the most terrifying of revengeful ghosts (*onryō*) (Borgen 1986:325). The evil doings of these 'great ones' when they turned their savage anger back upon civilization were indubitably read from disastrous happenings which were visited upon human society after their deaths: disastrous fires, murderous plagues, multiplications of insects resulting in poor harvests, starvation, and so on. To ward off the immensity of these ill-effects and the danger they posed to social stability, the Heian authorities resorted to posthumous rehabilitations of the victimized dignitaries. They were declared 'Venerable Spirits' (*goryō*) and public, grand-scale rites of pacification (*goryō-e*) were organized in their honour. Later these gradually developed into the Gion festival. When even the *goryō-e* proved to be insufficient, some of the *goryō* were furthermore enshrined and declared major divinities henceforth to be worshipped at some of the most famous shrines in the city, such as the famous Tenmangū (Tenjin), and the twin shrines of Kami-and Shimo-Goryō *jinja*.

The Gion festival in one form or another then became a model for a large number of festivals all around the country (Yoneyama 1989:420), like the Gion at Yamana shrine in Iida. These two Gion festivals share the original aim of purification from the affliction of death. As they exist today, however, they differ radically not only in their scale, but also in their character. The Gion in Iida in Morimachi is a local festival organized by and for the inhabitants of six local hamlets around the middle of July. Every single soul in these villages is expected to be an active participant, while the role of the passive spectator-visitor, so overwhelmingly dominating at the peak of the festivities in Kyoto, hardly existed in this rural area (until, that is, the recent appearance of the anthropologist, and the occasional amateur photographer from the big cities).

The Gion at Yamana shrine has three components which together give spectacular weight to the two days of its duration. The first of these is common to the vast majority of festivals, urban and rural, all over Japan: the annual worship with the attendance and offerings from key representatives of the parishioners. This is followed by the descent of the divinity from its abode in the shrine onto the sacred objects, *shintai*, *mikoshi*, that are then carried around solemnly in a procession through the community to a specific location, from where it is again transported back to its shrine in a procession at the end of the festival. In Iida, the procession leads the divinity (Susano-wo-no-mikoto) from Yamana shrine, to a much smaller outer edifice at a distance of about 500 metres in the vicinity said to be occupied by an unnamed female divinity. This yearly one-night visit of the male to the female, a familiar theme from Japanese legends and lore, lends an overall aura of fertility worship to the festival. The composition of the procession and the order within it reflect admirably the way the local inhabitants like to think authority and prestige should distinguish and adorn their world. In the front are the elders who have already retired from the most important roles of leadership in the different villages, some of them dressed up as supernatural beings, or as dignitaries from feudal times. They are then followed by a crowd of middle-aged men – respectable citizens, local administrators and entrepreneurs – dressed as feudal soldiers and carrying the *shintai*. The rear, by contrast, is made up of the officially powerless younger generation of womenfolk. These, however, are carefully distinguished after their respective stations within the reproductive process: first, the ones carrying babies who were born during the year; behind them walk all those presently pregnant; and then at the very end, all newly-married couples so far 'unripe'.

The second most important component, and the one that to most of the local inhabitants gives the real festive flair to the occasion, is a sort of competition between the hamlets in 'travelling feasts'. Each of the six villages that unite for the festival has its own a huge festival float (*yatai*) in which they invest much of their pride, but also a lot of their money! It is normally acquired through important financial 'offerings' on the part of all of the village families who purchase it collectively. They compete with each other in decorating them with lacquered, sculpted and engraved surfaces, and scenes from famous Kabuki plays. The mammoth wagons are paraded through the community during the days of the festival. From the morning hours to midnight all the young men, children and teenagers uniformed in their traditional festival attire, boisterously shouting '*wasshoi, wasshoi*' while pulling the floats, their mountainous loads, zigzag here and there, preferably through each others' neighbourhoods. They are accompanied by a captivating tune which is endlessly repeated on a flute, and the young men of course are appropriately intoxicated from sake and beer. The stories of the encounters of these movable feasts recall the socializing that supposedly took place formerly among the different *Dainenbutsu*, or *kodomo-nenbutsu* related above.

The last of the three main components of the festival is a thoroughly traditional form of entertainment (*geinō*), offered to the divinity on an elevated stage in the precincts in front of the shrine. These are the so-called *gagaku* and *bugaku*, among the oldest forms of music and theatrical dances known in Japan. It is held that originally these were forms of court entertainment imported from the continent during Nara and Heian periods. According to local records the art of *bugaku* and *gagaku* was first introduced at Yamana shrine the fifth year of Meiō (1496) from Tennōji, the oldest Buddhist temple in the country located in Ōsaka, also renowned for safeguarding this tradition. At Yamana shrine, while the *gagaku* music is played by adults, all the dances are performed by children, which is contrary to *bugaku* as it is known in the city. A further remarkable thing about these dances is not only how they have been passed on as a part of the local tradition at this small shrine for nearly 500 years, but also how in the process they have been partially adapted to the local Gion mentality, or rather, to the world-view of this rice-growing peasant society. Among the eight dances transmitted there is for example one, danced second-to-last, late in the night, called '*Tōrō*', or The Praying Mantis, unique to the *bugaku* of Yamana shrine. In it the dancers perform in costumes of these predatory insects which are believed to keep at bay a variety of other more destructive insects. Such imagery was not born in the aristocratic circles which first introduced the dances into the country. It gives expression to a deep-rooted insecurity before the forces of nature which has haunted the imagination of Japanese farmers since antiquity.

While the '*Tōro*' and the last dance, 'The taming of the bad lion' ('*Udenjishi*') are being played and danced, the six floats that had so far moved erratically around in the community in their competitive merriment now start entering the precincts of the shrine one by one for a concerted climactic end to the festival. It takes the form of the young men frantically dashing forward in a deafening, indistinguishable hubbub of the different festival noises pulling their floats at a frightful speed, one behind the other around the elevated stage where the posed calm of the *gagaku* and the *bugaku* by contrast attain a strikingly other-worldly appearance.

## CONCLUSIONS

Rituals are commonly characterized by a subtle interplay of bifurcation in their socio-cultural nature. In other words, they not only serve social functions but also carry symbolic meanings. 'Rituals are events that combine the properties of statements and actions' (Bloch 1986:181). In this chapter I have attempted to relate some of the collective actions engaged in by people in the rural communities where I did my fieldwork in Japan. It now remains to decipher the statements implied.

The totality of death rituals in Morimachi seems to arrange itself into two distinct systems. First there is the contemporary system of rites of death which engages people as representatives of their households all over Japan. It focuses on the articulation of individuality in death, and its progressive integration into an idealized image of the family and the descent-group. It permits individual members of the family in their death to progressively feed into the ancestors represented by their tablets in the family altar, their collective grave, and in an outer shrine as tutelary divinity (*yashikigami*), etc.

The other system is made up of the rituals that have been the subject of this paper. It demonstrates a concern for the collectivity of the dead in the hamlets. Through it they are integrated into a distinct global category identified with the local community, and that very identification is associated with the idea of death being under collective control. Here, 'death' is conceived of as a fearsome intruder gradually infiltrating the community from the ominous other-world of defilement ('*tokoyo*', '*nenokuni*'). Only the most 'diplomatic', concerted response to the insidious character of death's onslaught among the living can protect the collectivity and assure the victory of the regenerative forces of life. People do 'welcome' the dead all over Japan at the opening of the *bon* festival ('*mukaebi*','*bondana*', '*bonkazari*', etc.), but that sort of unambiguously positive gesture is reserved for 'their dead', the dead spirits of their particular household. All the death rites reported in this paper on the other hand seemed to be coloured primarily by a collective riposting to the forces of death. The significant accent falls primarily on 'pacifying', 'entertaining', or 'consoling' the spirits of the dead with the help of these rituals, and thereby sending them off cordially, if not expelling them out of the community at the end of the festivities.

Sir Edmund Leach (1961) wrote in the early 1960s a memorable paper on the social construction of 'time'. He pointed out that practically everywhere two different notions were operative, picturing 'time' as irreversible or as a repetitive duration. The conceptions underlying the entire system of Japanese death rituals can be outlined as two alternative elaborations permitting a synthesis of Leach's elementary notions of time.

Funerary rites in Japan are most commonly concerned with the death of individual members of households in local communities. These gradually accumulate their spiritual merit through the passage of time, and finally converge with the anonymous plurality of deified ancestors. They become tutelary gods ('*uchi-gami*', '*yashiki-gami*', '*ji-no-kami*', etc.) watching over the seasonal regeneration of the resources of life at the disposition of each household (linear time 'bent' into cyclical time).

The particular nature of the Japanese rites of death presented in this paper appear as a negative inversion of the sentiments ideally invested in the household rites for the dead now observed all over Japan. From the perspective which embraces the whole of the hamlet the nefarious destruction of death is conceived of as accumulating within the 'total' history of the community, particularly 'bad deaths' brought about by social and natural disasters leaving their scars on collective memory. Contrary to the view of the gradual evolution and transformation of death within the household here its impact is perceived of as accumulating in the *courte durée* of the annual cycles.

Death takes its toll from the community by striking here and there within it throughout the successive seasons of the year. The midsummer *bon* festival is the moment when the accumulative process is interrupted through the ritual intervention of the collectivity (or its representative members). By joining in rituals that give cognizance to the onslaught of death amongst themselves, it is as if the villagers domesticate and expel it momentarily beyond the boundaries of their finite world. Death is seen as a burden that accumulates through time calling for a collective effort for throwing it off, thereby assuring a healthy respite for the growth of life. But it is a Sisyphean undertaking since no sooner is the festival over than 'death' starts creeping in again, stroke by stroke, for a whole new round.

In Japanese rural communities such as Morimachi two opposed but complementary statements about the nature of death seem thus to be implied in ritual action. The one is primarily of a positive nature idealizing the household unit through a cycle of rituals that I call 'cycle of deification'. The other gives expression for a primarily negative conception of death engaging the entire community in a seasonal action that I prefer to call 'cycle of purification'. Where these two cycles intersect ('*hatsubon*'/'*bon*') the Japanese system of death rituals in its entirety is brought into view.

Finally, a few words on the historical context of the global structure of Japanese rites of death outlined above. Following the example of some recent studies on rituals (Tambiah 1979; Ariès 1981; Bloch 1986) it is worth asking whether the social functions and the symbolic meanings relevant to collective rites of death in Morimachi have changed through time.

Historians have worked on the pre-Buddhist period in Japan showing how an elaborate system of imperial funerary rites was the focal point for political, administrative, and even artistic life in the archaic empire (Macé 1986; Ebersole 1989). Then this ancient regime in Japan, organized around the gigantic burial mounds (*kofun*), disintegrated with the advent of Buddhism and the introduction of a Chinese form of administration. The result was a most radical break, a metamorphosis of social and cultural life of the ruling class. Buddhism provided a captivating new cosmology and ritual sophistication, Confucianism taught the Japanese aristocracy, and the *samurai* elite, who had become the rulers of society, to invest their dead with the ultimate value of their progressively Sinicized culture: 'filial piety'.

As for funerary practices and conceptions of death among the common people of Japan prior to the Heian period (794–1185) nothing can be assertained. It has been convincingly argued (Komatsu 1989:104) that the tendency to associate the origins of evil in society with the workings of dead spirits has existed in Japan since antiquity. All through history, as a part of a cosmological undercurrent among the common people in Japan, the dead seem thus to have been projected as an ominous threat to the living. Such would have been the dominating image of the dead until the Meiji 'restoration' (1867), when the entire population underwent a massive 'samuraization'. A part of that process was the internalization for the entire population of the Confucian teaching to invest one's dead with ultimate values. But if the Meiji era brought about a turn of the tables in favour of the dead, now being adopted as venerable ancestors in even the most depraved of households, the darker, more archaic side to their character survived implicitly within a variety of seasonal rites all over the country. An example thereof is the dual system of rites of death in Morimachi.[11]

## NOTES

1  The research in Japan on which this paper is based was carried out at various times between 1982 and 1989. The first part of it was made possible by grants from The Japan Foundation and Japan Society for the Promotion of Science. I am grateful to both these bodies for their generous support.

2  For the ancient period, the major contributions in Western languages are Macé 1986, and Ebersole 1989. Smith's *Ancestor Worship in Contemporary Japan* (1974) contains a historical account and an analysis of ritual life based on the author's own anthropological research. A great number of Japanese scholars have written on the theme and much of that material has been collected and published in important series like *Sōsō bosei kenkyū shūsei*, and *Sōsō to bosei*. One more highly noteworthy collection of papers on ancestor worship and funerary rites is to be found in *Bukkyō minzokugaku taikei*.

3 Jūsan Butsu: 'Ichi ni Fudō/ – Namu amida bu, Namu amida butsu, Namuamida – / Ni ni Shaka/ – Namu amida bu, Namu amida butsu, Namu amida – / San ni Monju/–Namu. . . etc. / Yon ni Fugen/ – Namu . . . etc. /Go ni Jizō/Namu . . . etc. / Roku ni Miroku/ – Namu . . . etc. / Nana ni Rakushi/–Namu. . . etc. / Hachi ni Kannon/ – Namu . . . etc. / Kyū ni Seishi/–Namu . . . etc./ Jū ni Amida/ – Namu. . . etc./Jūichi ni Ashuku/ – Namu . . . etc. / Jūni ni Dainichi/– Namu . . . etc. / Jūsan ni Kokuzō/ – Namu . . . etc.

4 The Japanese National Encyclopedia has this to say about *goeika*:

> A form of Buddhist music. Also called *junreika* (pilgrims' songs), it is performed by devout pilgrims on their visits to a certain number of holy places. While shaking small bells, *rei*, *suzu*, they chant words of grieving in sorrowful voices. Like another closely related genre, the *wasan* (Buddhist religious songs of the common people, praising the merits of Buddhas and holy men), the verses of *goeika* are written in *wabun*, that is in Japanese writing without the Chinese characters. [They] . . . describe sentiments of belief and sorrow and visions occasioned by the separation from the deceased. The origins of *goeika* are in fact unknown, but they are believed to have developed along with the so-called Kūya-nenbutsu. In the widest sense of the term in common use, the *goeika* are not limited to the pilgrims' songs, but include also a mixture of popularized *wasan* blended with refrains from ballads, resulting in a genre sometimes so-called *utawasan* or *hanawasan*.

5 See D.P. Martinez's Chapter 8 in this volume.

6 Celebrations of Buddha's enlightenment (Jūdo-e), birth (Nehan-e), and death (Hanamatsuri), and the festival of *Kannon Bosatsu*.

7 In this part of the region people follow the practice common in the eastern part of Honshū to celebrate a *shin-bon*, or a 'new-bon' over 13–16 July in accordance with the 'new' calendar adopted in late Meiji period. The inhabitants in the southern part of Morimachi celebrate *kyū-bon*, or 'old-bon', over 13–16 August.

8 In fact, *bon odori* is a generic name for a style of dancing. It refers to a relatively free selection of combined bodily movements from a set of about ten possibilities. These are danced to the rhythm of simple melodies, some of which give their name to a corresponding dance form.

9 1 *Bungakyakka*; 2 *Zumbaondo*; 3 *Hana no bon odori*; 4 *Sakura ondo*; 5 *Hi no kunidaiko*; 6 *Akita bon uta*; 7 *Morimachi uta*.

10 'The word *gion* derives from a Chinese abbreviation for the Sanscrit word *jetavanavihâra*, which in India originally meant a temple built

for Siddhartha Gautama, the founder of Buddhism' (Yoneyama 1989:419).

11 As for the urban milieu, yet another chapter may have opened up in the history of the dead in Japan with the 'de-samuraization' of the population in the immediate post-war period and the progressive disintegration of the *'ie'*-institution as a building block of society. Many new religions' emphasis on acknowledging the punitive nature of unhappy spirits among the dead in the family, as well as the remarkable growth in the macabre worship of *'mizuko'*, the spirits of aborted foetuses, in latterday Japan are but the more explicit among many other signs of new perceptions.

## BIBLIOGRAPHY

Amino Yoshihiko, Manabu Tsukamoto, Hirofumi Tsuboi and Noboru Miyata (1989) *Rettōbunka saikō*, Tokyo: Nihon Editāsukuru.

Ariès, Phillipe (1979) *L'homme devant la mort*, Paris: Edition du Seuil.

Bloch, Maurice (1986) *From Blessing to Violence*, London: Cambridge University Press

Bloch, Maurice and Jonathan Parry (eds) (1982) *Death and and the Regeneration of Life*, London: Cambridge University Press.

Borgen, Robert (1986) *Sugawara no Michizane and the Heian Court*, Cambridge Mass.: Harvard University Press.

Chamberlain, Basil Hall (1982) *The Kojiki*, trans., Tokyo: Charles E. Tuttle Company.

Dobbins, James C. (1989) *Jōdo Shinshū: Shin Buddhism in Medieval Japan*, Bloomington: Indiana University Press.

Ebersole, Gary (1989) *Ritual Poetry and the Politics of Death in Early Japan*, New Jersey: Princeton University Press.

Gorai Shigeru (1966) *Bukkyō bungaku kenkyū, 'Asobobe-ka'*, Tokyo: Hōzōkan.

Haga Noboru (1987) *Sōgi no rekishi*, Tokyo: Yūsankaku Shuppan.

Hagiwara Hidesaburō and Sudō Tsutomu (eds) (1985) *Nihon Shūkyō minzoku zuten*, vol. 2, *Sōsō to kuyō* (Illustrated dictionary of Japanese religions, vol. 2, funeral rites and services for the dead), Kyoto: Hōzōkan.

Harootunian, H.D. (1988) *Things Seen and Unseen, Discourse and Ideology in Tokugawa Nativism*, Chicago: The University of Chicago Press.

Hertz, Robert (1960) *Death and The Right Hand*, trans. Rodney and Claudia Needham, Aberdeen: Cohen & West.

Hori Ichirō (1971) *Manyōshū taisei, 'Manyōshū ni arawareta sōsei to takaikan'*, Tokyo: Heibonsha.

Komatsu Kazuhiko (1989) *Akureiron, – Ikai kara no messeji*, Tokyo: Seidosha.

Konō Jun (1981) *Enshū Dainenbutsu – Toshishakai no shūkyō*, Tokyo: Tamarutokuzenhen.

Kokumin Hyakkajiten (1969) Tokyo: Heibonsha.

Leach, E.R. (1961) 'Two essays concerning the symbolic representation of time', *Rethinking Anthropology*, London: Athlone Press.

Macé, François (1986) *La Mort et les funérailles dans le Japon ancien*, Paris: Publications Orientalistes de France.

Ooms, Herman (1976) 'A Structural Analysis of Japanese Ancestor Rites', in William H. Newell (ed.) *Ancestors*, Paris: Mouton.

Sasaki Kōkan (1989) *Sei to juryoku: Nihon shūkyō no jinruigaku josetsu*, Tokyo: Seikyōsha.

Shibata Motomu (1988) *Sōsō bosei kenkyū shūsei, 'Kyori no nenbutsu'*, Tokyo: Meichō Shuppan.

Smith, Robert J. (1974) *Ancestor Worship in Contemporary Japan*, Calif.: Stanford University Press.

*Sōsō bosei kenkyū shūsei* (1979) (5 vols) I, Tokyo: Meichō Shuppan.

*Sōsō to bosei* (1979) (10 vols) I, Tokyo: Meigen Shobō.

Takeda Chōshu (1957) *Sosensūhai: Minzoku to rekishi* (Ancestor workship: An ethno-history), Tokyo: Heirakuji Shoten.

—— (1976) *Nihonjin no 'ie' to shūkyō* (The Japanese 'ie' and religion), Tokyo: Hyōronsha.

Tambiah, S.J. (1979) A *Performative Approach to Ritual*, London: Proceedings of the British Academy LXV:113–69.

Tsuboi Hirofumi (1979) [1931] 'Nohonminzoku no tagensei', *Nihonminzokugaku 124*.

*Yanagita Kunio (1978) [1929] Sōsō shūzoku goi*, Tokyo: Kokushokan Gyōkai.

—— (1946) *'Senzo no hanashi'*, *Yanagita Kunio* 10, Tokyo: Shode.

—— (1978) [1975] 'Sōsei enkaku shiryō', *Yanagita Kunio* 15:479–520, Tokyo: Kokushokan Gyōkai.

—— (1978) 'Sōsei enkaku shiryō', *Yanagita Kunio* 15:520–49.

—— (1978) [1931] *Sōei no enkaku shiryō* (Material for a history of funeral customs), Teibon Yanagita Kunio XV:520–49.

Yoneyama Toshinao (1989) 'Soothing vengeful souls: the origin of summer festivals', *Japan Quarterly*, XXXVI (4) 418–23.

# 5 Orchestrated reciprocity
## Belief versus practice in Japanese funeral ritual

*Jane M. Bachnik*

Ancestors seem far from the epicentres of economic – and even socio-cultural – attention on contemporary Japan. But as the primary religious focus for the vast majority of Japanese (Smith 1974; Hamabata 1990), the ancestors – and the rituals given them by the living – are undeniably important. One clue to the relative lack of attention paid to this topic by researchers may be in the kind of communication the subject of ancestors seems to evoke. A disconcerting gap is often evident in researchers' questions about the meaning of ancestors, and the house-holders' professed lack of knowledge about that same meaning. House-holders very commonly claim to know nothing about the ancestors (Ooms 1967; Smith 1974; Plath 1964; Hamabata 1983; 1990). As a householder remarked to Ooms

> We are deeply bound by custom; the meaning escapes us and neither good nor bad results follow from the veneration or neglect of the ancestors.

And another:

> It is a bother and does not have any special meaning, but I probably will make the offerings. Doesn't one do these things naturally?
>
> (Ooms 1967:298–300)

Householders also profess to know little about the meaning of their spiritual practices. Hamabata reports that when he asked what the various plants arranged in the *bon* altars signified, 'no one was quite sure. They just "did it," year after year. Hasegawa *sensei* told me that if I really wanted to know, he would introduce me to folklorists' (1990:72).

But we must ask whether the householders truly do not know about the meaning of their beliefs and practices, or whether researchers are missing the point of the householders' answers. It appears that researchers and householders are speaking past one another, and Hamabata himself comes to this realization:

> After they performed some rite pertaining to death and ancestorhood, I would collar my informants and ask, "Do you really believe that the dead still continue to exist, that they are around somewhere?" Invariably, the answers would be to the effect: "Gee, I wonder." Or, "I don't know." Makoto Moriuchi's irritable reply, however, seemed right on target: "It really doesn't matter, does it?" Makoto was absolutely right. I was barking up the wrong tree.
>
> (Hamabata 1990:83)

Hamabata views this problem as a disparity between *objective* standards for knowledge about belief or disbelief versus the *subjective* reality of ritual experience.[1] Plath (1964) similarly links the ancestors to polarities of emotion, which he opposes to beliefs. But the problem may not be attributable simply to a focus on one versus the other term in a dualized set. Rather, we should instead problematize the way in which 'beliefs' and 'emotions' have been dualized in the first place. The meaning of ancestor rituals has largely been pursued through objectified accounts of the beliefs and meanings represented by the ritual practices, and the householders have not been able to supply these accounts. But the possibility also exists that the reason householders cannot supply objective meanings for their beliefs and practices is not because the rituals have no meanings for them, nor because they are 'subjective', but because ancestor rituals for them depend on a different kind of meaning, which does not rely on polar dualities.

Meaning in ancestor ritual has been largely approached through an objectified, semantic perspective to identify a core of belief systems *behind* the ritual practices. In this paper I will approach Japanese ancestor ritual through a focus on a different kind of meaning – known as pragmatic or indexical meaning – developed in the course of the ritual practices themselves. At issue are two different approaches to meaning, which have significance beyond the perspectives themselves, for these in turn can be linked to different organizational perspectives on social life, and different relations to dualisms.

Pragmatic meaning represents a focus on relationships long considered as central to Japanese social life. Relationships have been linked to 'betweenness' (Nakane 1972); and to the components of *ningen* glossed as 'space between', 'space', 'interval' (Bachnik 1986). Instead of 'entities' that form the constituent parts of a ritual, or 'mechanisms' for carrying out social functions, I argue that relationships can be viewed as *the organizational dynamic that produces such rituals*. To put this another way, relationships can be linked to the organization of 'habitus' and 'practice' (Bourdieu 1977; 1990) to 'agency' and 'structure' (Giddens 1979; 1984) to pragmatic, or indexical meaning (Jakobson 1960 Silverstein 1976; 1979; Hanks 1990; 1992; Brenneis 1994) to phenomenological perspectives of being-in-the-world (Merleau-Ponty 1962; Heidegger 1962), and through these perspectives to the organization of context (Duranti and Goodwin 1992; Bachnik and Quinn 1994).

Consequently the orchestration of relationships in ancestor ritual requires a shift in focus to householder's perspectives on the ritual – perspectives that have been largely overlooked in the focus on eliciting beliefs, but which indicate exactly what they say – that meaning for them lies in performance of a ritual. Their statements on 'doing' the customs pose further questions: namely, exactly how do householders view ancestor ritual, and how do they relate meaning to performing (or 'doing') the ritual?

I am proposing a shift of focus towards meaning that centres on relationships and prioritizes 'betweenness' (and ambiguity) over perspectives on relationships as discrete 'entities' or categories. Such a shift can be linked beyond Japanese households and beyond Japan itself to a shift of focus that prioritizes pragmatic over semantic meaning. Hendry's discussions of 'wrapping' in Japanese society (1993; 1990; 1989) provide an excellent illustration of pragmatic meaning.[2] Hendry points to the extreme care Japanese take in wrapping objects – from groceries to gifts – and draws parallels between the wrapping of material objects and wrapping in myriad other aspects of life. Polite language (*keigo*) wraps social interactions; architecture wraps space; ritual wraps transitions from mundane to transcendent, and in the other direction, from polite and formal to mundane and even raucous. Hendry also cautions that attempting to penetrate a labyrinth of layers to reach the content behind the form is to utterly miss the point.

In effect, two approaches to meaning are at issue here: one which views the meaning of gifts, language, social order, and rituals in terms of a 'centre' or 'core' beneath the wrapping; and a second approach which focuses on the activity of wrapping itself, and the relations wrapping defines between social participants and their context.

In the first approach wrapping obfuscates content, as paper covers the gift, and must therefore be removed and discarded to reach the gift, as core meaning. But Hendry's point is that for Japanese, wrapping as a form of polite language, ritual, dress, architecture, hierarchy and so on – is itself closely linked to meaning. This approach regards meaning not as the core behind the wrapping but as linked with the wrapping itself; not as a 'thing' – a gift, a speech 'level', a 'layer' of clothing – but as 'an almost literal embedding of the "contents", whether of a gift or of talk [that] may well be more significant than the contents themselves' (Brenneis 1994:x). Wrapping focuses on the process of locating the social participants in the social context, and *of delineating the context itself in terms of the 'wrapping'*.

(Bachnik 1994a:4–5)

To return to the discussion of ancestor ritual above, the researchers were focusing on 'core' meanings or belief systems in their questions, while the householders spoke of meaning in relation to doing. They just 'did it', year after year. Let us explicate these two perspectives on meaning further.

The first approach follows a tradition in logic and linguistic semantics, in which meaning can be treated as an inherent property of a proposition regardless of its context of use. This approach also contributes to a focus on the 'core' meaning that is external to context, and underlies words and actions. The second approach, of pragmatic or indexical meaning, takes the situationally located relationships between speaker, hearer and scene as a starting point (Brenneis 1994:ix–x). Meaning is located in, rather than being 'about' the external. Rather than a 'core' meaning *behind* the context, indexical meaning actively constitutes the context (Silverstein 1976). Therefore, social life is not so much reflected in social practice as it is – at least partially – constituted through it (Bachnik 1994a; Brenneis 1994; Duranti and Goodwin 1992; Hanks 1992; Silverstein 1976). I emphasize that it is impossible to use language without both describing general meaning *and* relating what we describe to social context; the foci of both must be taken into account. The question here is how these perspectives are prioritized.

In considering pragmatic meaning the index is crucial.[3] Indexes are highly contextual, signalling spatiotemporal distance between two points in a context. Indexes do not name objects; they are used to identify and *measure* degrees, magnitudes, and numbers of specific observations. 'The barometer, plumb line, spirit level, weather vane, pendulum, and photometer are cited by C.S Peirce as respective indices of observed specific pressure, vertical and horizontal directions, wind direction, gravity, and star brightness' (Singer 1980:490).[4] Moreover, indexical meaning relates dualistic oppositions prominent in Western thought, which is why Peirce considered it fundamental in his attempts to move beyond these oppositions (1931–5).[5] In this sense 'betweenness' in

Japanese relationships can be viewed as indicating relationships 'between' polar dualisms as well as connections between individuals (Bachnik and Quinn 1994).

Also important to the process of indexing is the situated nature of pragmatic meaning, organized by deixis. Deixis comes from the Greek word *deiknumi* 'to point' or 'to indicate'.[6] 'Deictic expressions are terms such as "here" and "over there" which point to features of the surrounding contexts' (Duranti and Goodwin 1992:43). But Hanks (1992) points out that terms like 'here' and 'there', are made comprehensible by their relationship to an anchorpoint or 'ground' from which the relationship is being gauged. The latter is the zero-point from which all of the conversational indexes are anchored ('here', 'there'; 'now', 'then'; 'you', 'he', 'she', 'it'; and the use of past tense). In English, 'I' thus anchors the discourse, allowing the participants to follow the pointers. Deictic expressions are also known as 'shifters', since 'within a conversation the person identified as "I" changes as speakers change' (Hanks 1992:43).

Hanks specifies that each deictic word minimally has two components: the referent, which is the thing, individual, event, or spatial or temporal location pointed out, and the anchor point relative to which the referent is identified (1992:51). From his extensive research on the Yucatec Maya, Hanks further specifies that these two components are in a figure/ground relationship, so that 'deictic reference organizes the field of interaction into a foreground upon a background, as figure and ground organize the visual field' (1992:61).

While Hanks is primarily focusing on deictic organization in language, he nevertheless considers deixis a 'social construction par excellence' (1990:7), meaning that deixis is based on a shared construction of social reality between the participants.[7] Consequently, the concept of 'ground' can be expanded to include background knowledge the speakers share which allows them to understand the reference that is pointed out. As I have already discussed elsewhere, Hanks's work on deixis is highly relevant to Japanese household organization (Bachnik 1994b).

In this chapter I will argue that a household's universe of social ties play a crucial role in its rituals; in fact, the ties themselves *can be viewed as a focus of the ritual*. It is possible, then, to view Japanese relationships from a perspective of indexical meaning, so that instead of 'here' or 'over there' the focus on 'other' becomes one of indexing the relationship of the other (as figure) from the vantage point of self (as ground). This is one way of seeing 'betweenness' as a process of indexing self/other relationships, from the vantage point of distance.

That this process of indexing 'betweenness' in self/other relationships exists in Japanese is indicated by the fact that it is named.
Indexing of self/other relationships can be linked to a paired set of
terms, *omote* and *ura* ('in front', 'surface appearance', and 'behind',
'what is kept hidden from others').[8] These terms have been linked
specifically to the indexing of distance in language (Ikuta 1980) and
social life (Bachnik 1994a; forthcoming). Furthermore, the same figure/
ground aspects of indexical meaning and deixis that Hanks elaborates
can be explicitly linked to another paired set of terms, *uchi* and *soto*
(inside and outside). These terms have been linked to the organization
of deixis in both Japanese language (Wetzel 1984; 1994) and social life
(Bachnik 1982; 1994b). We can begin to trace the relationship between
pragmatic meaning and ancestor ritual in household (*ie*) organization
by examining these terms more closely, beginning with *uchi*. Among
the meanings for *uchi* at least three important meanings can be
identified: (1) 'we', 'us', 'our group', 'I', 'me', 'my group'; (2) the
living generation (or 'this' generation) of the household, and (3)
'inside', which must be understood in relation to *soto*, 'outside'.

The first set of meanings links *uchi* to deixis, as a deictic anchor point
for discourse. *Uchi* has in fact been defined and discussed as a discourse
anchor point in Japanese (Wetzel 1984; 1994; Bachnik 1982; Quinn
1994). Moreover, *uchi* is a collectivity, rather than an individual,
meaning that the anchor point is collectively (and socially) defined.
Because the speaker is located within a collectivity the locus shifts
contextually from a collective 'we'/'us' to an individual 'I', 'me' –
albeit within the collectivity. I have therefore argued that the implications of deixis, and its anchored perspective in space/time are crucial
to Japanese group organization (Bachnik 1990), and especially to the
organization of the *ie* (Bachnik forthcoming).

Since *uchi* is a named aspect of *ie* organization, the latter also has a
deictic component, manifested by the fact that the members of 'this'
(anchored) generation (Bachnik 1994b) are named, as '*uchi*'. Thus the
second set of meanings for *uchi* specifically locates *ie* organization in
time and space. Such 'locatedness' is not passive but active; for *uchi*
members are not 'situated' – it is more accurate to say that they situate
themselves vis-a-vis their context. The process involves a mutual
construction of *uchi* and context *vis-à-vis* one another.[9]

The third meaning of *uchi* locates *uchi* (inside) in relation to *soto*
(outside). In meaning, 'inside' and 'outside' are fundamentally interconnected and situationally defined, since each is constituted in relation
to the other.[10] Inside and outside are indexes. The implications of an
indexical perspective on *uchi/soto* are that the *uchi* anchor point, or

members of 'this' *ie* generation, are closely interconnected with *soto* households and their members, through relationship ties (which are defined through indexing of *uchi* and *soto*). This perspective re-orientates the focus of household organization; rather than an isolated, objectified 'unit' – the household – I have argued that the *ie* should be viewed as a focal point for its universe of ties. The ties link the *ie* beyond itself to other *ie*, and are a fundamental part of its organization (Bachnik 1994b).

To turn back to the ancestor ritual, because household members must interact simultaneously with a large number of their relations, a ritual provides opportunities for viewing the process of indexical meaning as it is carried out. In a sense, a virtual orchestration is required by the house putting on the ritual, because an extensive 'universe' of its social ties participates in the ritual. 'Orchestration' requires indexing of all of these ties in relation to its own anchor point, by the house putting on the ritual. A variety of different categories of ties often participates in a single ritual – including those established by marriage/adoption (*engumi*), parent/branch (*honke/bunke*), an organization of parent/branch ties (*dōzoku*), neighbourhood (*kumi*), kinship (*shinrui/shinseki*). Until now, from a perspective prioritizing semantic categories, it has been difficult to grasp how a household actually manages to relate its different categories of ties to one another. From a perspective of indexical meaning, however, the comparison of similarity and difference among many ties can be seen as a primary focus of a household ritual. This is not only indicated in the process of carrying out the ritual; it becomes a focus of the ritual.

In its sense of *uchi* as inside ('we', 'us') versus *soto* as outside others ('they'), *omote/ura*, and *uchi/soto* provide a perspective on Japanese relationships as pragmatic indexes, through which participants can specify 'betweenness' by indexing 'degrees' of 'close/farness' or 'similarity/difference' in agreed-upon ways. As indexes, *omote/ura* and *uchi/soto* define basic distinctions between interconnection and otherness; in this sense they can be viewed as revolving around 'betweenness' and basic ambivalence.[11]

The orchestration of relationships in a ritual requires a shift in focus: for not only does a household's universe of social ties participate in its rituals; the ties themselves *can be viewed as the focus of the ritual*. Viewing the relationship ties themselves as the focus of the ritual markedly shifts the perspective on the ritual, and its meaning. Instead of 'core' meanings, delineated as beliefs that are objectified from the practices, the 'core' meanings in the ritual are actually sets of relationships, which are delineated by indexing distance along a variety of axes from the household anchor point. Rather than a core set of 'beliefs' (whose meaning escapes us) meaning can be found in the *practice* of doing the rites, in 'custom', which comes 'naturally.' To put this another way, the focus of the ritual is on the process of carrying it out – or to be explicit, on the indexing of relationships as 'figures' (gauged according to distance as 'close/far', 'similar/ different'), from the vantagepoint of the anchor 'ground'. Such gauging of distance in various ways is also linked or 'mapped' to other indexes, including the intensity of one's involvement in the ritual, both in terms of duration and one's degree of obligation to participate.[12]

Householders themselves view their ritual in a way that is quite similar to the focus outlined above, and the ritual I am about to discuss has been intensively gone over with the householders; in my discussion I have translated their words and used their terms whenever possible.[13]

The process of indexing relationships also allows us to grasp the transition made by the deceased from a living member of the *uchi* to ancestorhood. Buddhism has been adapted to Japanese indigenous practices by the linking of death to a transition, and the conceptualization of this transition as a journey to the 'other shore' or a state of enlightenment, in which the deceased is regarded as a potential Bodhisattva. Yet while the focus in Buddhism is the *attainment* of this state of Bodhisattvahood, the focus in Japanese ancestor practice is almost entirely on the journey itself, which fits the same focus on pragmatic meaning outlined above.

The ancestors constitute relationships rather than a 'belief system'; these relationships index a transition between worlds, which can also be viewed as a continuum between profane and sacred, between the human existence and attainment of the 'other shore' of the ancestor-to-be.[14] The indexing revolves around the ancestor 'going from' the *ie* – 'go' (*iku*) is a deictic verb along with 'come' (*kuru*) since they require an anchor point to be understood (Lyons 1977).[15]

I point out that a fundamental ambivalence is also present in the rituals surrounding death. This ambivalence finds expression in the possibility that the deceased will *not* become an ancestor, because he/ she will not 'go from' the *ie*. This possibility is expressed in terms of the deceased never beginning the 'journey', but remaining near the scene of death. Such spirits are viewed as ambivalent (in fact ambivalence is what they represent), and potentially dangerous; they may possess and afflict the living.

The movement of the deceased away from the house is effected solely by the caring and attention given to the ancestors by the living, since as both Smith (1974) and Hamabata (1990) have pointed out, the dead cannot reach their rightful state without the efforts of the living. In fact, the ambivalent spirits who hover near the scene of death are called *muenbotoke*, literally, those without relationships.[16]

## A RITUAL CONTEXT: BACKGROUND TO THE KATŌ SOCIAL UNIVERSE

I will now develop a sustained discussion of a specific household, whom I call the Katōs, focusing on the process of their putting on a funeral ritual.[17] The Katō house, located in eastern (Tōshin) Nagano prefecture, was the anchor point for me in a longitudinal, 25-year investigation of *ie* (household) organization, involving six years of research between 1967 and 1992.

The ritual on which I focus is the funeral of Jūnosuke, the household head in the previous generation of the Katō house. Jūnosuke died on 29 March 1969, and his funeral took place over four days, from 29 March through 1 April. Since the ritual focuses on *uchi/soto* 'relationships', which require knowledge of the Katō *ie* and its 'universe' of ties, I must briefly sketch in some necessary understanding of the Katō *uchi* organization, as well as their *uchi/soto* ties. A brief background of *ie* organization is also necessary. Figure 5.1 includes the genealogy of the Katō *ie* over time, from generations one to nine; its *uchi* organization in time, generations eight to nine, and 'close' *uchi/soto* relationships which formed a series of cores in the funeral.

To first give an overall perspective on *ie* organization, the *ie* is viewed by its members as continuing over time, from its beginning in generation one, to the present generation nine. Its members also carry strong expectations of continuing the organization into the future (generation ten). Only two successors exist in each generation: a married couple who occupy permanent positions (Kitaoji 1971; Bachnik 1983). Members who are not recruited to one of the two permanent positions are ordinarily recruited outside the *ie*, to occupy either of the successor positions in an ongoing *ie*, or to become the first generation of a new *ie*, which is called a branch (*bunke*), and which continues its own generational line over time.

Those who leave the *ie* change their *uchi* anchorpoint, but their move creates a relationship link between their old and new anchor points. The circles in Figure 5.1 represent anchor points of those who came and went to and from the Katō *ie* through recruitment for *engumi*, marriage/ adoption. These ties gradually fade as the person through whom the tie was established dies and is forgotten. Thus none of the ties in the first five generations of the Katō *ie* are remembered by its *uchi* members. In generation six the Katōs know that a wife for the successor was recruited into the house from the Kake house, and that three children were born into the *ie*. The only son succeeded, and the two daughters were recruited outside. One was married into the Kikuchi house in the same village. The other was established with a husband in a Katō branch as its first generation, also in the village. This same branch also established its own branch in the next generation (Figure 5.1), and the latter is located very near the Katō house.

Six children were born in generation seven, and the oldest son succeeded the natal household. His wife was recruited from another Katō house, while two other sons were established in branches, and two daughters went in marriage, respectively, to the Hayami and Kake houses. The youngest son Jūnosuke, who is the focal point of this funeral, married, divorced shortly afterwards and never remarried.

The successors in generation seven, Jūtarō and Misako, had no children, and when Jūtarō died suddenly in the late 1940s, no successor had been decided upon. A council of relatives (consisting largely of the sixth and seventh generation ties just outlined) met and decided to let Jūnosuke succeed temporarily. Since he was divorced, elderly, and had no children, after his death the *ie* would be succeeded by the son and wife of the second Katō branch in generation seven. This meant that branch seven would sacrifice its own succession for that of the Katō parent house (*honke*) that had established the branch.[18] This couple would be adopted into the Katō *ie* after Jūnosuke died.

Generation eight consists of this couple, the present successors, Shigeo (*otōsan*) and his wife (*okāsan*) Mitoshi and their five children, of whom the oldest son is the next successor. They constitute the Katō *uchi*. The most important and 'closest' ties to *uchi* are those made through the marriage of the *otōsan*'s only sister to the Hase house, and to the Miuchi house through the marriage of the *okāsan*. The oldest son's marriage and birth of children, as well as the daughter's marriage and children in the Kamibayashi household, have not yet taken place at the time of Jūnosuke's funeral.

The selection of Jūnosuke as successor created all-too-human problems, for he was unable to manage the household assets and, in need of funds, he gradually began to sell off the *ie* property. Relatives became alarmed, particularly Shigeo and Mitoshi, who worried about having no *ie* to succeed. The relatives met again, and this time decided that Shigeo and Mitoshi would take over management of the *ie*. Jūnosuke retired voluntarily, thus barely avoiding disinheritance. At this point Shigeo and Mitoshi moved from their branch house into the main house, and Jūnosuke went to Tokyo to live.

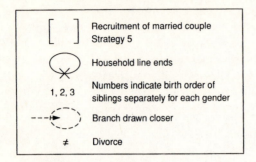

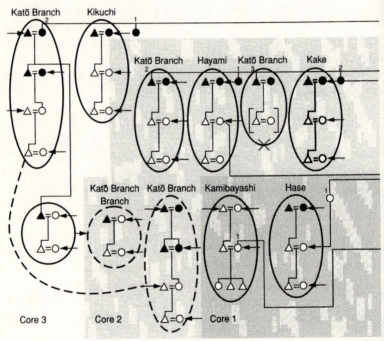

*Figure 5.1*  The Katō universe: permanent and temporary ties

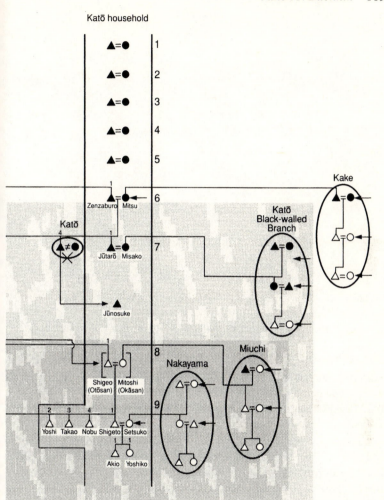

Katō household

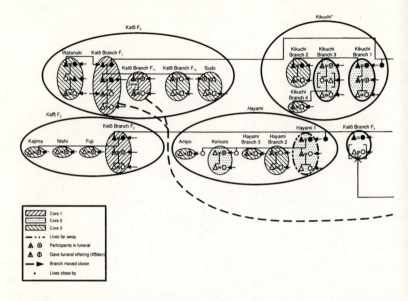

*Figure 5.2* Katō family universe: Jūnosuke's funeral

In the several years before his death Jūnosuke had become ill, and had been cared for, first by Shigeo and Mitoshi, and then by a nursing home when he became too ill to remain in the house. This is why Shigeo and Mitoshi had already become successors of the house before the time of Jūnosuke's death.

When Jūnosuke died in 1969 the Katōs had the major responsibility both for putting on the funeral, and for the ancestor ritual that would assist the departed in making his journey to the 'other shore'. The Katōs viewed their relationship (and obligation) to Jūnosuke as one stemming from his position as a former successor in their *ie*, so that the fact of his succession loomed larger for the Katōs than his misdeeds. The Katōs maintained that they saw no relationship between Jūnosuke's deeds in his life and his status as an ancestor; they were caring for Jūnosuke out of social obligation to the *ie*. Smith (1974) also makes this point.

## BEGINNING THE JOURNEY OF THE ANCESTOR: THE FIRST DAY

Each ritual involves a unique focus, and is constituted through a uniquely defined set of ties, gauged from the house anchor point.[19] The focus of the ritual was defined somewhat ambiguously, from two

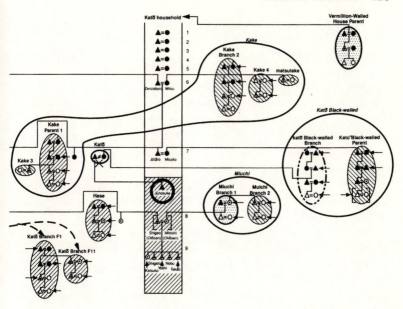

vantage points in *uchi*: (1) Jūnosuke (who was 'leaving' the *ie*), and (2) the *otōsan* and *okāsan* (Shigeo and Mitoshi), who were the present successors of the *ie*. Because of the focus from Jūnosuke's perspective, the seventh generation relatives were gauged as 'closer' than they would have been if the ritual focus had been in generations eight or nine of the *ie*.

Immediately upon being informed of Jūnosuke's death, the Katōs notified their 'close' relatives (*chikai shinrui*), and their children, two of whom were working in Tokyo. Those informed of the death, and drawn into the ritual first, were the 'closest' ties; and these people participated intensively throughout the ritual. Thus a link or 'mapping' was made between the indexing of 'close' and 'intensive' participation. As time went on more people were informed of the death and drawn into the ritual until the fourth day when the *kokubetsu shiki* or final ceremony was held, and the largest gathering of the household universe assembled. Following this the burial took place.

The core of 'closest' ties (shaded as 'Core 1' in Figure 5.2) who were notified first, were the Katō branch/branch ($F_{11}$), the *otōsan*'s only sister in the Hase house, and two ties in Jūnosuke's generation: the Kake house, and the Katō seventh generation branch ($F_2$), both househeads of whom were nephews of Jūnosuke. The sixth generation Katō $F_1$

branch was also notified, (the Katō branch/branch $F_{11}$ is actually a branch of this household). I should note that the Katō $F_1$ branch has moved to Yokohama, yet commonly maintains its relationship ties; thus the househead was able to reach the village before evening.

Only the individual linked to the deceased from each of these households came immediately to the Katōs. The *otōsan*'s sister came, but not her husband; Jūnosuke's nephews but not their wives. Only from the branch/branch house ($F_{11}$) were there two people – and the Katōs justified this through 'closeness' on two axes: that house is located immediately across the road, and it is the Katō's branch/branch (regarded as a close tie). All of these 'closest' ties except the sixth generation branch were located within 12km of the village, although none was in the village except the branch/branch.

So far the ritual involved a gauging of closeness between anchor points (and earmarking persons within anchor points). Closeness is mapped to intensity here, so that more members participate from anchor points gauged very close. The reader should also be able to notice a juxtaposition of 'closeness' along two axes: most of the core 1 ties were socially close relationships, whose location was distant. Yet all of these ties, including the farthest in Yokohama, came immediately. Only one household was close on both physical and social axes; and this house produced double the number of participants.

These closest 'core' ties centrally participated in the ritual, occupying the 'close' positions and continuing 'from beginning to end' (*saisho kara saigo made*), as the Katōs put it. They are its core, in fact. This meant that 'intensity' was indexed with 'closeness'. Moreover, this was done in two ways: for duration (from beginning to end) and degree of involvement. After laying out the body of the deceased, the first and most crucial task faced by the Katōs and their closest 'core' ties, was to get the ancestor to begin his journey rather than hovering around the body or becoming an ambivalent *muen* spirit. Because of this the ritual practices which took place immediately after death and through the first night focused on directionality, for not only do the ancestors 'go' from the *ie*, they leave the house in a north or north-westerly direction, a direction which the living deliberately avoid using. Once again, *iku* and *kuru*, along with their English counterparts, 'coming' and 'going' – as deictic verbs – indicate the importance of the deictic anchor point, and of indexing.

The attempts to get the new ancestor to leave the house were manifested through a series of reversals of the directions utilized in everyday life. Immediately after death, the body (with cotton in all the orifices) was laid on one *futon* (rather than the usual two); with the head facing northwards (Japanese sleep facing either south or eastwards). (See Figure 5.3). One kimono was put on the body and tied backwards (facing leftward instead of right). At the head of the body was placed a plate of cakes made of rice flour (*dango*) which were raw, instead of cooked; and a screen (*byōbu*), which was placed upside down. That a ritual is indeed an intensification of everyday experience is indicated by the fact that most of the reversals taking place in the ritual are strongly avoided in everyday life.

A sword (or knife) was placed beside the body to ward off wandering spirits (*muen botoke*), and the living sat up all night beside the body, keeping incense burning (important because the wafting smoke is considered a vehicle for the spirit of the ancestor). Tired though they were, people managed to keep awake by chatting softly, then took turns dozing for short catnaps.

## THE SECOND DAY

Early on the morning of 30 March three of the women 'closest' to the deceased washed the body. This task (which is potentially polluting) was performed by the 'closest' women in the core of households: the *okāsan*, the *otōsan*'s sister in the Hase house, and the wife in the branch/branch across the road (Figure 5.2).

From here the ritual opened outward: another group of houses which I term Core 2 was notified at the same time as the Core 1 group, but these houses were considered more distant and were not drawn into the ritual until the evening of 30 March. Core 2 included the vermilion-walled house (as the Katōs' parent (*honke*) which established the house nine generations ago); the Hayami and Komura houses ('close' relatives from Jūnosuke's generation, who were both more geographically distant than the Katō and Kake houses in that generation); the Kikuchi house and its branch (who were geographically close but socially distant, because the link was made in generation six); Miuchi (the *okāsan's* mother from her natal household, who is geographically and socially close, but related to the deceased through the *okāsan* as an affine, making her slightly more 'distant' for this ritual). Miki, a former tenant of the Katōs living nearby was also notified, and came over immediately, to help with the work preparations for the funeral, but did not participate in the first-night vigil. The indexing of the Core 2 ties can also be seen as arrived at through gauging distance along different axes, with the net result that all of these ties were considered more 'distant' than those in Core 1.

On the evening of the second day the body was placed in the coffin

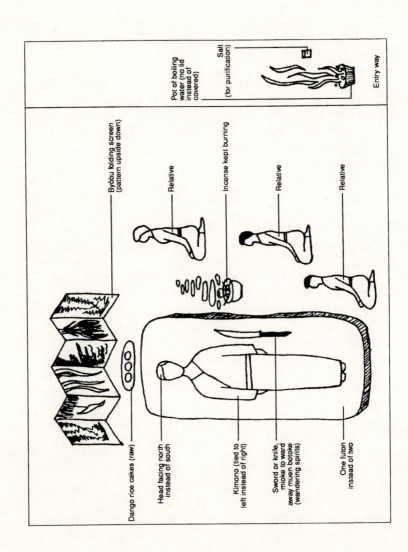

Byōbu folding screen (pattern upside down)

Relative

Incense kept burning

Relative

Relative

Dango rice cakes (raw)

Head facing north instead of south

Kimono (tied to left instead of right)

Sword or knife, mioke to ward away muen botoke (wandering spirits)

One futon instead of two

Pot of boiling water (no lid instead of covered)

Salt (for purification)

Entry way

(*kan*), a barrel-shaped affair in which the body sits upright. Both core groups listed above were present, along with a priest, but the groups were differentiated in what they wore and did. The 'close' Core 1 relatives wore simple white kimono (*yukata*) turned inside-out with straw ropes as belts, while the Core 2 group wore black mourning clothes. The 'close' relatives and the Katō household members put the body in the coffin, and the symbolism of the journey was strong here, as well as the emotional ties with the departed, for with the body were placed items to facilitate the ancestor's journey. The men (not women) put the lid on the coffin and tied the rope around it. This was the time of separation from the departed, and the saddest time for the 'close' relatives. From this point the deceased was called a *hotokesama* (Bodhisattva), and the 'close' relatives put the coffin near the alcove (*tokonoma*) in parlour four (Figure 5.6), and again slept fitfully next to the *hotokesama*, while the Core 2 relatives returned home.

## THE THIRD DAY

On the morning of 31 March the Katōs notified the people in their parent/branch organization (*dōzoku*) and the neighbourhood five-house group (*kumi*) – relationship categories that differentiated them from the Core 1 and 2 households (Figures 5.4 and 5.5). Representatives from these households now came to the Katō house and burned incense before the coffin. These *dōzoku* ties were distinct from the parent/branch, and branch/branch ties involved thus far, all of which were direct ties with the Katō house (F). The *dōzoku* ties were indirect parent/branch links, which were established by the Katō's parent (A), the vermilion-walled house. These branches were gauged as much more 'distant' because they were not directly established by the Katōs, but by the vermilion-walled house. The *kumi* relationships were defined by physical proximity and these commonly include all the households next to, behind, and in front of a house (all deictically defined, and indexing every direction from the anchor point).[20]

Each of these houses was asked for labour: from the five-house group the Katōs requested one person on 31 March and two on 1 April; from the *dōzoku* they asked for only one person on 1 April. These ties were asked to help prepare food for the largest part of the ritual, on 1 April, and to help make some of the ritual artifacts, carried in the funeral procession. The amount of assistance asked for indicated that the *kumi* ties are stronger than the *dōzoku* ones, since throughout the ritual, the intensity (and kind) of participation is indexed by the intensity of the tie itself. Both the entry of these ties into the ritual at this late point

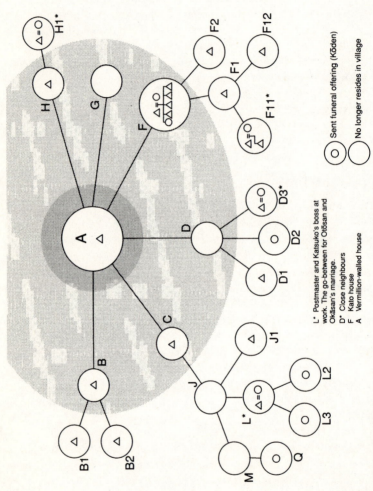

L* Postmaster and Katsuko's boss at
   work. The go-between for Otōsan and
   Okāsan's marriage.
D* Close neighbours
F  Kato house
A  Vermillion-walled house

○ Sent funeral offering (Kōden)

○ No longer resides in village

*Figure 5.4* Parent/branch participation in Katō funeral: third day

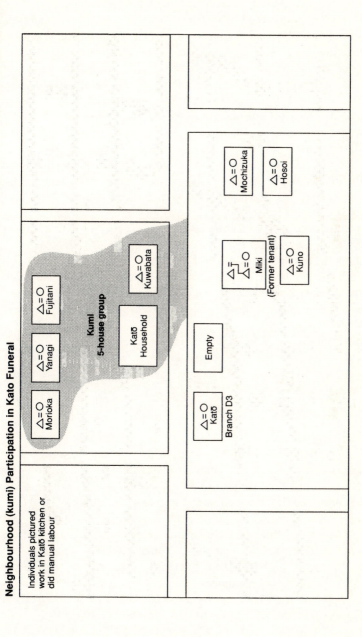

*Figure 5.5* Neighbourhood (*kumi*) participation in Katō funeral

in time and the kind of assistance asked for says much about the significance of both these kinds of ties: the five-house group (*kumi*) ties are locationally 'close', but they were not part of the 'core' ritual for the household, nor have they been asked to participate in any 'inside' events of the ritual itself; the *dōzoku* ties are even more distant.

On the morning of 31 March the cremation was held, in which only the 'core' households (plus the Kikuchi house) participated. These households, plus all the members of the Katō house went to the crematorium (*kasōjō*) for the cremation. This is the only part of the burial where the Katōs required the services of professionals. Cremation is recent, dating from the post-war period in this area, so that some aspects of the funeral ritual are still carried out as if the body is not being cremated (for example, placing the body in the coffin). The members of this party returned with a small box of ashes (the *ikotsu*), which was placed on a shelf (*saidan*) near the sacred alcove (*tokonoma*) in Parlour 4. The *saidan* replicates the ancestor shelf (*butsudan*), but is outside it, for the deceased, still in transition, is not yet able to be placed inside the *butsudan* as an ancestor. This *dan* is treated in much the same way as the *butsudan*, however, and flowers, heart-shaped ancestor cakes (*dango*), now cooked, are placed on it and incense is burned before it.

On the third day the house also sent notification of the death to the the Saku city office (*shiyakusho*) where it would be recorded in Jūnosuke's record (*koseki*). Everything was now ready for the final, and largest part of the ritual.

## THE FOURTH DAY

On 1 April the *kokubetsu shiki* – literally the announcement-of-leave-taking ceremony – was held. Here the universe expanded to its broadest point; and all those not yet drawn into the ritual, but who gauged some relationship with the deceased, now came to the Katō house. A few of these people lived too far away to come to the ritual before now. But most of those who came now were distant/weak ties, such as guests or neighbours who were outside the five-house group, but still close enough to know the Katōs well. Some were also ties of the core or extended core households, who were either 'close' branches, or siblings recruited out of the 'core' *ie*. Figure 5.2 indicates that each of the relationships of the Katō *ie* is itself an anchor point, with its own universe of ties, the closest of which were now drawn into the ritual along with their anchor points. All the houses in the core group now included their close one-step universes. The *dōzoku* and *kumi* ties now

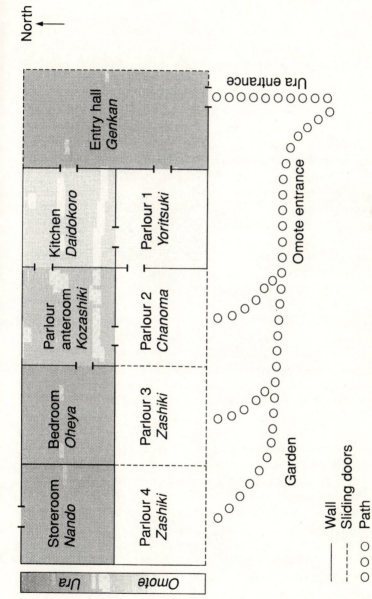

*Figure 5.6* Katō house plan

participated as well. The *kokubetsu shiki* involved the fullest orchestration of the relationships.

Three of the four Katō parlours (see house design, Figure 5.6) had now been opened up into one large room, and the sliding panels to the outside had also been opened in Parlour 4. The ceremony itself was held in Parlour 4, while the relatives spilled over into Parlours 3 and 2. The Katō household members were seated in a row at the entry to Parlour 3, with the *otōsan* (wearing a ribbon around his neck, indicating he was the successor of the household of the deceased) closest to the *dan*, followed by the *okāsan*, then the children. Behind the Katōs, in Parlours 2 and 3 were the Core 1, Core 2, and Core 3 relatives, all of whom sat quietly, dressed in black mourning clothes, watching the priests in the still-chilly spring while sitting carefully on their heels.

The ritual began with chanting before the *saidan* by the priest from the household temple, accompanied by a priest from the neighbouring village. After the priests finished, guests started coming, entering through the garden of the Katō house, then walking up the stone stairway to Parlour 4, and stepping into the house. Each walked up to the *saidan*, lit incense, bowed, then turned, knelt on the *tatami* and bowed deeply to the floor, offering condolences in polite language to the Katō house members, who bowed deeply to the floor in response, then responded with the equivalent of 'thank you'. The guest next turned to the assembly of relatives and bowed deeply to them, offering condolences again, and receiving a bow and thank you in response. Each guest brought an offering of money (*kōden*) which was taken (and the amount recorded) when he/she entered; and each received a gift-bundle upon leaving, which contained tea and salt (to dispel pollution by the proximity to death).

This part of the ritual soon acquired a rhythm, as the guests came, bowed and prayed briefly before the *saidan*, then turned and greeted first the household members, then the rest of the relatives. There were two waves of bows and murmured thank yous; the small wave of the seven Katō members and the low murmur of their answers; then the larger wave of all the relatives bowing in unison and the much larger swell of their answers. The chill of the early spring day and the need to sit precisely on one's heels eventually brought numbness and stiffness, so that finally, after the last guest had left, when Nobu hoisted himself up, groaning, along one of the house posts, a murmur of sympathetic laughter went through the room of relatives.

From here a procession was formed, which went from the house to the Katō graveyard behind the vermilion-walled house, carrying the remains of the deceased, and all the paraphernalia for the ancestor to be placed at the grave. The procession was led by a priest, followed by a line of relatives, each carrying something for the deceased, which had been decided beforehand by the Katōs and Core 1 relatives. The place of each person in the procession combined with what he/she carried spelled out a series of relationships to the deceased, which began with 'far' ties, moved to 'close' – then 'closest' – and again back to 'far', and it was widely known what these places spelled out.

When the procession reached the newly dug grave, the burial proceeded quickly. The priests chanted prayers, then put the box of ashes into the grave. Next the hole was filled in, the temporary gravemarker put in place, and a tray of food, water, tea and incense all put before the new grave. More prayers were chanted by the priests, then the temporary tablet and the picture are taken back to the house and placed into the *butsudan*. The living had now accomplished the first and most important task: assisting the deceased to accomplish the first part of his transition to ancestorhood – the beginning of his journey.

The living now returned to the house for the third and final part of the ritual. During the burial, the three parlours had been transformed by the *kumi* and *dōzoku* women, who had been cooking and helping with other preparations for two days. Two long low tables spanned the length of the room, and these were joined together at one end to make a three-sided table. Now, finally, everyone who had participated throughout the long process of separation from the first-night vigil to the leave-taking ceremony, could sit and relax, enjoying a meal and sake. Soon the room was buzzing with talk and subdued laughter, as the Katōs moved around the table, filling the cups with sake.

After the relatives left, a second sitting was held for all the women who had helped prepare the meal, plus the *dōzoku* members. The atmosphere at both meals was relaxed; the Katō members, as hosts who had no places at the table, helped fill the sake cups of the guests, who finally relaxed and enjoyed a well-earned rest. For the Katō's and the 'closest' core relatives it had been a long time of tense planning, making sure that everything would go right. They still had not had a chance to relax and eat. But they could now breathe a sigh of relief that the ritual had been carried out successfully, without major conflict.[21]

## IMPLICATIONS OF PRAGMATIC MEANING: APPROACHING THE ORGANIZATION OF PRACTICE THROUGH PRACTICE

To go back to the two approaches to meaning at issue in the organization of this ritual, one could view the meaning of gifts, language, social order, and rituals in terms of a 'centre' or 'core' beneath the wrapping; while the second approach, which we related to the Japanese emphasis on wrapping, focuses on the process of organizing the ritual itself, which is linked to a focus on indexing the relationships putting on the ritual.

The funeral ritual, then, is organized in the manner of a snake eating its tail – in that it focuses largely on the process of delineating its own organization. The focus on the process of creating the ritual *is* the ritual; this same process is also the ritual organization.

Not only does the focus on indexical meaning help in explaining the organization of the ritual, but the ritual also helps in explaining the organization of indexical meaning. This can be followed out in two ways, following out the two sets of paired terms, *omote/ura*, and *uchi/soto*. The ritual traces out two broad organizational processes, which are both differentiated from one another and linked together.

The first involves a differentiation of similarity/difference, or interconnection/otherness. Each of the relationships that took part in the funeral was indexed by distance, and this differentiation was crucial to the organization of the ritual. The fact that three 'core' sets of relationships were differentiated was a main feature of the ritual; each of the cores was defined by a different degree of distance. Distance itself was not gauged mono-dimensionally, but along a variety of axes. Rarely was a relationship close or far along only one axis; most often closeness along one axis (for example, social) was juxtaposed by distance along another (for example, physical). Sometimes houses were 'close' on more than one axis, which produced marked intensity.

The relationships in each household 'universe' and in each ritual are a unique set, making the focus highly contextual, particularistic, and infinitely variable. Yet the focus on particularism in opposition to generalized meaning which transcends context can be closely linked to the discussions of semantic and pragmatic prioritization of meaning above. In this sense both Bateson (1972) and Silverstein (1976) have noted that contextually defined, pragmatic foci are defined along lines of 'how' rather than 'what' questions. Consequently, although the particular universe of relationships in this ritual is unique, *the way in which the relationships were indexed was a focus of considerable sharedness*. In fact, each participant had to agree on his/her placing throughout the ritual, meaning that the indexing was a joint process. Planning a ritual involves gauging how the other party sees the anchor point, as well as vice versa. Disparities here produce conflicts, as illustrated by the case of the Katōs' next door neighbour, who was placed in the second sitting of the banquet as a 'close' tie gauged by physical proximity, and a distant *dōzoku* tie. The neighbour was offended, feeling that he should have been in the first sitting. He left the banquet early, although the Katō *okāsan* tried to persuade him to stay.

That the indexing of relationships in a ritual actually indexes these relationships in practice is confirmed by the facts of this conflict. When a relationship could not be mutually indexed, it could not be carried out, and the neighbour walked out of the ritual. Moreover, to this day the two houses have had no further contact.

The indexing of distance 'produces' the ritual (or its organization in practice) by the 'mapping' of the distance index onto a series of other indexes which related 'distance' specifically to various indexes for performance in the ritual. Thus 'closeness' was linked with intensity and duration; 'distance' with lack of intensity and duration. The number of members participating from each anchor point was also linked to 'closeness'. And throughout the ritual participants were 'placed' in relation to one another – for example, in the funeral procession, at the banquet table, etc. Here too, 'placing' was mapped to distance. Finally, funerary offerings (*kōden*) were given by each participant, and once again, the monetary amount was scaled along the same distance axis, and this knowledge was widely shared. The Core 1 households gave between 5,000–10,000 yen; Core 2 around 1,000 yen; and Core 3 300 to 500 yen.

The indexing of distance throughout the ritual can also be linked to an indexing of degrees of sharedness, or similarity versus otherness. Here the significance of 'betweenness' of *gen* or *kan* (meaning 'space', 'space between', 'space of time', 'an interval') in words for the conceptualization of human relationships (such as *ningen kankei*) means that the ambivalence of 'betweenness' is a central facet of relationships for Japanese. The focus on indexing of relationships is actually about trying to anchor this ambivalence – by attempting to agree on the degree of similarity (which is simultaneously gauged in inverse relation to the degree of difference). Thus the 'closest' ties (to those who have a greater degree of similarity and smaller degree of difference) have a greater degree of participation in the ritual, which requires their identification with *uchi* the 'inside', or anchor point of the Katō household. The indexing here too is enacted in a manner such that the closest ties are drawn into *uchi* (with the implication that they are the most similar). This can be viewed as a play on the shifting relationships between I and Thou discussed brilliantly by Buber (1958), and further elaborated by Levinas (1987 [1947]), and Derrida's discussion of Levinas (1978).

The movement of 'close' ties into *uchi* produces the second major dynamic of the ritual, which can be viewed *vis-à-vis uchi/soto* indexing. As mentioned previously, Hanks's differentiation of deictic organization into two components in a figure/ground relationship, has considerable bearing on the organization of the Japanese *ie* and, specifically, its funeral rituals. In fact, because of the snake-eating-its-tail quality of the ritual, not only does the figure/ground relationship help in explaining the organization of the ritual, but the ritual also helps in explaining the organization of the figure/ground relationship, because of the way it portrays this relationship throughout the enactment of the funeral. I will now elaborate on this.

Just as 'deictic reference organizes the field of interaction into a foreground upon a background, as figure and ground organize the visual field' (Hanks 1992:61), this funeral ritual in the *ie* can be viewed as a field of interaction with a foreground upon a background, which organizes the visual field, as figure and ground. 'Ground' is *uchi*, the anchor point of the living members of the *ie*. 'Figure' is constituted by the *soto* relations who are linked to *uchi* through a variety of ways: by a person recruited to or from the *ie* in marriage, the proximity of being neighbours, or a parent/branch relationship. Each of the *soto* relationships is indexed *vis-à-vis* the Katō anchor point. The figure/ground relationship is necessary to gauge each relationship as 'close' or 'far', (and this is the *omote/ura* indexing discussed above). This distance index is in turn mapped to index the degree of intensity and duration of each household relationship in the ritual. The beginning of the ritual is gauged as the point of deepest intensity, with the house drawing on a few relationships whose involvement will persist throughout the ritual, 'from beginning to end'. The house proceeds over time to draw in more relationships of lesser intensity, which are involved for shorter periods, until the *kokubetsu shiki*, which draws in the shallowest ties, who come briefly to the ritual event, and simply offer incense. But the anchorage of the *uchi/soto* dynamic also creates a process of reciprocity, in which those participants who were involved with the earliest, deepest, and longest participation, become the recipients of a banquet prepared by representatives of *dōzoku* and *kumi* ties, (who were drawn in later, with shallower and shorter participation).

*Uchi/soto* indexing involves a particular kind of directional deference with strong parallels in language and social life. In language, humbling of self and deferring to another is exemplified in the use of honorific forms, such as *irassharu* ('come, go') in reference to a *soto* person, and humble forms *mairu* ('come, go'), in reference to self or another *uchi* member. This directional movement is expressed interpersonally in the dynamic of *amaeru/amayakasu* (Doi 1973a; Lebra 1976), in which one person indulges the other. This has been specifically linked to *uchi/soto* by Rosenberger (1994). The *amayakasu* person is *uchi*, in humbling, or reserving self-expression, while facilitating the expression of the other as *soto*. The latter is deferred to, or indulged, by being catered to. The *uchi/soto*, *amaeru/amayakasu* relationship is also the model for Japanese host/guest relationships. The host, as *uchi*, reserves self-expression and caters to the *soto* guest. We can say the guest is 'wrapped' or cocooned, in this indulgence (Bachnik, forthcoming). We can also say that the focus of all attention is on *soto* who represents the 'figure' in this relationship, while *uchi* is the 'ground'.

The point is that this *uchi/soto* figure/ground relationship is not static, and the funeral ritual in fact delineates the dynamics of this relationship. Three 'core' groups of houses are delineated: the first comes immediately and participates from day one through day four. These people help prepare the body, attend the crucial all-night vigil on the first night, help put the body in the coffin, and go with the Katōs to the cremation. They help plan the ritual, help the Katōs greet the more distant guests at the final ceremony, and have places in the procession leading to the graveyard and burial.

But the participation of these Core 1 ties also *draws them into the Katō uchi*. This is actually one of the major implications of household 'assistance'; the Core 1 ties are drawn into *uchi* because they are participating in *uchi*, and in doing so incur pollution involved in helping to get the body ready for burial. They are also participating in *uchi* in assisting the Katōs to relate to their more *soto* ties who will be coming to the *kokubetsu shiki* and the burial. By 1 April the boundary of the Katō *ie* has been shifting outward, temporarily including those who assist the Katōs in a gradually expanding series of waves (Figure 5.7). At the final ceremony both the spatial positioning and the interaction with the guests who come to offer *kōden* make it clear that in opposition to these (more distant) guests all three cores of relatives are now *within the house boundary*. They are on the side of the hosts, 'catering to', rather than 'being catered to'. The guests are bowing to *them* and offering condolences; they are responding along with the Katōs.

But since the Core 1 participants are not really *uchi* members of the Katō *ie*, they are only temporarily performing these *uchi* tasks. Consequently, a reciprocity is introduced through the dynamics of the incorporation of the *soto* ties into *uchi*. The Core 1 and 2 households have given more to the Katōs than their help – they have also given 'coming into' the *uchi* itself – for they are not members of the Katō anchor point. The Katōs now reciprocate by reversing the directionality

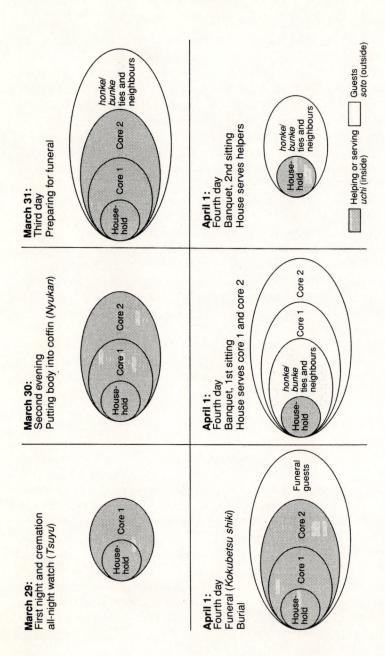

**March 29:**
First night and cremation
all-night watch (*Tsuyu*)

Household — Core 1

**March 30:**
Second evening
Putting body into coffin (*Nyukan*)

Household — Core 1 — Core 2

**March 31:**
Third day
Preparing for funeral

Household — Core 1 — Core 2 — *honke/bunke* ties and neighbours

**April 1:**
Fourth day
Funeral (*Kokubetsu shiki*)
Burial

Household — Core 1 — Core 2 — Funeral guests

**April 1:**
Fourth day
Banquet, 1st sitting
House serves core 1 and core 2

Household — *honke/bunke* ties and neighbours — Core 1 — Core 2

**April 1:**
Fourth day
Banquet, 2nd sitting
House serves helpers

Household — *honke/bunke* ties and neighbours

Helping or serving *uchi* (inside)

Guests *soto* (outside)

*Figure 5.7 Uchi/soto reciprocity in Katō funeral*

of their coming into *uchi* and shifting them to *soto* by *giving deference to them* – in honouring them with the best places at the banquet given immediately after the burial.

The Katōs cannot reciprocate to Cores 1 and 2 without drawing still more ties into *uchi*. At this point they call on their *dōzoku* and *kumi* ties. These help the Katōs give deference to the first sets of core ties, by preparing the house and the food for the banquet following the ritual, and they in turn are drawn into the physical *uchi* section of the house – the kitchen – when they do so (see Figure 5.7). Subsequently, these *dōzoku* and *kumi* ties also receive reciprocity from the Katōs, for coming into the *uchi*. Once again, they are shifted to *soto*, and the direction of deference is reversed, so that these ties receive, rather than give deference at the second sitting following that of the core participants in the ritual banquet.

Thus the figure/ground relationships in the ritual take on a wave-like dynamic, in which the incorporation of the Core 1 and 2 ties who share the tasks of *uchi* hosts with the Katōs, produces a shift in direction of deference. The first set of ties is shifted from *uchi* to *soto*, host to guest, and from ground to figure at the banquet after the ritual. But this can happen only with the aid of the second set of *kumi* and *dōzoku* ties who next shift from *soto* to *uchi* to help the Katōs give deference to the first set of ties. These ties are also shifted from *uchi* to *soto*, from host to guest, and from ground to figure as well in the second sitting of the banquet.

But these two waves of *uchi/soto* reciprocity were not identical, and the differentiations between them were based on differentiations between the categories of relationship ties. Grasping the indexing of this reciprocity also allows us to see how the ties are differentiated *vis-à-vis* one another by the householders. The closest cores consisted solely of ties established through children recruited through marriage/adoption (*engumi*) or established as branch houses. The second 'wave' of ties consisted of neighbourhood houses (*kumi*) and *dōzoku* ties. They were informed of the funeral later, and were not included in the ritual itself on the side of the Katōs as hosts. They gave incense as guests, both at the time the body was put in the coffin, and at the final ceremony. Their inclusion came when the Katōs had to repay the group of ties who were included. The neighbourhood houses were asked for labour (not for decision-making assistance); they came into the *uchi* of the physical space of the kitchen rather than the *uchi* of the funeral ritual; and they were repaid by receiving a meal *after* the others. The indirect *dōzoku* ties (all of which were also located in the village) were even more distant than the *kumi* ties, since they were asked to contribute fewer people and less labour.

This ritual illustrates a distinction which occurred consistently in all the rituals and general *tsukiai* among the households (and their ties) which I investigated. A differentiation through indexing is made between social 'closeness' (through a marriage/adoptive or a direct parent/branch tie) and physically defined closeness of 'living close by', as the neighbourhood and indirect parent/branch ties. Just as these relationships are indexed differently, their participation is different as well. Socially close participants are drawn into the 'core' (or *uchi*) of the ritual, as well as its decision-making processes. Physically close participants are asked for physical labour, but they do not participate in the social core of household crises or decision-making. Furthermore, as in this case, the physical labour is for the purpose of repaying the ties on the social axis.

The 'core' circle of ties (who come 'from beginning to end') are those who can be called upon in any crisis. They will come and 'help' in person, and their giving is multi-levelled, including both emotional and social dimensions on a personal level, and extending to giving of their own universe ties. These people enter farthest into the *inside* of a household's core affairs because they know and understand much about each other's 'inside' affairs, and in fact some of them (for example the *otōsan*'s sister in the Hase house) grew up inside the same house.

The ritual demarcates a time continuum 'from beginning to end', which is matched up with the distance axes of each household in the universe. The table for the banquet divided into two sittings illustrates the indexing for both distance (*omote/ura*) and directional deference (*uchi/soto*). The two priests and the head of the vermilion-walled house are placed at the head of the table, indicating deference. But nearest the priests are the core 'close' members – those who have participated in the ritual 'from beginning to end.' They have been given 'high' places precisely because they are very 'close', indicating the highest deference and a degree of 'catering to' which equates 'close' with greater, rather than less deference. This constitutes repayment by the house for the 'close' part these relatives have played in the ritual. Following these are seated the Core 2 and then the Core 3 relatives, so that the *dōzoku* members are at the lower end of the table.

These two axes are actually in operation along a single physical table-length. The indexing of distance (which can be equated with *omote/ura*) equates 'close' with the lower and 'far' with the upper places at the table. But the indexing of directional deference (as *uchi/soto*) includes the flip-side dynamics of exalting those who are outsiders, and humbling one's self and group. Thus precisely those ties which had been drawn farthest 'into' the Katō household during the ritual can now be acknowledged as outsiders by a degree of *soto* deference precisely commensurate with the degree of their shift into *uchi*.

The significance of the Katō funeral ritual involves more than ancestors, ritual, or Japanese social organization. As an example of an organization defined by the process of delineating that organization, the actual funeral ritual represents the organization of practice in the only way possible: through the detailed explication of that very organization in practice. In this sense the householders' practices are actually more enlightening than solely philosophical accounts of practice, agency, pragmatic meaning, and phenomenology because of their embedded focus (and they are far more enlightening than I could capture in this account). We can now turn back to their answers on ritual meaning with a new eye, for 'just doing' the practices is no mere process of social action by reflex. Their practices indicate that pragmatic meaning has much to contribute to our understandings of context – and of 'self-conscious', or agency-focused social order – meaning in this case, a social order consisting of the very process of constituting itself.

## NOTES

1 However, Hamabata also moves away from these dichotomies in his next sentence:

> What is felt to be true in ritual experience may not correspond to what is thought to be true in mundane experience. But the point is: one form of understanding does not negate the other. For example, when Makoto Moriuchi opened his family's *butusudan* and introduced me to his deceased father, even I participated in the ritual experience by bowing and saying, 'Nice to meet you'. I felt Mr. Moriuchi's presence. When Makoto snickered, I was brought back from the ritual to the mundane and *thought* that Mr. Moriuchi's presence couldn't be real. Did I or didn't I believe? I don't know.
>
> (Hamabata 1990:84)

2 This use of 'pragmatic' differs from its everyday usage (which has utilitarian connotations); I am using pragmatic in a way similar to Peirce's discussions of indexical meaning. This will be elaborated below. For further discussion of pragmatic meaning see Levinson (1983) and Silverstein (1976). For further discussion of pragmatic (indexical) meaning in Japanese language and society, see Bachnik and Quinn (1994). Wrapping is also the focus of a collected volume edited by Ben-Ari, Moeran, and Valentine (1990).

3 Peirce's three different kinds of signs: icon, index, and symbol, are each characterized by different relations of the sign to its object: 'resemblance, contiguity, and association by convention, respectively' (Singer 1980:491).

An iconic sign resembles its object (as a diagram or picture, which may even momentarily make us forget the distinction between the real and the copy). An indexical sign has a direct relation to its object and qualifies its object by being really connected to it (Freeman 1937:31). Symbols are triads because they have a joint relationship between the object denoted and the mind. The relationship is established by convention (e.g. the word 'dog') and its relationship is arbitrary. For Peirce, symbols are the residual class of signs, where neither physical similarity nor contextual contiguity hold between sign vehicle and entity signalled. Thus 'sign' and 'symbol' are not interchangeable terms for Peirce; for a symbol is merely one of the many sign types.

4  Smoke is an index of fire; a rap on the door is an index of someone seeking entry (Peirce CP, III). A pointing finger is an index which 'is based upon the idea of identification, or drawing attention to, by pointing' (Lyons 1977:II:637).

5  Dyads, which consist of 'two subjects brought into oneness', are crucial for Peirce because they allow possibilities for overcoming the dualities between self and the external world. Specifically, 'These subjects have their modes of being both in themselves and in their connection with each other . . . The dyad is not the subjects, *but the relation between them*' (Freeman 1937:18, emphasis added).

6  I am grateful to Steven Klein (personal conversation), for this information. Lyons's definition of deixis is a handy one:

> The location and identification of persons, objects, events, processes and activities talked about, or referred to, in relation to the spatiotemporal context created and sustained by the act of utterance and the participation in it, typically, of a single speaker and at least one addressee.
>
> (1977:II:637)

Such indexes do not contribute to the referential speech event because their function is different: *they signal the structure of the speech context* (Silverstein 1976).

7  As Hanks puts this: 'When speakers say something like, "Here it is", he or she unavoidably conveys something like, "Hey, you and I stand in a certain relation to each other and to this object and this place, right now".' (1990:7).

8  Doi (1973b; 1986) stipulates that the meanings of each of these paired terms overlap, so that aspects of self cluster at one pole, as *uchi*, *ura*, while aspects of social life cluster at the other pole, as *soto*, *omote*. Doi uses inside and outside (linked to *omote* and *ura*) as central concepts for the organization of a Japanese self, which is characterized by situational shifting between the two 'modes' (1986; 1973b). Lebra (1976) considers inside/outside dimensions (linked to *uchi/soto* and *omote/ura*) as central to her treatment of 'situationalism' in Japanese culture and behaviour. Doi's observation is important, since it directly links aspects of self and society to degrees of in- and outside-ness. The paired sets of terms also link emotional 'inside' aspects of self to 'outside' aspects of social obligations, ritual and order. These terms have been considered an organizational focus for Japanese language, self, and social life (Bachnik and Quinn 1994).

9  Both Nakane's discussion of *ba* as 'location' – a translation of the term 'frame' which she uses to define the Japanese group – and her discussion

of 'the ready tendency of the Japanese to stress situational position in a particular frame' (1970:2), are readily explainable by deixis. Yet both *ba* and situational position in a particular frame are problematic as structural concepts. The common usage of the term *uchi* in '*uchi-no* or *uchi-dewa* referring to one's own people and work place' (Nakane 1970:120), is better explained through the widespread use of *uchi* as a deictic anchor point, than through positing 'familialism' throughout Japanese society.

10  Such meaning is pragmatic, or indexical, and it must be pointed out that the indexing of inside/outside dimensions is a necessary part of being human (Straus 1967), while it is widely recognized that all natural languages have deictics (Lyons 1977; Anderson and Keenan 1985; Weinreich 1980).

11  The same ambivalence is expressed in a number of other paired sets of terms, including *tatemae* (the surface reality) and *honne* (the world of inner feelings) (Hamabata 1983:7–8); *giri* (social obligation) and *ninjō* (the world of personal feelings) (Hamabata 1983:22); *soto* (outside) and *uchi* (inside); *ōyake-goto* (public) and *watakushi-goto* (private); *hara* (sacred, extraordinary, formal) and *ke* (profane, ordinary, informal), *omote/ura* (Doi 1973b; 1986); *tatemae/honne*; *giri/ninjō*; *hare/ke*.

12  Here I am referring to Ochs's discussion of mapping.

> Indexical relations are more complex than one-to-one mappings between linguistic forms and contextual features. They cannot be fully understood without additional mappings – between a particular contextual dimension and sets of linguistic forms, and between a particular contextual dimension and sets of linguistic forms, and between a particular linguistic form and several contextual dimensions.
>
> (1990:293)

Ochs is here referring to indexing in the process of language socialization, but mapping is applicable beyond this process.

13  The major difference between their perspectives and the one I detail in this paper is in the degree of detail and fine-tuning, in which they truly excel.

14  The ancestors are viewed from the anchor point of the living *ie* members, and it is *their* changing perspectives on distance between the ancestor and themselves which brings about the ancestor's transition between worlds. At the point of death each ancestor is 'close' to the *ie*. Death starts the ancestor on a trajectory on which he/she moves gradually away from the *ie*, until the ancestor becomes 'far', then fades off the horizon altogether. The movement can be punctuated by a series of stages (for example Smith's *shirei, nī-botoke, hotoke, senzo, kami* (1974:56), but the stages are not uniformly defined by households. For further discussion see Bachnik (forthcoming) Chapter 13.

15  In fact, all of the major household rituals focus around coming and going to and from the anchor point, and thus involve deixis. These include 'coming' (or 'going') in marriage/adoption, or 'coming into' the *ie* through birth. (See Chapter 8 of Bachnik forthcoming for further discussion of deictics of 'coming' and 'going' in *ie* organization.)

16  As Robert Smith notes: 'An outstanding feature of the ceremonies for the dead is that from start to finish they are primarily the responsibility of the household and its members' (1974:69–70). Hamabata agrees:

> Household members *alone* are responsible for maintaining the realm of

the sacred: members set up the altars, make offerings of food and prayer, secure the presence of a priest to chant sutras. Members of the household not only maintain but create the sacred. In fact, members of the *ie* are active participants in creating ancestors-cum-gods.

(Hamabata 1990:72)

17  A more detailed discussion of this ritual occurs in Bachnik, forthcoming.
18  This is possible because the houses share ancestors, and because the parent Katō household had a much longer genealogy.
19  For example, in the marriage of the oldest son, Shigeto, the wedding ritual was indexed from the perspective of both the son, and the *otōsan/okāsan*, which occasionally created conflicts, and raised protests from the son. It should be said that each household ritual focuses on a member who is making a transition, and in this sense someone from within the anchor point (*uchi*) is highlighted. The *soto* relationships of that member also become a focus of the ritual. But those putting on the ritual (the successors in the next generation – the *otōsan* and *okāsan*) also inevitably focus the ritual from the perspective of their own ties as well.
20  A discussion of parent/branch, and *kumi* ties from the vantage point of deixis appears in Bachnik, forthcoming, in Chapters 9 and 10 respectively.
21  The ritual was not actually over, though. The following day all close Core 1 relatives again gathered, and together visited the grave, bringing food and tall thin slats of wood representing stupas, which they left at the grave. Although one should visit the graves every day for seven days, no one has such time anymore, so they brought all seven days' worth at once. Following this, they returned and had another meal (*gokurō oiwai*) at the Katō's, and the Katōs redistributed the flowers, rice cakes, and food which were displayed in the house during the leave-taking ceremony, among these guests.

# BIBLIOGRAPHY

Anderson, S. R., and E. L. Keenan, (1985) 'Deixis', in *Language Typology and Syntactic Description*, Vol. 3: *Grammatical Categories and the Lexicon*, T. Shopen (ed.) Cambridge: Cambridge University Press, pp. 259–308.

Bachnik, Jane (1982) 'Deixis and self/other reference in Japanese discourse', *Working Papers in Sociolinguistics* 99:1–36, Austin, Texas: Southwest Educational Development Laboratory.

—— (1983) 'Recruitment strategies for household succession: rethinking Japanese household organization', *Man* (n.s.) 18:160–82.

—— (1986) 'Time, space and person in Japanese relationships', in Joy Hendry and Jonathan Webber, (eds) *Interpreting Japanese Society: Anthropological Approaches*, Oxford: JASO, pp. 49–75.

—— (1990) 'Being in the group: spatio-temporal "place" in Japanese social organization', in M. Raveri and A. Boscaro, (eds) *Rethinking Japan*, vol. II, London: Paul Norbury Pub.

——(1994a) 'Introduction' in J. Bachnik and C. Quinn (eds) *Situated Meaning: Inside and Outside in Japanese Self, Society, and Language*, Princeton: Princeton University Press.

—— (1994b) 'Indexing self and society in Japanese family organization', in

J. Bachnik and C. Quinn (eds) *Situated Meaning: Inside and Outside in Japanese Self, Society, and Language*, Princeton: Princeton University Press.

—— (forthcoming) *Family, Self, and Society in Contemporary Japan*, Los Angeles and Berkeley: University of California Press.

Bachnik, Jane, and Charles J. Quinn (eds) (1994) *Situated Meaning: Inside and Outside in Japanese Self, Society, and Language*, Princeton: Princeton University Press.

Bateson, Gregory (1972) *Steps to an Ecology of Mind*, New York: Ballentine Books.

Ben-Ari, Eyal, Brian Moeran and James Valentine (eds) (1990) *Unwrapping Japan*, Manchester: Manchester University Press.

Bourdieu, Pierre, (1977) *Outline of a Theory of Practice*, Cambridge: Cambridge University Press.

—— (1990) *The Logic of Practice*, Stanford: Stanford University Press.

Brenneis, Donald (1994) 'Foreword: Inside and Outside', in J. Bachnik and C. Quinn (eds) *Situated Meaning: Inside and Outside in Japanese Self, Society, and Language*, Princeton: Princeton University Press.

Buber, Martin (1958) *I and Thou*, New York: Charles Scribner's Sons.

Daniel, E. Valentine (1984) *Fluid Signs: Being a Person the Tamil Way*, Los Angeles and Berkeley: University of California Press.

Derrida, Jacques (1978) 'Violence and metaphysics: an essay on the thought of Emmanuel Levinas', in *Writing and Difference*, University of Chicago Press. (First published as *L' écriture et la différence*, Editions du seuil, 1967.)

Doi, Takeo (1973a) *The Anatomy of Dependence*, Tokyo: Kōdansha International Ltd.

—— (1973b) '*Omote* and *ura*: concepts derived from the Japanese 2-fold structure of consciousness', *Journal of Nervous and Mental Disease* 155(4):258–61.

—— (1986) *The Anatomy of Self*, Tokyo: Kōdansha International Ltd.

Duranti, Alessandro and Charles Goodwin (eds) (1992) *Rethinking Context: Language as an Interactive Phenomenon*, Cambridge: Cambridge University Press.

Edwards, Walter (1989) *Modern Japan Through its Weddings*, Stanford: Stanford University Press.

Evens, T.M.S. (1990) *Transcendence in Society: The Comparative Study of Conflict and Sacrifice in Social Movements*, Greenwich CT: JAI Press.

Freeman, Eugene (1937) *The Categories of Charles Peirce* Chicago: Private Edition, Distributed by the University of Chicago Libraries.

Fukutake Tadashi (1967) *Japanese Rural Society*, Ronald P. Dore, trans., Ithaca: Cornell University Press.

Giddens, Anthony (1979) *Central Problems in Social Theory: Action, Structure and Contradiction in Social Analysis*, Berkeley and Los Angeles: University of California Press.

—— (1984) *The Constitution of Society*, Berkeley: University of California Press.

Hanks, William (1990) *Referential Practice: Language and Lived Space among the Maya*, Chicago: University of Chicago Press.

—— (1992) 'The indexical ground of deictic reference' in A. Duranti and C. Goodwin (eds) *Rethinking Context*, Cambridge: Cambridge University Press, pp. 43–76.

144    *Ceremony and Ritual in Japan*

Hamabata, Matthews (1983) 'From Household to Economy: the Japanese Family Enterprise', Ph.D. dissertation, Harvard University.
—— (1990) *Crested Kimono: Power and Love in the Japanese Business Family*, Ithaca: Cornell University Press.
Heidegger, Martin (1962) *Being and Time*, trans. John MacQuarrie and Edward Robinson, New York: Harper and Row. (First published as *Sein und Zeit*, Tübingen: Neomarius Verlag, 1926.)
Hendry, Joy (1989) 'To wrap or not to wrap: politeness and penetration in ethnographic inquiry' *Man* (n.s.) 24(4):620–35.
—— (1990) 'Humidity, hygiene, or ritual care: some thoughts on wrapping as a social phenomenon', in E. Ben-Ari, B. Moeran and J. Valentine (eds) *Unwrapping Japan*, Manchester: Manchester University Press.
—— (1993) *Wrapping Culture: Politeness, Presentation and Power in Japan and Other Societies*, Oxford: Oxford University Press.
Ikuta Shōkō (1980) 'Ethnography and Discourse Cohesion: Aspects of Speech Level Shift in Japanese Discourse', M.A. Thesis, Cornell University.
Jakobson, Roman (1960) 'Concluding statement: linguistics and poetics', in T. Sebeok (ed.) *Style in Language*, Cambridge, MA: MIT Press, pp. 350–73.
Kitaoji Hironobu (1971) 'The structure of the Japanese family', *American Anthropologist* 73:1036–57.
Klein, Steven (1988) 'Individual and Community in an Adolescent Group Home', Ph.D. Dissertation, University of North Carolina.
Lebra, Takie (1976) *Japanese Patterns of Behaviour*, Honolulu: University of Hawaii Press.
Levinas, Emmanuel (1987) *Time and the Other*, Pittsburgh: Duquesne University Press. (First published as 'Le temps et l'autre', in J. Wahl (1947) *Le Choix, Le Monde, L'Existence*, Grenoble-Paris: Arthaud, 1947.)
Levinson, Stephen C. (1983) *Pragmatics*, Cambridge: Cambridge University Press.
Lyons, John (1977) *Semantics*, Vols I and II, Cambridge: Cambridge University Press.
Martin, Samuel (1975) *A Reference Grammar of Japanese*, New Haven: Yale University Press.
Merleau-Ponty, Maurice (1962) *Phenomenology of Perception*, Colin Smith, trans, London: Routledge & Kegan Paul.
Miller, Roy Andrew (1967) *The Japanese Language*, Chicago: University of Chicago Press.
Nakane, Chie, (1967) *Kinship and Economic Organization in Rural Japan*, London: Athlone Press.
—— (1970) *Japanese Society*, Berkeley and Los Angeles: University of California Press.
—— (1972) *Tekiō no jōken* (Conditions of adaptation), Tokyo: Kōdansha.
Ochs, Elinor (1990) 'Indexicality and socialization' in G. Herdt, R. Shweder J. Stigler (eds) *Cultural Psychology: Essays on Comparative Human Development*, Cambridge: Cambridge University Press, pp. 287–307.
Ooms, Herman (1967) 'The religion of the household: a case study of ancestor worship in Japan', *Contemporary Religions in Japan* 8(3–4): 201–333.
Peirce, Charles Sanders, (1931–1935) *Collected Papers*, vols. I–III, C. Hartshorne and P. Weiss (eds), Cambridge, Mass.: Harvard University Press.
Plath, David (1964) 'Where the family of god is the family', *American Anthropologist* 66:300–17.

Quinn, Charles J, (1994) '*Uchi/soto*: tip of a semiotic iceberg?', in Jane Bachnik and Charles J. Quinn (eds) *Situated Meaning: Inside and Outside in Japanese Self, Society, and Language*, Princeton: Princeton University Press.

Rosenberger, Nancy R. (1994) 'Indexing hierarchy through Japanese gender relations', in Jane M. Bachnik and Charles J. Quinn (eds) *Situated Meaning: Inside and Outside in Japanese Self, Society, and Language*, Princeton: Princeton University Press.

Silverstein, M. (1976) 'Shifters, linguistic categories, and cultural description' in K. Basso and H. Selby (eds) *Meaning in Anthropology*, Albuquerque: University of New Mexico Press, pp. 11–55.

—— (1979) 'Language, structure, and linguistic ideology', in Paul R. Klyne, *et al.* (eds) *The Elements: A Parasession on Linguistic Units and Levels*, Chicago: Chicago Linguistic Society, pp. 193–247.

Singer, Milton (1980) 'Signs of the self: an exploration in semiotic anthropology', *American Anthropologist* 82:485–507.

Smith, Robert J. (1974) *Ancestor Worship in Contemporary Japan*, Stanford: Stanford University Press.

Stark, Werner (1962) *The Fundamental Forms of Social Thought*, London: Routledge & Kegan Paul.

Straus, Erwin (1967) 'On anosognosia', in E.W. Straus and R.M. Griffith (eds) *The Phenomenology of Will and Action*, Duquesne: Duquesne University Press, pp. 103–26.

Weinreich, U. (1980) *On Semantics*, W. Labov and B. Weinrich (eds) Philadelphia: University of Pennsylvania Press.

Wetzel, Patricia Jean (1984) '*Uchi* and *Soto* (In-group and Out-group): Social Deixis in Japanese', Ph.D. Dissertation, Department of Linguistics, Cornell University.

—— (1994) 'A moveable self: the linguistic indexing of *uchi* and *soto*', in Jane Bachnik and Charles J. Quinn (eds) *Situated Meaning: Inside and Outside in Japanese Self, Society, and Language*, Princeton: Princeton University Press.

# 6 Memorial monuments and memorial services of Japanese companies

## Focusing on Mount Kōya

*Hirochika Nakamaki[1]*

## INTRODUCTION

In the 1970s, especially after the oil shock, interest in Japanese business administration grew enormously. Various systems, such as the seniority system, lifetime employment, and company labour unions, which Japanese intellectuals had regarded as obstacles to Japan's economic growth, began to be evaluated, mainly by foreign economists and scholars. Since then much has been discussed and published on these topics, but there has been little research on the religious aspects of Japanese business administration.

The company or corporation is commonly called *kaisha* in Japanese. In contrast to the West, where the company is most definitely viewed as a secular entity engaged in economic activities, in Japan many major companies have a more or less religious dimension, which is Shintoic and/or Buddhist. This seems to be a characteristic common to Japanese companies, in contrast with those on the European and American continents.

Let me give some examples before embarking on the topic of memorial monuments. Small Shintō shrines are constructed in the compounds or on the roof of a company's head office building and religious ceremonies are regularly conducted to pray for continued prosperity and for the workers' safety (Jinja Shinpōsha 1986).[2] For example, Matsushita Electric Corporation (Panasonic) has a shrine in each factory and a monthly ceremony is conducted by a company priest in Ōsaka and its surrounding area. This priest is employed by the company and belongs to the managerial department. For the New Year ceremony, the company's first product is donated in place of the traditional first fruit, e.g. a new washing machine from the factory may be offered. In some other companies the company president includes a business report in his prayer to the tutelary deities in an annual ceremony.

If a company president dies, his funeral service is usually conducted as a company ceremony. All the employees who have died during the year are honoured together in an annual memorial service. This, of course, is normally associated with Buddhist rather than Shintō ceremonies. It is not uncommon for companies to hold memorial services as an established annual event. Some companies include employees who have died after the fixed age of retirement. A monument may be erected at the company headquarters itself, but some companies maintain tombs or memorial monuments for their employees at such sacred places as Mount Kōya or Mount Hiei.

## COMPANY MEMORIAL MONUMENTS

In this chapter I will focus on *kaisha* which maintain monuments on Mount Kōya on Honshū, the main island of Japan. I have chosen Mount Kōya because it represents the most important location for monuments of this type, containing over 100 such monuments, constructed so as to compete with one another. The term '*kaisha*' used here includes banks, department stores, and various associations related with *kaisha* such as the Lions Club. It does not include schools, schools of the traditional arts (*iemoto*), or senior citizens' clubs. Also, although I have used the general term 'memorial monuments' (*kuyōtō*), this is meant to include such structures as mausoleums (*byō*), stone monuments (*sekihi*), ossuaries (*nōkotsutō*), and tombs (*haka*). At Mount Kōya the terms 'enterprise tomb' (*kigyōbaka*) and 'company tomb' (*kaishabaka*) are commonly used, but there is not yet a general term for company memorial monuments.

Mount Kōya serves as the headquarters for the Kōya sect of Shingon Buddhism and is also the sacred location of the tomb of the sect's founder (at Oku no in). It is located in the mountains of Wakayama prefecture south of Ōsaka city. Beginning with the monuments to the *daimyō* (feudal lords) lining both sides of the main street for worshippers to Oku no in, the innumerable memorials stand clustered together inside a dense grove of cedars. Among them those devoted to companies amount to no more than a few scattered structures. According to a record of 1822, there were 110 feudal domains (*han*) which had memorial monuments for their feudal families in Oku no in. This amounts to approximately 42 per cent of the total number of feudal domains in that area (Hinonishi Shintai 1990:148).[3] However, a forest of company memorial monuments is plainly visible within the cemetery park.[4] In June 1991 there were about seventy-five in the Oku no in cemetery (including those in the cemetery park) and about twenty-eight in the Mount Kōya memorial park (Daireien) which was established in 1969. The memorial monument built in 1927 by a small newspaper distributor for its deceased employees seems to be the oldest so far found; representative of the earliest company monuments is the one erected by the Matsushita Electric Corporation in 1938. It was followed during the war years by others such as Maruzen Petroleum in 1941. During the first half of the 1950s companies such as Ōsaka Gas and Nankai Electric Railway were added. In the latter half of the decade, however, memorial monuments were constructed by several other companies, including the Photography Association, Nissan Automotive, Ezaki Glico, Sharp, Yakult, and Chiyoda Mutual Life Insurance. The construction of new monuments increased rapidly throughout the period of high economic growth during the 1960s. At present their numbers continue to increase, but at a more gradual rate.

## CULT FOR THE 'DECEASED SOLDIERS' AND 'ANCESTORS' OF THE COMPANY

Company memorial monuments usually bear an inscription. The sentiments expressed vary with the company, but the most common themes include:

> the occasion of the monument's construction;
> gratitude for the prosperity of the company;
> veneration of the spirits of predecessors (executives and employees);
> prayers for the prosperity of the company;
> prayers for the prevention of work-related accidents;
> thanks for customer patronage;
> praise for Mount Kōya.

The original intent behind the erection of memorial monuments was simply to commemorate deceased employees. Inscribed on the memorial monument of the Matsushita Electric Corporation is the phrase that the souls of dedicated employees who unfortunately have died through sickness or accident while working, or before retirement, shall be commemorated forever. This is similar to the cult of the 'deceased soldier' (*eisei*) and this fictive character was a strong theme on the early memorial monuments. Yanagita Kunio (1976:71), a prominent folklorist, wrote about the deceased soldiers who were enshrined at Yasukuni shrine. He remarked on the fact that the spirit of soldiers in the front line was enhanced by the prospect of being enshrined as gods of the nation after their death.[5] This also applies to the deceased spirits of 'company soldiers' (*kigyō senshi*).

In 1957 Nissan Automotive inscribed this on a memorial stone: 'to commemorate and console the souls of the deceased of our company'. In 1964, Yakult and Chiyoda Mutual Life also chose not to refer specifically to those who had died whilst working, rather, they emphasized the commemorative elements of the company's predecessors, and referred to how the company was founded and how its prosperity had increased. In other words, they pray to the 'company ancestors' for protection and prosperity. This is fictive ancestor worship. From the 1970s, this type of inscription has become conspicuous at Mount Kōya.

The change of emphasis from 'deceased soldiers' to 'ancestors' is occurring slowly. Early monuments, such as that of Matsushita Electric, are next to memorial tombs of company founders. The majority of recent monuments, however, have no founder's tomb. They are more concerned with the prosperity and perpetuity of the company itself, and with the cult for the deceased company 'soldiers' and 'ancestors'.

## AN INVESTIGATION OF MEMORIAL SERVICES FOR THE DECEASED

Memorial ceremonies at company monuments are usually conducted from spring to autumn, mostly as annual events. An examination of the date of the construction of memorial monuments reveals that most are put up during the months from April to November, thereby avoiding the snowy winter months.

I would like to outline the particulars of these memorial services through the use of five examples, followed by a comparative analysis. The subjects are the Nankai Electric Railway, Matsushita Electric, Kokuyo Office Supplies, Chiyoda Life Insurance, and the Ōsaka Council of Allied Printing Associations.

These five examples were chosen for a number of reasons. First, Nankai Electric Railway provides the main access to Mount Kōya; while Matsushita Electric is a typical representative of a giant corporation; and the Ōsaka Council of Allied Printing Associations is a group of medium- and small-sized companies. Second, the ceremonies of Kokuyo and Chiyoda happened to be held on the same ceremonial occasion as those of the Ōsaka Council and were selected for comparison. Another reason is that the memorial ceremonies of Matsushita Electric and Ōsaka Council of Allied Printing Associations are considered to be the largest in Oku no in and Mount Kōya memorial park, respectively.

## 1  Nankai Electric Railway Corporation.

The Nankai Electric Railway operates the rail lines south of Ōsaka, including the line which functions as the main artery for pilgrims between Ōsaka and Mount Kōya. Its monument in Oku no in cemetery park was constructed in 1953, and a memorial service is held every year in June.

The memorial service for deceased company officers and employees began at 10:00 a.m. on 7 June 1988 in the council room of the Nankai Electric Railway headquarters in Ōsaka. The altar contained memorial tablets (*ihai*) devoted to the souls of deceased company members, a register of the names of all the deceased up to that time, and a copper tablet engraved with names of company officers and employees who had died during the previous year. The attendants consisted of fourteen members from the families of the eleven recently deceased individuals, sixteen company officers and directors including the company president (*shachō*), a representative of the labour union, and forty-six representatives from the various departments and sections, for a total of seventy-seven persons. The general executive of the Buddhist sect on Mount Kōya served as the ritual's officiating priest. He was accompanied by seven additional priests and five musicians. The chief of the general affairs division assumed the role of company chairman.

Following the opening address by the chairman and the chanting of sutras by the priests, the chief priest and company president delivered eulogies. The priest prayed for the souls of the dead – particularly those who had passed away during the previous year. He told of their efforts on behalf of the company and of their service to society, and requested their protection for both the good fortune of their survivors and prosperity for the company. The company president expressed similar sentiments, but added a report on recent work-related matters, referring in particular to the proposed construction of the New Kansai Airport on a landfill site in Ōsaka bay and the company's efforts to take advantage of this opportunity.

Next came an offering of incense, first by the company president, then by a representative of the bereaved families, accompanied by the chanting of Buddhist sutras. The representative of the bereaved families, himself a vice-president of the company, was the eldest son of the former president who had died several months before. They were followed by the rest of the surviving family members, officers and directors, the union representative, and the representatives of all the various departments and sections. The incense burning was followed by a salutation from the chairman and some closing remarks. The priest and musicians led the departure, followed in order by the bereaved family members, officers and directors, the union representative, and department and section representatives. About fifty minutes had elapsed between entrance and departure, the service itself lasting forty minutes.

In examining the special features of this ceremony, I would first like to focus on rank. The order of entrance and departure were directly related to an individual's position within the company hierarchy. The bereaved family members were arranged according to the date of death of the deceased, but their representative was chosen based on his deceased father's former status in the company.

Early in the morning on the following day, 8 June, a party of company representatives set out from Ōsaka on the Nankai Railway to place the memorial tablet in the company monument, arriving at the monument at about 10:00 a.m. The group consisted of two Buddhist priests and nine other attendants, including the vice-president serving as representative for the bereaved families, followed by the general department chief, the general section chief, the chief of the secretariat, and general affairs division chiefs, all from the company headquarters. They were joined at the site by the Mount Kōya railway stationmaster, the head of the Mount Kōya Automotive Business Office, the chief of the cable car division, and a driver. The memorial service lasted for fifteen minutes, but although sutras were chanted there was no offering of incense by the attendants. Following the service, the vice-president placed the tablet inside the memorial. The party then left to worship at Oku no in, after which the caretakers poured water over the monument dedicated to the spirits of those who had died in traffic accidents.[6] This monument was erected in 1968 to commemorate the lives of the many victims of three train accidents which had occurred in 1967. The graves of several company officers are lined up around the company memorial monument as well.

## 2 Matsushita Electric Corporation

Matsushita Electric is a large enterprise, which was founded by Matsushita Kōnosuke in 1918. Its products are well known in Japan under the brand name 'National', and overseas as 'Panasonic' and 'Technics'. Its headquarters is in Ōsaka.

The company cemetery is located at the midway point along the main street to Okunoin, with the Kubota Steel cemetery plot just across the road. The deceased employees memorial monument was constructed in September 1938 at the request of Matsushita himself. This was one of the original company memorials, and served as a model for later monuments. The annual memorial ceremony is held in September, the month in which the monument was erected.

On 20 September 1988 the participants set out from Ōsaka's Nanba station by Nankai limited express, arriving at the Mount Kōya Station an hour and a half later. There they boarded three chartered buses and proceeded to Saizen'in, their company temple. The memorial service began at 11:20 a.m. at the main hall of the Saizen'in. The participants consisted of the bereaved families of those employees or retired employees who had died during the previous year, along with company executives including the company president, labour union representatives, and representatives from the *Sōaikai*, a friendship society for retired employees, making a total of 157 participants. The resident priest of Saizen'in served as the officiator, and was assisted by nine other priests. After the sutras had been chanted, the officiating priest read out the names of the recently deceased. Next the company president delivered a memorial address. Recounting the Matsushita company's seventy-year history, he noted that it had prospered through the efforts and enthusiasm of their predecessors in spite of the hardships and suffering they had to endure. He recalled the virtues of those who had died due to misfortune, illness, accident, or war, as well as those who had died after retirement. He then expressed condolences to the bereaved family members, reported on the recent condition of the company, pledged his efforts to improve management, asked for the protection of the spirits of the predecessors for the prosperity of the company, and finally closed with a prayer for the happiness of the souls of the deceased in the next world.

The offering of incense was conducted at four separate locations, with the chairman calling the participants forward in turns, beginning with the company president. At this same moment, just before noon, all Matsushita offices and factories observed a minute of silent tribute as the entire company prayed for the souls of the deceased. The priest withdrew following the offering of incense and chanting of sutras, and the ceremony ended at about 12:15 p.m. The order of departure began with the company officer representatives, followed by the bereaved family members, section representatives, and other attenders.

The group then moved to the educational training centre of the Layman's Association (*Daishi Kyōkai*) headquarters for a communal meal. In the afternoon a ceremony was held before the graves at the Matsushita cemetery plot. With three priests reading the sutras, the company president led the company officers, bereaved family members, and attendants in an offering of incense. The group left Mount Kōya at 4:00 p.m.

# 3 Kokuyo Corporation

Kokuyo is a leading manufacturer of office supplies. Its monument to the souls of the deceased was built in Mount Kōya memorial park (Daireien) on 20 August 1974, to commemorate the company's seventieth anniversary. At 11:30 on the morning of 20 August 1987, a memorial service was held at the Tentokuin, the company temple, and, following a break for lunch, another memorial service began at 1:00 p.m. in Daireien. The ceremony was led by the resident priest of Tentokuin with one assistant. The participants consisted of the company president, labour union representative, and twenty bereaved family members, and in that order they made the incense offering. Following this, the base of the five-story monument was opened and wood chips resembling wooden grave tablets were placed inside. On them were written the posthumous Buddhist name (*kaimyō*), secular name, and the date of death of each of the deceased.[7] After the priests withdrew there were salutations from representatives of the bereaved families which ended after about thirty minutes. Finally the group gathered in front of the symbol of Daireien for a commemorative photograph, then disbanded.

Over 200 deceased individuals are commemorated at the Kokuyo monument. These are limited to employees who passed away either during their tenure at the company or following retirement. Their names are engraved on the stone monuments beside the memorial. There are two such monuments; one is dedicated to employees, the other to the presidents of primary wholesaler agencies. However, worship is rarely performed at the president's monument.

# 4 Chiyoda Mutual Life Insurance Company

Chiyoda is one of Japan's most prominent life insurance companies. Its 'Predecessors' Monument' was erected in the cemetery park on 15 April 1964 to mark the company's sixtieth anniversary. The inscription reads as follows:

> In gratitude to our predecessors [deceased contractors, company founder, executives, and senior employees] for their support and meritorious service, and in remembrance of the benefits we have received from them, we erect this monument and respectfully pray for their happiness in the next world.

The names of these predecessors are recorded there on the 'List of the Deceased'.

At 11:05 on the morning of 21 August 1987, the head priest of Ryūkōin (the company temple) and four other priests arrived, together with the Ōsaka division chief and ten other attendants. They began the memorial service immediately . Following an offering of incense by all the attendants, the officiating priest recited some phrases of mourning. He then delivered a sermon which lasted about five minutes. The entire service took 45 minutes. There were no bereaved family members in attendance.

## 5  The Ōsaka Council of Allied Printing Associations

The Ōsaka Printing Industry Ossuary Monument was constructed in Mount Kōya memorial park on 20 August 1973. The Ōsaka Prefectural Print Manufacturer's Association sponsored an exhibit of the art of printing and international printing machine parts at the Ōsaka World Exposition in 1970. According to the inscription, 'To commemorate [the exhibit's] unprecedented success, this monument was constructed with the cooperation of the Ōsaka Council of Allied Printing Associations'. The Council was founded in 1967. At that time its membership stood at about 3,000, but at present it has grown to about 6,000. It has purchased 200 burial plots, totalling about 165 m$^2$, for over 70 million yen and has constructed the ossuary monument. This is the largest monument in Daireien, and the Council's association to mobilize participation in the memorial services is also the strongest.

The following is a summary of the memorial service held on 20 August 1987. There is a reception post in front of the Daireien business office, showing a list of contributors along with the amount of money they have donated. The service began at 11:30 a.m. There were about 300 participants, about sixty of whom were recipients of the association retirement fund who had arrived the day before and spent the night in the temple lodgings. During his salutation, the president of the Ossuary Monument Association referred to the historical background of the structure and the number of recently deceased, and recommended that their remains be placed in the monument. After the chairman had explained the order of the ceremony, ten priests arrived. In addition to the officiating priest, this number included the resident priest of the temple lodgings where the overnight guests and the chief director of Daireien had stayed. After the chanting of sutras by the priests and a 'memorial address for the souls of the recently deceased and those whose ashes have been laid to rest' delivered by the association president, there was an offering of incense. The order began with the chairman and proceeded with the allied associations representatives

representatives of the bereaved families, and ordinary worshippers. At 12:15 p.m. the memorial service ended and the head priest began his sermon, speaking very simply for twenty minutes on two themes: the immortality of the soul and gratitude to others. After the priests had departed, most of the attendants entered the ossuary monument to visit the remains of the deceased. The monument at present contains the remains of about 400 individuals, but is capable of accommodating about 20,000. Following this there was a communal meal, after which the participants went their separate ways.

The memorial service the next year followed approximately the same itinerary. This time, however, there were 390 attenders and the number of priests had increased to twelve. The officiating priest was the former director general of Mount Kōya. The sermon was delivered by the chief of the general affairs division, himself a Buddhist priest. The sermon was abbreviated to thirteen minutes due to sudden rain.

In 1987 and 1988 the recipients of the retirement fund numbered about eighty. In 1988, the group set out from Ōsaka on two chartered buses to Mount Kōya the day before the service, stopping at Daireien for a commemorative photograph with its director. They then checked into their temple lodgings at the Yōchiin, had their evening meal together, then passed the rest of the evening as they choose. The next morning a Buddhist service was conducted at Yōchiin and the entire group attended. The service consisted mainly of six priests chanting the sutras and the participants lighting incense. At 7:00 a.m. the service ended and was followed by a simple explanation about the temple. After breakfast, the group boarded buses and headed for the main entrance to Okunoin. There they split into two units and were led on a guided tour of Okunoin, after which they participated in the memorial service at Daireien. In addition to this group, about ninety individuals related to the Allied Printer's Association were lodged at the Ichijōin and Fumon'in temples and joined the others at the memorial service.

## 6 Comparison

This completes the description of five company or association memorial monument rituals. I shall now try to place them into some kind of order. Looking first at the place and importance of memorial services, it appears that Chiyoda Life Insurance and the print manufacturers emphasize the service conducted at the monument itself, while Matsushita Electric tends to attach greater importance to the temple ceremony. In the case of Nankai Electric Railway, the memorial service conducted at the company headquarters is on a significantly greater scale than that held at the memorial. In the case of Kokuyo, the temple and monument services form a chain of events.

The number of priests employed also varies with the company. For the print manufacturers, the officiating priest occupies the highest rank possible for Buddhist clergy; at Nankai Electric Railway he holds the status of executive director of religious affairs of the sect; while for the others he occupies the position of resident priest. The number of priests ranges from two to twelve.

In the case of Ōsaka companies and associations, it is the president who leads the procession of participants. For companies whose head-quarters are in Tokyo, the lead position is taken by the chief of the Ōsaka division. It is common for the bereaved families to participate, but there are also cases, such as that of Chiyoda Life Insurance, where they do not attend. Looking at the order of offering incense, the company or association president, as a representative of the sponsors, comes first. He is normally followed by the bereaved families or their representatives, but at Kokuyo the labour union representative preceded them. Usually all the attendants participate in the incense offering.

A characteristic feature of all the ceremonies is that not only the members of the executive class, but also representatives of the labour union, participate in the memorial services. In the case of Nankai, Matsushita, and Kokuyo, the labour union representative preceded the department and section chiefs. Since the print manufacturers group consists only of owner-managers, rank-and-file employees are not involved.

## COMPANIES AND FEUDAL DOMAINS

According to Umesao Tadao, the model for large commercial enter-prises (*kaisha*) in Japan was the feudal domain (*han*) of the Edo period rather than European companies. Umesao (1980:224–6) argues that the qualities necessary for managing a large enterprise organization – responsibility, leadership, strategic thinking, and the ability to com-promise – were already possessed by the *samurai*, the military admin-istrators of the pre-industrial period. The hierarchical relationship between feudal lord, principal retainer, and ordinary *samurai* corres-ponds to that of company president, director, and employee, and many terms such as director (*jūyaku*), supervisor (*torishimari*), head director (*tōdori*), account (*kanjō*), stock (*kabu*), and bill of transaction (*tegata*), have survived from feudal times. Moreover, the relationship between domain (*han*) and retainer has been reproduced in the company lifetime employment system, and loyalty to the domain has manifested itself in the employee's selfless devotion to the company.[8] Actually, during the Edo period some *han* began to actively promote the development of industry and established the economic foundations of *han* management, which were carried over into the company organization after the Meiji Restoration. After the political revolution of Meiji, the *samurai* lost their position and salaries. Some became merchants and in many cases company owners, as well as soldiers, policemen, and teachers.

The roots of the so-called 'salary men' go back to this *samurai* class. *Samurai* were soldiers, dedicated their lives to their lords, and in return, received salaries in measures of rice. They became, however, administrators or bureaucrats during the peaceful period of Edo, which lasted for about 250 years from the beginning of the seventeenth century. The castle thus became an administrative centre. During the Edo period there were about 250 *han* throughout Japan. Sometimes the feudal lord who led the *han* was ordered to move to a new domain, in much the same way as the transfer of the present-day 'salary men', who are often referred to as 'company soldiers'.

Though the *samurai* class was abolished, the ethics of the *samurai* remained and began to disseminate through the population at large. The ethics of *samurai*, such as selfless devotion to the feudal lord, were dominant in the formation of modern Japanese culture. In this culture, the feudal lords and *shōgun* were replaced by company owners and emperor. The family code of the *samurai* was declared universal for the whole population through the Civil Code of 1898, which remained in force until the end of the Second World War. Juridically at least, the male head of household and his successor dominated the household just as the former *samurai* had dominated theirs. In the company, the relationship between employer and employees was also grasped as reflecting that of a patriarchal family. And in the cases of big companies, their model of management was greatly influenced by that of *han*, as Umesao argues.

At present it is through commercial enterprise that Japan maintains its economic prosperity. For this reason, human relations within the company are extremely important. This has led Yoneyama Toshinao (1981:111–37) to suggest that, in addition to blood ties and local community ties, we must focus also on the concept of association (*sha'en*).[9] From overseas, Japan is often characterized as a single large corporation (Japan, Inc.). According to Umesao Tadao's interpretation, this is because the incorporation of *han* (the *bakuhan* system) was transformed into an organizational pattern for the modern Japanese business corporation. Explaining the memorial monuments on Mount Kōya as symbols of the transition from domain to corporation and feudal lord to company president is not incongruent with this interpretation. The emphasis, however, is not on the individual *shachō*, but on the *kaisha* itself.

## NOTES

1 This chapter was translated by Scott Schnell.
2 See Jinja Shinpōsha (ed.) (1986) *Kigyō no jinja* (Commercial enterprise shrines), Jinja Shinpōsha.
3 Hinonishi Shintai (1990) *Kōyasan oku no in minzokushi* (Folklore on Mount Kōya), Tokyo: Kosei shuppansha.
4 The term memorial monument is used throughout, with the understanding that, in general, there are no bodies, bones or ashes interred in the place. Memorial tablets are the main features of these monuments. An exception to this is, of course, the Ōsaka Printing Industry Ossuary Monument described below.
5 See Yanagita Kunio (1976) *Meiji-Taishō-shi sesōhen* (Social life of Meiji–Taishō period), Tokyo: Chūō Kōronsha.
6 Pouring water is an act of purification associated mostly with Shintō rites, but important here in a Buddhist context of caring for the dead (Japanese text).
7 The posthumous Buddhist name is given to the deceased by a Buddhist priest. This name is written in several Chinese characters, which are engraved on the gravestone or on a wooden memorial tablet.
8 See Umesao Tadao (1980) *Chikyū jidai no nihonjin* (Japanese in the global era), Tokyo: Chūō Kōronsha. Originally published in 1974.
9 Yoneyama Toshinao (1981) *Dōjidai no jinruigaku* (Contemporary anthropology), Tokyo: NHK Books.

## BIBLIOGRAPHY

Hinonishi Shintai (1990) *Kōyasan oku no in Minzokushi* (Folkflore on Mt. Kōya), Tokyo: Kosei Shuppansha.
Jinja Shinpōsha (ed.) (1986) *Kigyō no jinja* (Commercial enterprise shrines), Jinja shinpōsha.
Umesao Tadao (1980) *Chikyū jidai no nihonjin* (Japanese in global era), Tokyo: Chūō Koronsha.
Yanagita Kunio (1976) *Meiji–Taishō Sesōken* (Social life of the Meiji–Taishō period), Tokyo: Chūō Koronsha.
Yoneyama Toshinao (1981) *Dōjidai no jinruigaku* (Contemporary anthropology), Tokyo: NHK Books.

# Part III
# The tools of ceremony

# 7    A Japanese Shintō Parade

## Does it 'say' anything, and if so, what?[1]

*Arne Kalland*

This chapter deals with a local Shintō festival which is held once every eighteen years,[2] and in which the central event is a parade through the community of Shingū.[3] None of the participants in the 1988 festival could give the anthropologist the 'meaning' of all the paraphernalia carried in the parade or of all the rituals performed during the festival, although a few could articulate what some of the objects and rites 'meant' to them. Only one participant – the Shintō priest – could give an interpretation of most of the festival's many different parts, although frequently only after looking them up in some authoritative handbook for Shintō priests.[4] Most people had only vague ideas about the significance of the festival, and those who voiced an opinion were by no means agreed as to its interpretation. This bears out Caillet's observation (1986:35) that a ritual day in Japan 'does not seem to have a finite, limited meaning in itself. It is just a moment where human and divine worlds come into contact, a moment the significance of which is not clearly stated'.

This brings me to one of the central issues in much of the recent writings on rituals, namely: what does a ritual – and all the objects or symbols used in the ritual – mean to the holders of a particular culture, and what do we as anthropologists do when the informants – as often is the case – cannot put into words all the emotions, associations and memories a ritual brings forth in their minds?

Two contrasting views have influenced this debate. In 1953 Nadel claimed that meanings which cannot be explained by natives are private and non-social and thus irrelevant (1953:108). Victor Turner (1969), among others, has, on the other hand, argued that it is the task of the social anthropologist to grasp these 'hidden' meanings in order to provide etic interpretations in addition to the native points of view. Lévi-Strauss (1963) goes even further in an attempt to find deeper structures universal to myths and rituals.

There are problems with symbolist and structuralist approaches. For, as Keesing has pointed out, how do we know if our interpretation is correct if these meanings are unconscious (1982:180)? Given the definition of culture as a system of shared knowledge, Keesing has also asked whether hidden meanings – which are seen by the anthropologist but not shared by the informants – are part of the latters' culture (1982:192). In its ultimate consequence this approach operates at such a high level of abstraction that we are in danger of learning more about the workings of the human brain than about cultures.

Lewis gives a similar warning saying that 'we can read meaning *into* what we see (where it does not belong) and this may tell more about ourselves than about what we have seen' (1980:18, italics in original). He goes on to argue that rituals are a form of performance or art rather than a form of communication (1980:6–9). Keesing also takes issue with ritual as a system of communication, saying that '*communication* predisposes us to seek meanings, where native participants are primarily engaged with ritual as a mode of *action*, a form of collective work for social ends' (1982:186, italics in original).

Therefore, more than simply saying something, rituals also do something (Barth 1975), and people perform religious actions in order to achieve good health, economic success, and so on. This view is supported by observations made by many of the participants themselves stating that the importance of the festival is not so much its intrinsic meaning as what it actually does.

To the inhabitants of Shingū, the Gosengū festival – or *Shikinen-gosenza-sai* to give it its full name – does not only say different things, it also does different things. To some it is performed in order to secure divine protection for the community and its inhabitants, while others expressed the opinion that the purpose of the festival is merely to carry on a tradition: 'we do what our ancestors always have done.' But it is an expensive tradition as each household contributed on average 70,000 yen (at a rate of 230 yen to the pound sterling) to the rebuilding and construction work at the shrine in addition to private expenses incurred during the festival. Certainly, expensive traditions are only continued if they serve a wider purpose. Some people hold a Durkheimian view, claiming that this wider purpose is to bring about community solidarity. It is an opportunity to meet and do something together, and to the participants the purpose (*mokuteki*) of the festival *is* communication (*komyunikeeshon*), not so much between man and deity as between men.

This communicative aspect of the festival is important – and it will be discussed at some length below – but as a matter of fact, the festival is not well suited to bringing about village solidarity as it alienates about 10 per cent of the population for religious reasons. The members of the Sōkagakkai Buddhist sect refuse to have anything to do with the festival, so in a sense the village solidarity is challenged and endangered by it. Communal clean-ups of the beach, sports days, and activities at the community hall are probably much more efficient – and cheaper – ways to help bring about an integration of the village (see Reader's chapter, this volume).

In order to grasp the reason why so many people spend so much money and energy on this festival, we have to seek other interpretations. It is, on the one hand, possible to focus on the *participants*, and in particular to look at the social organization and management of the festival and see this as a mirror of the village organization as a whole. A number of recent papers have analysed Japanese festivals in this way (e.g., Akaike 1976; Ashkenazi 1985, 1990; Bestor 1985; Littleton 1986). On the other hand, it is possible to focus on the ritual *objects* used during the festival. Why are they used and what do they stand for, or 'mean'? Finally, it is possible to analyse the festival as a *process* whereby participants and objects interact.

The latter approach will be attempted here, and in so doing I will limit myself to an analysis of one element of the festival, namely the parade.[5] I will, as a first step, discuss in some detail the various positions in the parade. What does a particular object mean (if it means anything at all to any of the participants) and why is it carried by a particular person? Keeping the warnings of Keesing and Lewis in mind I will limit myself to a discussion of views and interpretations as they have been expressed locally.[6] I should stress, however, that this is a composite view in that no single person possesses the sum of this knowledge. From this it will be possible to discern certain themes in the parade; the objects do not only have a meaning in themselves, but gain their fuller meaning in association with other objects. The parade can be viewed diachronically; the sequence of the objects is important. Taken together, the objects, the participants and the progress of the parade comprise an entity which also has a significance of its own. The interpretations offered are again based on the informants' interpretations, although often made only implicitly by them. Finally, some of the objects are also central elements in other annual festivals held in Shingū, and these can thus be viewed as pointers to these festivals. Gosengū can therefore to a certain extent be conceptualized as a 'meta-festival' which places the annual festivals in a broader perspective and thus structures time.

## LAYOUT OF THE PROCESSION (*GYŌRETSU*)

Layouts of the Gosengū parades – indicating positions of each object as well as names of the persons carrying them – exist for most of the Gosengū festivals held since 1755. The layout for the 1988 parade is given below in the left-hand column. The objects are described in the right-hand column, with symbolic meaning as given by local inhabitants. Names of persons have been omitted, but social positions of participants will be given when relevant.[7] The parade was divided into 'sections', members of the organizing committee being in charge of each of them.[8] These sections are arbitrarily partitioned.

## SECTION I

| | |
|---|---|
| 1　Two lanterns　(*chōchin*) | These are white paper lanterns, each decorated with a red-painted *gohei* on one side and a person's name painted in black on the other. The members of the executive committee and shrine committee as well as those who have donated more than 1 million yen are honoured by having their names painted on such lanterns. The 'meaning' of the lanterns is to convey a message that these persons have been the 'cornerstones' for the festival. |
| | It is particularly honourable to have one's lantern at the front of the parade. Two lanterns take this position and they bear the names of the head of the shrine committee and the vice-chairman of the organizing committee. |
| | A *gohei* is a staff with sacred cut paper (which also may be termed *gohei* or *nusa*) attached to it. To the priest it symbolizes a sacred tree into which the deities can descend, although it must not be confused with a *shintai*, the object in which a deity resides. The *gohei* thus indicates the presence of a deity and can – like trees, mountains and pillars – be looked upon as a bridge between heaven and earth, although this interpretation was not explicitly made by the priest. (See also Ono (1962:24); Herbert (1967:116–17).) |
| 2　A white flag　(*seidō*) | Upon the flag are written the characters for 'pure' and 'road' written in black. This flag |

signals that this is the route upon which the deities are going to proceed, and that it is therefore pure, or alternatively, that the road is purified.[9]

| | |
|---|---|
| 3 A Shintō priest (*shinshoku*) | The priest comes from another town and is dressed in white. He carries small pieces of cut sacred paper (*kiri-nusa*) which he tosses around, particularly at corners and crossings – which are regarded as dangerous areas. Like the *gohei*, the *kiri-nusa* indicates purity and sacrality, and that the road is purified. |
| 4 Sarutahiko | This deity is believed to have served as a guide to Niningi, the son of the sun goddess Amaterasu, when he descended to Earth. Thus, the pair of Sarutahiko may serve as guides or vanguards to the parade. Sarutahiko is, moreover, regarded as a deity of the crossroads and thus of procreation (Herbert 1967:496). |
| | Sarutahiko is here depicted as a long-nosed goblin (*Tengu*), but the connection between the two is uncertain. They are represented by wooden masks on top of poles and with three-forked gaffs at the very top. The one carried on the right-hand side is painted blue and the other red. |
| 5 Two pine torches (*taimatsu*) | These torches were originally lit, but this is no longer done due to the polluting smoke. They consist today of straw wrapped around poles. Symbolically they still illuminate the road.[10] |
| 6 *Oshioi* (literally 'the well of tide)' | *Oshioi* is a box of sand which is taken from the wet part of the beach early in the morning of the festival day. This is one of the most important positions in the parade, and the carrier (who is selected with great care) throws – as a form of purification (*kiyome*) – sand on the road, and particularly at the corners and crossings. *Shio* also means 'salt', which is another important purifying agent much used in Shintō rites. |
| 7 Two lanterns | These bear the names of two members of the shrine committee. |
| 8 A large branch of *sakaki* | This is a branch of the *Cleyera ochnacea*, decorated by sacred paper. The whole branch is regarded as a *haraigushi*, a sacred wand with |

long strips of paper used for purification rites and which the priest regards as a kind of *gohei*.

The priest had several suggestions as to why *sakaki* is so special. His first explanation was that the word for the tree is written with a Chinese character which combines the elements 'tree' and 'deity'; then he added that it is shining evergreen which always grows upwards.[11]

## SECTION II

| | |
|---|---|
| 9 Bow and arrows (*yumidai*) | The priest suggested that the bow and arrows signal the power of the deity, but he agreed that they could also mean protection and thus be connected to the deity Hachiman (see also position 16 in Section III of the parade). |
| 10 Two lanterns | These bear the names of the chairman of the arranging committee (right) and one large donor (left). |
| 11 *Nikki* and *gekki* | These two 'flags' symbolize the sun and the moon, respectively. The yellow 'sun-flag' is carried on the right, whereas the silver-coloured 'moon-flag' is carried to the left. The meaning of these flags is uncertain, and the priest said that they are included to make the procession joyous. |
| 12 *Shishi* | *Shishi* are two 'lion' heads, one red and the other blue. They are placed on a white-covered carriage with the red lion head placed on the left-hand side and the blue one on the right. The priest believes that the lions are messengers from the deities and that they protect against illness and accidents. These heads point to the Gion festival (9 July) when the fire brigade put on the heads and run from house to house, extracting bad influences – and obtaining lots of alcohol – on their way through the village. |
| 13 Two lanterns | The lanterns in this position bear the names of the largest donor (right) and another donor (left). |
| 14 and 15 *Nikki* and *gekki* | These are flags as in position 11 above. |

**SECTION III**

| | |
|---|---|
| 16 Eight white flags (*hachiki*) | The flags are decorated with stylized *gohei* painted in black. 'Eight' means 'good luck' and also 'many'. The white symbolizes – according to the priest – both ritual purity and shining light, and the flags may thus symbolize a penetrating light which purifies. |
| | With another character for '*hata*' (flag) the compound can be read as 'Hachiman' (eight flags) who is the war deity, alias Ōjin-Tennō, and the flags can thus also symbolize the War God protecting the parade and the deities therein. (For other interpretations of Hachiman, see Herbert 1967:433–8.) |
| | These flags signify several annual festivals when they are hoisted outside the shrine building. |
| 17 A small halberd (*ko-boko*) | According to the priest this has the same meaning as the bow and arrows: a show of power as well as protection. |
| 18 *Engi* | This is the shrine chronicle written in the early eighteenth century. As a matter of fact, only the empty box in which the chronicle is usually stored is carried in the parade because the priest is afraid that it will be lost.[12] |
| 19 'The thirty-six great poets' (*Sanjūrokkasen*) | This describes a collection of paintings made by Katō Shōun – who was in the *daimyō*'s service – to illustrate thirty-six famous ancient poems copied by court nobles. The collection was donated to the shrine early in the eighteenth century in gratitude for a pregnancy which occurred after worshipping at the shrine.[13] This collection is the pride of the village and it has attracted some media attention. Again, only the box is carried. |
| 20 Two lanterns | These bear the names of two more members of the shrine committee. |
| 21 Zuijin | This consists of a pair of sitting figures with bows and arrows. Locally they are known as Yagorō, who is believed to have been a giant. They are placed on a white-covered carriage, the red figure to the left and the black/blue to the right. |

According to the priest '*Zui*' means 'protection' and these figures protect the shrine. Zuijin is generally regarded as a guardian of gates and is therefore also called 'Kado-mori-no-kami' (Herbert 1967:98). But written with another character for '*kado*' the latter name can mean 'The Protector of Corners'. This may explain why the priest associated Zuijin with Dōshōshin, who is a deity of crossroads and is thus similar to Sarutahiko as well.

22 *Okumai* ('long-continued rice')

Sacred raw rice is carried in the procession. This is one of the most important positions in the parade. Rice is indispensable in all Shintō festivals and this rice symbolizes that Japan is the 'Land of Abundant Rice' (Mizuho-no-kuni).

This rice has 'always' been donated by one particular household in Shingū.

## SECTION IV

23 *Hōgyoku* (treasure gem)

This a round golden ball, *tama*, made of bronze. *Tama* is a very complex concept, generally meaning jewel as well as spirit/soul, and the priest associated this ball with the Dragon King, Ryūjin, although it does not specifically symbolize this important deity. In his opinion the ball symbolizes the heart (*kokoro*).

The *tama* points to the New Year festival 'Tama-seseri' when teams of youths used to fight each other to get hold of the ball. The winning team was supposed to be well-protected during the following year.

The main fishing festival of the year, *Ryūgū-matsuri*, is held in honour of the Dragon King, Ryūjin, who also might be worshipped as the deity of rain, which partly explains the golden ball (*tama*) he carries and which sparkles like lightning. As a bringer of rain Ryūjin thus has importance also to the farmers.

24 *Gokubitsu* ('offering chest')

This box contains a portable altar used for two ceremonies held during the parade. It also includes two sets of offerings, *sonaemono*, used during these ceremonies: sake (right), raw rice (centre), raw fish (left), and *tamagushi* (a sprig of *sasaki*). The portable altar is wrapped in sacred rope made of rice straw, *shimenawa*.

25 Two lanterns     In this position the lanterns bear the names of the cashier in the organizing committee (right) and a generous donor (left).

26 *Yaotome* (literally 'the eight (or many) virgins')     This part of the procession may be exactly what it says. Alternatively, this part is called *chigo* ('small children'). About 300 children – girls and boys – dressed in colourful clothes participated, the youngest accompanied by their mothers. Ideally, they ought to be under twelve years of age (or fifth grade), although the priest denied that this had anything to do with menstruation. The children walk in two rows, holding long 'ropes' made of white cotton cloth. Originally the rope was tied to the *mikoshi*.

The 'meaning' of the *chigo* is – according to the priest – to make the parade colourful and joyous. Moreover, this part indicates that the deity has many supporters. It is to show off.

27 Two 'golden *gohei*' (*kinpei*)     These have the same meaning as an ordinary *gohei*, which is both a symbolic offering and an indication that the deity is present. They keep impure substances at a distance and thus protect deities. There is one *kinpei* for each deity. There are symbols of the imperial jewel (*magatama*) on them and this symbol is used as a crest (*shamon*) by Hachiman, thus indicating his presence as well.

28 The musicians (*gakujin*)     These are boys between the fourth and seventh grade. They are dressed in white and play *entenraku* music on flutes. The 'meaning' is to follow tradition.

## SECTION V

29 *Osaisenbako*     This portable offering box, into which worshippers can toss coins, is also used for the Tsujigitō festival held annually in July.

30a *Tamagake-sakaki*    This is a long pole with something which resembles a mirror (*kagami*) and a jewel (*magatama*) hanging from the top, with the *magatama* highest.

30b *Tsurugigake-sakaki*    Again this is also a pole, but with a model of a sword at the top. Strips of paper in five colours (*goshiki*) hang down both poles which are also decorated by artificial *sakaki* branches.

Together these two poles comprise the three imperial regalia: the mirror, jewel and the sword. According to the priest, these symbols carried in the procession show that the deity also possesses these, and not only the imperial household. Moreover, through these symbols the festival is linked to a national cult.

31  A Shinto priest    This priest, who comes from another shrine, should have carried a *haraigushi* in order to purify the road, particularly corners and crossroads. He was prevented from participating, however. This position was dropped at the final moment since the priest was unable to attend, and the priest at the front of the parade (position 3) did this task as well.

32  Two lanterns    These bear the names of a member of the shrine committee (right) and the deputy hamlet headman (left).

33  A shield (*tateita*)    As a protective 'weapon', this protects both the deities and the parade.

34  The third 'golden *gohei*'    See position 27 in Section IV.

35  A large mirror    The mirror is dragged on a carriage also used for the Tsujigitō festival. The mirror, which was donated in 1882, signals the presence of the deity, although it does not function as the place where the deity dwells (i.e., *shintai*).

## SECTION VI

36  The portable shrine (*mikoshi*)    This enshrines the three deities who make up the *ujigami* of Isozaki *jinja*, i.e., Ebisu, Daikoku, and Susano-wo-no-mikoto. Their three *shintai*, which are wooden figures wrapped in white

cloth, were moved from their temporary residence in Ebisu-do to the *mikoshi* before the procession started. The *mikoshi* – which was carried by young men aged between eighteen and thirty years old and who had gone through special purification rites – was black-lacquered and covered with thirty-six mirrors (actually there were two missing). The mirrors made sounds, which the priest was unable to interpret. On the roof of the *mikoshi* was a figure of the phoenix (*hōō*). This bird, which originally comes from China, is in Shintō associated with heaven, and thus may symbolize the dream which people have of flying to heaven.

37 Two lanterns  These bear the names of the hamlet headman (right) and the hamlet cashier (left). This is a particularly honourable position in the procession.

38 The (three) fans (*sashiba*)  These are meant to cool the *shintai* and thus the deities. The fans have pictures of a phoenix on one side and of a dragon on the other. The dragon may symbolize the deity Ryūjin, who was discussed above.

39 Two lanterns  These bear the name of two donors, one male (right) and one female (left).

40 The silk parasol (*kinukasa*)  The parasol, a sign of respect, is meant to shade the resident priest.

41 The shrine priest  He will be wearing white and violet formal dress to show his rank and the importance of the event. White means purity in this context, the priest said. Beside the priest walked the following persons: His son (on his left), the chairman of the organizing committee and one member of the shrine committee (on his right). These are honourable positions.

## THE 'MEANINGS' OF THE PARADE

I have so far limited myself to a synchronic description of the various objects carried in the parade and what they, in isolation, mean to some of the local villagers. It is time to look upon the parade diachronically: in other words, we have to look at the connection between the various elements in order to analyse the parade as a *process*.

It will immediately be apparent that there are several themes that are repeated in the parade. First, there is the theme of purification. The white flag (position 2), the priest throwing cut paper (3), the sand from the beach (6), the *sakaki* branch (8), the eight white flags (16) and the priest waving a *haraigushi* (31) are all interpreted as purifying agents by the priest. Moreover, the *gohei* that are depicted on all the paper lanterns and the *kinpei* (27 and 34) are also objects which keep pollution at a distance. These elements purify the route – and the village – before the coming of the deities.[14]

Another theme is guidance. As has already been mentioned, the two pine torches (5) can be interpreted as purifying agents, but to the priest they are first and foremost included in the parade to illuminate the road (although the parade is always held at the middle of the day), thus showing the way and securing a safe passage for the deities. The paper lanterns may serve the same function while Sarutahiko (4) – and possibly Zuijin (21) – seem to have served as guides and guardians.

A third theme is strength. Bow and arrows are carried (position 9), as are a halberd (18) and a shield (33). Moreover, the giant Zuijin (21) is regarded as a strong 'soldier' and is depicted carrying bow and arrows; the eight white flags (16) can be interpreted as a symbol of the war deity Hachiman; and the pair of lions (12) protects the village from evil influences.

While the first section of the parade (positions 1–8) can be looked upon largely as a sequence of spiritual protection and guidance, physical protection is more prevalent in the following two sections (9–22). It should, however, be stressed that there are overlaps between the sections with regards to the main themes. Together, the first three sections can be seen as an 'army' giving spiritual and physical protection to the deities and the participants.

As the procession proceeds other themes become more prominent. Three objects carried close to the centre of the parade facilitate offerings to the deities. The offerings chest (24) contains the offerings of rice, fish, sake and sprigs of *sakaki*, all of which are practically indispensable in any Shintō ritual. Money offered by worshippers during the two ceremonies held on the way can be tossed in the offerings box (29). The raw rice carried in position 22 is regarded as an important offering to the deities, but it also symbolizes the importance of rice in Japanese culture in general. The *gohei* and *kinpei* may also be symbolic offerings to the deities (Herbert 1967:117).

The *gohei* and *kinpei* indicate the presence of the deities as well. The large mirror (35) and the thirty-six mirrors hanging on the portable shrine (36) are even more powerful symbols of the presence of divine powers who are enshrined in this, the most important object of the parade. The *kinpei* and the mirrors are all located close to the *mikoshi*.

The deities are surrounded by their believers, or 'court'. First comes the group of children dressed in colourful costumes (position 26) followed by young boys playing flutes (28). The portable shrine itself (36) is carried by a group of thirty young men. At the rear we find the most prominent persons of the 'court': the village priest (who is the high mediator between the villagers and the deities), the leader of the organizing committee and one representative from the shrine committee (41). In the old days the village leaders (*shōya* and *kumigashira*) used to walk in this position as well. In a sense then, in these positions (i.e., 26, 28, 36 and 41) we find a cross-section of the male population in the village. Only middle-aged men in their thirties and forties are poorly represented in these 'positions of the court', but then they carry most of the objects in the procession. Sections IV–VI can thus be viewed as made up of the tutelary deities and their court.

A few more themes should be mentioned. The silk parasol (40), which is an important symbol in Buddhist iconography, is carried close to the village priest and conveys respect, as do the three fans (38) cooling the deities. The shrine chronicle (18) and the 'thirty-six pictured poems' (19) are important treasures to the shrine. The former was donated by a group of prominent villagers in 1721 while the latter was donated by the feudal lord. These objects give legitimacy to the shrine and its priest. Moreover, they also give an aura of greatness to the shrine and thus to the deities. This focus on greatness or importance is also the theme of the two poles carrying the sacred imperial regalia: the mirror, jewel and sword (30). The golden ball (23) symbolizes to some of the participants the Dragon King, and this gives added significance to the shrine and the community as well. 'This shows', according to the priest, 'that we have the protection of this deity also'.

## THE PARADE AND THE SOCIAL ORDER

This 'aura of greatness' is an important consideration in the planning of the parade, and at one level of interpretation the whole parade is seen as a show of strength – the priest likened it to military parades staged by many regimes on national days.[15] And like military parades, the procession is aimed at both 'domestic' and 'foreign' consumption. The many objects carried show, according to the priest, that the deities have great powers and deserve respect from the villagers. At the same time, however, they are also signals of great power *vis-à-vis* the outside world, as are the many villagers participating in the parade – and in particular the many children – who indicate the great number of supporters the deities have. In that sense the procession does not only indicate the importance and strength of the deities, but also the strength of Shingū itself.

One might well ask at whom this show of strength is aimed, and again there are two targets. On the one hand, there is the world 'out there'. Japanese villages have been described as 'autonomous' (Befu 1968) and they were often in conflict with each other. To be backed by deities with strong powers gave villagers strength and confidence for these conflicts.[16] On the other hand, to be associated with a strong shrine also gave prestige to the village and the village leadership and this is still an important factor contributing to local pride and identity. People who have moved into Shingū take it as a final confirmation for their acceptance when they are asked to participate in the parade. The combination of deities worshipped, the village festivals held and the way these festivals are organized all tend to be unique to a community. People are quite conscious that 'this is the way we do it, others do it differently'. Through local beliefs and rites 'we' are separated from 'them' and socio-cultural boundaries are drawn. These boundaries are not necessarily congruent with the geographical ones (Yagi 1988), but in the Gosengū case Shingū as a geo-political unit receives attention in two ways: only residents of Shingū are allowed to participate in the parade (with two exceptions to be dealt with below) and the procession proceeds along the geographical boundaries.

It is also possible to discern different age groups in the parade. Children precede the young musicians who, in turn, are followed by the young men in their twenties carrying the *mikoshi*. The old village leaders form the rear. Using walkie-talkies, men in their thirties take care of traffic and supervise the movements of the parade, while middle-aged men carry the paraphernalia. All age groups in the community are thus involved, and the mutual dependencies that exist between age groups are stressed. This interpretation was quite widely expressed in Shingū. Alien to the local exegesis – but nonetheless captivating to an anthropologist – is the corollary of this view, e.g., that the festival can be seen as a *rite de passage* in which people are brought from one age group to another.[17] Seen as a *rite de passage* the festival marks the liminal phase, which begins with the transfer of the deities from the main shrine building (in 1988 on 22 September) and ends with the parade and the deities being re-installed into the shrine (in 1988 on 9 October).

The cohesion of the village is thus stressed in several ways. But, simultaneously social differences are also pointed out. A number of paper lanterns bearing the names of the festival leaders and generous donors are carried in the parade, informing all participants and onlookers about who have formed the 'backbone' for a successful festival. Moreover, some of the positions in the procession are more prestigious than others. The parade is divided into sections, with members of the organizing committee being in charge of each. It carries higher prestige to be in charge of the first and last sections than the others. Likewise, it is more prestigious to have lanterns carrying one's name in these positions than in the middle. Some of the paraphernalia have been donated by individuals, and these are carried by someone from the donors' households or their descendants thus prolonging the effect of past glory. A few paraphernalia, such as the sand and the uncooked rice, are of particular importance and special attention is given to these positions.[18] The separation of age groups has already been pointed out, and females are excluded except as children or as mothers leading their youngsters. The role of the women as socializers is thereby underlined.

If we compare the names written on the lanterns, which are always carried in pairs, we will see that lanterns with names of the most generous donors are carried to the right of those of smaller donors; lanterns with names of male donors are carried to the right of those with female donors; lanterns with names of festival officials are carried to the right of those of donors; and lanterns with names of the shrine committee members are carried to the right of those carrying the names of village officials. In other words, large donors rank over smaller ones; shrine officials over village officials (in the festival context); officials over donors; and men over women.[19] The whole parade then, is loaded with messages of social hierarchy. Through the parade the social structure of the community is metaphorically expressed.

The 1988 procession passed through all the three parallel streets in Shingū (first Uramachi, then Nakamachi and finally Honmachi) before it proceeded to the beach. The general direction of movement was with the sun which, incidently, is the opposite direction of the movement in the annual *Tsujigitō* festival. By this route the boundaries towards the hamlets Minato and Shimonofu as well as towards the sea were marked. At each crossing the priest (3) waved his *haraigushi* and threw some pieces of cut sacred paper in all directions. The carrier of the box with sand likewise tossed sand in order to purify these dangerous spots through which bad outside elements tend to come.

The procession made two stops on the way: first at the centre of the village and then on the beach. The only explanation I got for making these stops was that they were 'convenient' places for both the deities and people to take a rest. Rituals were performed at both places, however, and these rituals were to a large extent identical but for one significant difference: the prayers offered to the deities were different.[20] If we take a closer look at these ceremonial places and at the prayers read, it will emerge that there is greater significance to these stops than just taking a rest.

The first ritual was performed practically in the centre of Shingū, near the place where a lane intersects Nakamachi. The location of ritual space, although only temporary, is of great importance to people.[21] The purity of the deities radiates into the neighbourhood and the honour to have 'housed' the deities, albeit only in one's compound, lingers on and is but one of the many symbolic expressions of social status. From this central place in Shingū the power of the deities also radiates to all corners of the village. The village is brought together, and this idea receives added significance through the prayer (*norito*) read. In the prayer the accomplishment of the villagers (i.e., *ujiko*) are stressed: that they have been loyal to the deities and have conducted the festival in the traditional way; 'that they have offered food from the sea and the land'; and that they have played drums and flutes so that 'the sound will flow to heaven'. In return they petition for a peaceful mind and divine protection so that they can be 'prosperous as the oaks and the mulberry trees'.

On the beach, however, there is no mention of the accomplishments of the village. Instead the deities are asked to take in the scenery of the ocean, to calm the wind and waves and to help the fishermen to harvest products from the sea so that they can be prosperous and happy. What is at stake here is Shingū's relationship with the sea. This theme is repeated when the procession passes under a makeshift *torii* on its way from the beach back to the shrine,[22] thus symbolically recreating the old myth of the tutelary deity's first arrival.[23]

## CONCLUSION

The priest once said that the purpose of Gosengū is to keep the shrine clean, in both the spiritual and physical sense of the word. This is obvious, and it is, in my opinion, equally obvious that the festival, through the parade, also serves to purify the village. The parade with all its purifying paraphernalia – as well as the rituals performed on the way – brings about a thorough purification of the community. Although purification rites are held in most houses daily and in the community several times annually through the festivals connected to the village shrine, 'dust' accumulates. Periodically it is therefore necessary to perform more penetrating 'house-cleaning' rites. Gosengū is such a rite, which thus will secure divine protection in the future.

But the parade is much more than this. Through a diachronic analysis of the parade as a process it is possible to isolate several themes. The composition of the parade tells us that the deities provide both spiritual and physical protection to the community. The grand scale of the affair indicates that the deities and their 'court' are able to perform these tasks successfully. The deities are present in the midst of their following, and through offerings the community communicates its willingness to continue its relationship with the deities.

Through the parade the social structure of the community is also expressed. In general only villagers are allowed to participate. Outsiders are only allowed as onlookers. People who have moved into the village take participation as a proof of their acceptance as co-villagers. The internal structure based on sex and age also finds its expression through the layout of the parade, as does, to a certain extent, the social hierarchy. Since paraphernalia donated by individuals are later carried by their descendants, such donations is a way to invest in long-term prestige. The festival provides a historical as well as contemporary legacy to influence. It places Shingū in a historical perspective and through the many 'pointers' in the parade it is a kind of 'meta-festival' ordering the annual festivals into a coherent whole.

The modern Durkheimian notion that the ritual is communication between people, and not necessarily between men and deity, is also present and is actively voiced in the community. To these people the festival might be a profane event and is 'a mode of *action*, a form of collective work for social ends' to paraphrase Keesing (1982:186).[23]

The festival thus 'does' a lot of things and can be used for many purposes, but, as pointed out by Gerholm (1988:198), rituals 'are *ways of doing things with symbols*' (italics in original). This brings us back to the meaning of the objects carried. Some are multi-vocal in that they convey several meanings simultaneously. Moreover, since several objects convey identical meanings, they are redundant. Finally, an object evokes different associations among actors. Any individual can only grasp a small portion of the whole; 'meanings' are to a great extent subjective. Admittedly, no single person in Shingū shares all the interpretations offered in this paper, although all the interpretations are certainly to be found within the community. Individuals know only bits and pieces, and it has been my aim to put these bits and pieces together in order to present the local reservoir of ritual knowledge.

# NOTES

1  The data for my paper was collected in Shingū during fieldwork in 1988 (September and October), supplemented in 1989 (15 June–15 September).

2  Nobody could offer a satisfactory explanation as to why the festival is held every eighteen years. The only explanation I got was that this is about the length of time that the building material of cypress (*hinoki*) keeps well. Other shrines in the vicinity hold such festivals with different intervals, however.

   It may be significant that eighteen is one and a half times the cycle of twelve years, or that eighteen multiplied by two is thirty-six – a number which also figures in the festival. Eighteen years might also once have been regarded as the length of one generation. Such speculations have no part in the villagers' worldview, however.

3  Shingū which has about 240 households, has given its name to the township Shingū machi which is located in Fukuoka prefecture (Kalland 1981). I have had close contacts with Shingū since my first fieldwork there in 1975/6. Financial support from the Institute for Comparative Research in Human Culture and from the Nansen Foundation (both Oslo) enabled me to undertake fieldwork there in September and October 1988 in connection with the festival.

4  In many respects the local priest was to me what Muchona was for Turner (1959); not only was he an articulate exponent of his own culture, but he was a scholar in his own right.

5  The Gosengū festival was held on 9 and 10 October 1988, but preparations started a few years earlier. The festival has been held fifteen times since the relocation of the village and shrine in 1685. A new building housing the priest's office (*shamusho*) and a hall for exhibiting votive paintings (*emadō*) was built in connection with Gosengū in 1988. About 30 million yen was collected from within the village as well as from those living elsewhere who still regard Shingū as their hometown (*furusato*).

   On 22 September the images (*goshintai*) representing the three deities enshrined in Isozaki Shrine were moved with great caution to a temporary place of residence in another shrine building within the same compound. They remained there until noon of 9 October when they were transferred to a portable shrine (*mikoshi*) which was the central object of the parade. After circling the village the *mikoshi* returned to Isozaki Shrine where the deities were again installed.

6  Interpretations offered by other sources will be used to a limited extent in order (1) to make explicit what has only been made implicit by informants, or (2) to give added weight to local interpretations.

7  The allocation of positions in the parade was an elaborate process in which the committee had to consider the social structure of the village, and a full treatment of this process is beyond the scope of this paper. But, in principle, objects which were donated by individuals should be carried by those individuals, their relatives or their descendants. It is also prestigious to carry some of the other objects (discussed below) and the bearers of these were chosen with great care. Members of the organizing committee had special roles in the parade. Furthermore, in general, no household should have more than one member participating in the parade and each of the nineteen neighbourhoods should be represented with an equal number of persons (except for one largely depopulated neighbourhood). Sex and age are also important considerations.

8  The organizing committee (*hōsankai*) included the six members of the shrine committee (*sōdaikai*), the three village officials (*ku-sanyaku'in*), the

head of the community hall association, one representative from each of the nineteen neighbourhoods, three selected festival leaders (chairman, vice-chairman and cashier), and – according to some informants but not all – the Shintō priest. Among these there was an executive committee (*yakuninkai*) consisting of eight people: the three selected festival leaders, the three community leaders, the chairman of the shrine committee, and the priest.

9  This flag was new in 1988. In the plan for the 1970 festival the term *seidō* was written with the characters for 'spirit' and 'road', leaving out the explicit reference to purity.

10  Torches are frequently linked to fire festivals, but there seems to be no awareness in Shingū of such a connection. Nevertheless, it might perhaps be possible to argue that the burning torches consume all impurities in the village and thus act as another purifying agents, such as the sacred artificial trees that are set alight in the Goshonai area (Egenter 1981).

11  For a general discussion of the importance of this kind of tree in Shintō see Herbert (1967); Bernier (1975:52–3). Another evergreen (*shiba*) is in fact used in Shingū since *shiba* grows faster and is more abundant.

12  The shrine possesses two such *engi*. The oldest was donated in 1721 and the second in 1735.

13  Within the shrine compound there are two round stones encircled by fences. The one to the left (when approaching the shrine) is the female stone and the one to the right is the male one. The female stone, called *Komochiishi* ('the stone of having a child'), is known for its powers to make barren women pregnant. Indeed, a couple came to be blessed by the stone (the wife actually sitting on the stone while the priest purified her) during the festival as they thought the stone particularly powerful at festival times. Unfortunately, she was still not pregnant one year later.

14  Redundancy is common in rituals everywhere, but repeated purification has a special flavour in Japanese culture where neither purity nor pollution is an absolute concept. What is important is not the *state* of purity but the *process* of purification. This applies to religious as well as to secular behaviour, as anyone observing Japanese washing apparently spotlessly clean floors can testify. But of course, the two processes of cleaning – the religious and the secular – are not separated in Japan. To clean the floor implies a clean-up of the mind: both are intended to restore order from chaos.

15  The procession might also be compared to the train of a feudal lord on his way to and from Edo during the Tokugawa period (Brian Moeran, personal communication).

16  In the medieval times many shrines possessed territorial fiefs and then this backing might have been very real (Kalland 1984).

17  Most people can hope to live through four festivals in their lifetime. They will experience their first festival as a child/teenager participating as *chigo* or musician. At the next festival the child has grown into a young adult, newly married or about to marry. A young men will at this stage carry the *mikoshi* or supervise the progression of the parade. At his third festival he will have grown into a mature man with grown-up children. He is in his prime and is now the household head participating in the community affairs. Such men carry the many paraphernalia in the festival. Finally, at his last festival he is a grandfather who has retired as the head of his household.

But age brings prestige and his contemporaries are now the festival leaders.

This interpretation gives credence to the view that periods of eighteen years have became an institution because this was regarded as the length of one generation. The locally held view that this period was chosen because it matched the endurance of the building material can then be understood metaphorically. It is an empirical fact that *hinoki* can last longer than eighteen years, but the important point in Japan is that it has lost its freshness. It takes on an aura of decay and death, which of course is anathema to Shintō.

18  The person who carried the sand in 1988 was the former leader of the shrine parishioners (*sōdai-chō*). He is a descendant of one of the original settlers in 1685, and in 1988 he was old and well respected. That he had been a fishermen and the head of the fishing cooperative was an added advantage. The raw rice has always been carried by a member of the same household.

19  The opposition between left and right is less clear in other positions of the parade. The 'sun' flag is placed on the right side of the 'moon' flag, indicating that the sun is above the moon. On the other hand, the red lion is on the left side of the blue. The same was the case with the pair of Sarutahiko and the pair of Yagorō. Usually, red is regarded as superior to blue, however. I have the suspicion that they had in fact been misplaced, but the question regarding right–left and red–blue was of little or no importance to the priest, and the whole question is further confused by left being superior to right in certain ritual contexts.

The parade was video-taped by a hired professional film crew in order to record for the future the way in which the festival should be conducted. It is my guess, therefore, that what might have been the 'wrong way' in 1988 will be the 'correct way' in 2006, which is of course an important warning to structuralists working with neat schemes of oppositions.

It should be obvious that new ways to record festivals – such as through videos – will have important effects on the future of the same festivals. There are reasons to believe that this will slow down changes made in the performance of festivals and reduce the importance of the ritual experts as keepers of ritual knowledge.

20  I will not describe these rites in detail here since they follow the general pattern in Shintō rituals, but a few words are in order. At both places a sacred square had been marked off by *shimenawa* ropes strung between four fresh branches of bamboo. The ground of the square was covered by sand recently fetched from the moist part of the beach. The portable shrine was put to rest before the square (the *shimenawa* accidentally was hung so low that the *mikoshi* could not enter the square). The portable altar with the offerings was placed at the opposite side of the square. The ritual sequence followed the general order: the assistant priest read the prayer to the deity of purification, Haraedono-ōkami, before he waved the *haraigushi* and thus purified first the *mikoshi*, then the village priest and finally the festival committee which was standing in the background. Thereafter the village priest stepped forward and read the main prayer before he offered the first sprig of *sakaki*. Representatives of various groups then donated other sprigs.

21  There were some discussions about the location for this ceremony. Previously it was held inside the compound of a Shintō priest who used to live at this crossing. Because this household has now left, it was suggested

that the ceremony be held at a large parking lot on the other side of the lane. However, it was decided instead to have it performed at the opposite corner where the much smaller parking lot owned by the honorary chairman of the arranging committee is located. Some people hinted that the ceremony was moved because the large parking lot was located in front of the house of the deputy hamlet chief, who for many years had been a communist member of the town council.

22 There is a stone *torii* located on the beach, and the processions used to go under this. Recently, however, fish-curing plants have for some reason been allowed to enlarge their facilities in such a way that it is impossible to pass under this *torii*. The organizing committee therefore insisted that a makeshift *torii* made of *shimenawa* hung between two bamboo poles be erected across the road leading from the beach to the village.

23 According to this myth the storm god Susano-wo-no-mikoto came drifting on a wooden board. He was unconscious when he was washed ashore. He came to his senses, however, when he heard a cockcrow, and going after the sound he came to the village, where he was enshrined. This legend is given locally as an explanation for an old taboo against eating chicken in Shingū, particularly among the fishermen and in the priest's household, but this has now broken down. Nevertheless, during the festival, a dish, *aji-gohan*, which is usually served with pieces of chicken, was served without meat.

24 Consequently, there is a continuous local debate whether some of the items carried in the parade, e.g., the thirty-six pictures, are religious objects or not. This is a very important question, for if the objects have no religious meaning, they can be symbols for everyone, also for the Sōka-gakkai members. The Sōka-gakkai believers claim that the pictures are not religious *per se*, but put in a religious context they acquire religious meanings. They cease to be symbols for the community and become symbols for the shrine.

## BIBLIOGRAPHY

Akaike, Noriaki (1976) 'Festival and neighborhood association', *Japanese Journal of Religious Studies*, 3(2–3):127–74.

Ashkenazi, Michael (1985) 'Priests, carpenters, and household heads: Ritual performers in Japan', *Ethnology*, 24(4):297–305.

—— (1990) 'Festival management and the corporate analysis of Japanese society', in E. Ben-Ari, B. Moeran and J. Valentine (eds) *Unwrapping Japan: Society and Culture in Anthropological Perspective*, Manchester: Manchester University Press: 205–20.

Barth, Fredrik (1975) *Ritual and Knowledge Among the Baktaman of New Guinea*, Oslo: Universitetsforlaget.

Befu Harumi (1968) 'Village autonomy and articulation with the state', in J.W. Hall and M.B. Jansen (eds) *Studies in the Institutional History of Early Modern Japan*, Princeton: Princeton University Press.

Bernier, Bernhard (1975) *Breaking the Cosmic Circle: Religion in a Japanese Village*, Ithaca: Cornell University East Asia Papers No.5.

Bestor, Theodore C. (1985) 'Tradition and Japanese social organization: Institutional development in a Tokyo neighborhood', *Ethnology* 24(2):121–35.

Caillet, Laurence (1986) 'Time in the Japanese ritual year', in Joy Hendry and

Jonathan Webber (eds) *Interpreting Japanese Society: Anthropological Approaches*, Oxford: JASO Occasional Papers no. 5:31–48.

Egenter, Nold (1981) 'The sacred trees around Goshonai/Japan', *Asian Folklore Studies*, 40(2):191–212.

Gerholm, Tomas (1988) 'On ritual: A postmodernist view', *Ethnos* 53(3–4):190–203.

Herbert, Jean (1967) *Shintō: The Fountain-Head of Japan*, London: George Allen & Unwin Ltd.

Kalland, Arne (1981) *Shingū: A Study of a Japanese Fishing Community*, London: Curzon Press.

—— (1984) 'Sea tenure in Tokugawa Japan: The case of Fukuoka domain', in K. Ruddle and T. Akimichi (eds) *Maritime Institutions in the Western Pacific*, Ōsaka: Senri Ethnological Studies 17, National Museum of Ethnology: 11–36.

Keesing, Roger M. (1982) *Kwaio Religion: The Living and the Dead in a Solomon Island Society*, New York: Colombia University Press.

Lévi-Strauss, Claude (1963) *Structural Anthropology*, Harmondsworth: Penguin Books.

Lewis, Gilbert (1980) *Day of Shining Red: An Essay on Understanding Ritual*, Cambridge: Cambridge University Press.

Littleton, C. Scott (1986) 'The organization and management of a Tokyo Shinto shrine festival', *Ethnology* 25(3):195–202.

Ono Sokyō (1962) *Shinto: The Kami Way*, Tokyo: Tuttle.

Nadel, S.F. (1953) *The Foundations of Social Anthropology*, London: Routledge & Kegan Paul.

Turner, Victor (1959) 'Muchona the Hornet, interpreter of religion', in J. Casagrande (ed.) *In the Company of Man*, New York: Harper: 333–55.

—— (1969) *The Ritual Process*, Harmondsworth: Penguin Books.

Yagi Yasuyuki (1988) '*Mura-Zakai* – The Japanese village Boundary and its symbolic interpretation', *Asian Folklore Studies*, 47:137–51.

# 8 Women and ritual[1]

*D.P. Martinez*

## INTRODUCTION

In some ways, as will be seen below, this chapter might best be entitled 'gender and ritual' since my main argument is that we can understand little, in any society, if we focus only on male or female roles. Despite the emphasis on women, this chapter does refer to what men do as well. In fact, it could be said that this chapter is also about structures of power and knowledge, insiders and outsiders, rather than just age and gender. However, for our purposes, power and knowledge must be taken as constituting a given, which, in Japan, is linked to age and gender *and* to one's position along the continuum from outside to inside. Thus, in beginning with women, I am just exploring a different facet of established ritual and ceremony not, as might be assumed, because of a focus on women, phenomena such as spirit possession, witchcraft, etc. I am well aware that this approach, as with all anthropological descriptions and analyses, is subject to a variety of qualifications, the most important being that 'things change'. Not only do things change for the actors, but the actors change, societies change, and so on. In order to understand the present, however, it is important to understand the past. Thus, the rites of a fishing village held to be more traditional than most of the rest of Japan can give us some insight into what modern rituals are about.[2]

Moreover, in giving this chapter a title as general as 'women and ritual', it should be clear that I had in mind a very wide discussion of the situation relating to women and religion in Japan. It also implies, of course, that I must discuss the issue in the broader cross-cultural context of theories on women and ritual, and it is here that I would like to begin before moving on to describe the relation between women and ritual in one particular place – Kuzaki village where I did my fieldwork in 1984–6 – and then, more generally and briefly, within the context of urban Japan and its new religions.[3]

## WOMEN AND RELIGION IN ANTHROPOLOGICAL THEORY

Very little has been written specifically about women and ritual. In noting this, I am not denying that there has not been a large body of ethnographic description of women's involvement in ritual: Victor Turner, as is well known, used examples of rites involving women in his discussion of African ritual (1957); interesting for the Japanese case is Kerns's(1983) analysis of the women/ancestor relationship in a matrifocal black Carib society; for Nepal there is Lynn Bennett's (1983) excellent *Dangerous Wives and Sacred Sisters*; Christine Hugh-Jones tackled some aspects of Amerindian women's ritual roles in *From the Milk River* (1979); and there are various essays on Korean female shamans which outline life histories that fit I. M. Lewis's typology for the connection between gender inequality and possession (Kendall and Peterson 1988; Wilson 1983); and there are, certainly, numerous articles along similar lines. However, it is rare to find any theoretical models for the role of women in the rites of established religions save that of the feminists who argue that the combined effect of religious ideology and the male domination of orthodox ritual is to keep women 'in their place'. The emphasis on women's marginalization and on the control of female sexuality (see Ranke-Heinemann 1990) is important and cannot be ignored, especially in the Japanese case, where the history of women's involvement in religion is both complex and unusual.[4] This, however, tells us little of how to approach the ritual roles, unimportant as they may seem, which are seen to be essentially female within a society. What does the inclusion – rather than the exclusion – of women in ritual tell us about them? I want to argue here that this has rarely been a central theme in work on ritual.

For example, in the introduction to the collection of essays entitled *Women's Religious Experience*, Pat Holden summarizes the feminist stance which includes the muted group model:

> Women are confined to the domestic sphere often in some form of 'seclusion'; and even if they are allowed to move in public spaces 'veiling' or the social conventions related, for example, to the dangers of their sexuality impose similar restraints on their freedom. They are excluded from formal religion, and from participating in important public rituals; they may be prominent in possession cults or healing rites but these can be seen as simply extensions of their traditional female roles . . .
>
> Men, on the other hand, are prominent in religious organization; they perform the important rituals, formulate dogma and hold the pens that write the 'divinely inspired' texts.
>
> (Holden 1983:2)

This does not deny, of course, that women can be an important part of a religion in symbolic terms, but it does argue that the creation and use of this symbolism is in the hands of men. Only the Indianist Catherine Thompson (1983) argues against this model by pointing out that, at least in Hinduism, women gain power from the fact that worship is only possible through an affinity with the powers of the divinity. Or, to put it as Mary Douglas (1966:174–5) once did – although she was not discussing women and ritual – in some societies women have power precisely because they are considered to be dangerous and polluting. In the Hindu case, it is women's symbolic sexual and polluting powers which make it possible for them to act as mediators for certain gods and certain rituals.

Thompson (1983), then, argues for an understanding of the sexual division of labour which is important in ritual in order to understand a society's religion. Thus, despite the fact that women and the rituals they perform often have low or secondary status, they are an essential part of the religious system and our understanding of the whole is improved by considering them. This point is extremely important for the Japanese case, for in Japan women have often been the charismatic leaders and founders of new religions which have become mainstream rather than marginalized (Hardacre 1986). I want to argue that in order to understand how, in Japan, religious ideology both can be written by and kept in the hands of women, we need to look at their roles in traditional rites and ceremonies.

## THE JAPANESE CASE

The argument that we need to study the sexual division of labour in ritual more carefully is based on the assumption that this has not really been done, or not been done often enough, in the case of Japan and its traditional religions. While this is true, I shall try at the end of this chapter also to argue that because the traditional division of ritual labour has not been analysed fully, our understanding of women's roles in Japan's 'new' religions is imperfect.

When the relationship between women and religion is discussed in the literature on Japan, the themes often fall into three broad categories: the importance of women in the pre-Buddhist past; issues of purity, pollution and dangerous female sexuality; and the female founders and followers of new religions, especially within the urban context. These themes are not mutually exclusive. All of them should sound familiar to Western scholars, and it should come as no surprise that some feminists have argued that there was a decrease in women's status as the more male-dominated Buddhist ideology was accepted in Japan (Paulson 1976). Echoes of Western nineteenth-century theories which postulated a pre-historic matriarchy centred around a mother goddess (Bachofen 1967; Engels 1891) are not, I think, coincidental. While it is true that there is evidence of a female shamanic cult in pre-Buddhist Japan (i.e., before the sixth century AD), which was similar to Korean cults (Wilson 1983) and which can still be found in the Okinawa islands (Bell 1984), this does not necessarily mean that all women held higher status at that time. While we can ask whether menstruating women at this time were regarded as pure and possessed by the deities, thus becoming living goddesses, as Yoshida (1990) and Symers (1983) argue, or whether they were deemed polluting in much the way Buddhism views them, this does not tell us much about the day-to-day lives of women or how they were treated.[5] That certain women were central to pre-Buddhist religious cults is all we know. While it cannot be denied that Buddhism, Confucianism and the increasing rigidity of feudalism (Ackroyd 1957) all combined to marginalize 'Shintō' shamanesses in particular and women in general, what I want to argue is that in accepting this reality, many specialists on Japan have gone on to ignore the significance of women in modern religious practices.[6]

In fact, what all current anthropological approaches to ritual in Japan convey is that ritual's structure and purpose, both in Shintō and Buddhist rites, is always a Durkheimian one: ritual both expresses and upholds the structure of the community. Thus the role of men in ritual is not really discussed either. Typical of the anthropological approach is to affirm, as Bestor does, that village and neighbourhood festivals especially '[validate] many of the social arrangements of the mundane secular world as it exists within [the community]' (1989:264). The fact that this basically functional approach is correct might lead the outsider to conclude that not much more can be said about ritual in Japan. Yet, I believe, such an approach only skims the surface of the meaning and importance of ritual for the Japanese.

Part of the problem, and one which I encountered frequently in my fieldwork, is not that foreign anthropologists of Japan do not look for deeper structures, but that the native informant often gives no other explanation for a ritual than the rather obvious one which even the casual observer might discern. In their reflexive book on ceremony and symbolism in the Japanese home, Jeremy and Robinson note:

> Our final impressions of the festivals and ceremonies which were recounted to us, is that they exist on a variety of different levels and fulfil a range of needs all at the same time. None that we can recall

can be entirely divorced from the mysteries of folk religions but all of them seem to serve a social purpose as well. These influences, though, are seldom overt. No one could tell us with authority, for example, how shishi odori [lion dance] developed or what particular meaning it has. It is connected with the rice harvest. It has always been so. It is an expressive plea, a form of thanksgiving, an invitation to the deities, and so forth. But for the participants, the meaning and excitement probably lie in the performance itself. For the observers it lies in the entertainment of an occasional spectacle. If there are deeper connections, then they remain deep for the ordinary folk, not open to articulation, but certainly not open to rejection by an outsider.

(Jeremy and Robinson 1989:92)

This passage is quoted in full because it clearly describes the way I felt about the rituals I observed during the period 1984–6 in Kuzaki: the meaning and importance of the rituals were not open to articulation by the villagers, but rituals did operate on many levels and not just on the single level of expressing and maintaining village hierarchy and autonomy.

This is related to the fact that most rituals in a village or neighbour-hood take place in two spheres: rites performed within the household by particular individuals and rites performed outside the household in which the participation of some – but not all – household members is required by the neighbourhood or the village associations.[7] It is absolutely essential, I believe, that an analysis of Japanese ritual be based on both these events: if we look only at village festivals or only at household rituals we get an incomplete picture and are left with the standard analysis of Japanese ritual as expressing and reinforcing Japanese group orientation. I am not saying that ritual in Japan is not about hierarchy, harmony, and co-operation – it is. But reasserting that this is what ritual is all about does not tell us anything about the manner in which the individual who exists within these structures partakes in this creation of hierarchy, harmony and co-operation. Such an approach still emphasizes the performance aspect of Japanese ritual, but this, as Ben-Ari (1991) has argued, can be fruitful if the performance is carefully dissected.

## THE EXAMPLE OF KUZAKI, A FISHING AND DIVING (*AMA*) VILLAGE

In a chapter as brief as this, not all the rituals which could be seen as central to such an analysis can be described. Readers must refer to Table 8.1, which might begin to give an idea of the ritual division of labour in the village of Kuzaki in Mie prefecture. While it could be argued that one village, and one famed for its intense religious life, cannot be considered representative for all of Japan, a comparison of Kuzaki's 'traditions' with what other villages in various parts of Japan were doing in the pre-war era shows that Kuzaki was at one time typical, rather than unusual, in its religious life.[8]

*Table 8.1* Roles and ages of women involved in various rites in Kuzaki-chō

| Rite | Main actors | Age grade (*fujin-kai*) |
|---|---|---|
| Caring for the household Shintō deities | women (daughters-in-law) | 20s to mid-50s |
| Caring for the household's ancestors (Buddhist) | women (grandmother) | mid-40s to death |
| Worship of the sea deities for safety diving, fishing and in thanks for large catches | women (all divers) | 20s to mid-50s |
| Worship of field deities | women | 20s to mid-50s |
| Worship of Jizō-sama, the protector of children (Buddhist) | mothers | 20s to mid-50s |

I believe also that Kuzaki is typical in its religious attitudes. All villagers participate in both Shintō and Buddhist rites. In general, Shintō rites are for life-cycle rituals, performed for births, marriages, bad-luck years, etc., while Buddhist rituals are for the dead (see also Ooms 1976). Yet despite the number and frequency of village rituals, the people of Kuzaki do not see themselves as especially 'religious' or pious.[9] As Jeremy notes for the village in which he worked, most villagers do not differentiate between 'normal' and 'sacred' events 'since these events are part of the normality of an unquestioned world of belief' (Jeremy and Robinson 1989:92). For the people of Kuzaki, 'religious' is what churchgoing Westerners are, what they do is just the way life is.

The village model of the ritual division of labour was an interesting and twofold one. It was believed that 'religious' people (such as foreigners and members of new Japanese religions) could not live in a village in which the fabric of life consisted of the co-operative worship of the deities of the fields, mountains, seas and the veneration of the village dead. This is a model which corresponds closely to the anthropological model of ritual in Japan. The other model held by the villagers, a more complex one for it seemed to belie the facts, was that

'Shintō was for women and Buddhism was for men'.[10] Let me describe how this model does not work and, yet, how it is true.

Ritual in and for the household is performed by different members of the household. For example, all children will help make the flags with the family name which decorate the family Buddhist altar (*butsudan*) during the summer festival when the household's dead return to visit (*bon*); but it is only the eldest male child who has a very specific role in the public ritual for an ancestor's first *bon*. In general, adolescents seem to be least involved with household ritual, although adult men also perform very few of the rites within the household. In fact, the bulk of household rites are performed by women. These rites include the daily offerings to the Shintō deities, which are often kept in the kitchen, as well as the daily prayers and offerings to the household ancestors. There is a minor division of labour here which is rather important: the young wives of the household are often responsible for the offerings to the Shintō deities, but it is the older women of the household who are responsible for the ancestors. In fact, the women in the age group of 43–60 are supposed to be learning and practising how to care for the ancestors and they are taught by their mothers-in-law.

Rituals performed for the household include the monthly climb up the sacred mountain, Sengen, which is next to the village, in which all working women (those under sixty) make offerings to the various deities enshrined on the mountaintop.[11] Women pray to the Shintō deities here for good luck in their diving, good luck in fishing, and good health for the family members. Although the mountain has a small area devoted to various Bodhisattvas, only women ever make this trip and when I asked if the men ever worshipped, I was told 'sometimes they do'. Yet, even the few male divers in the village never participated in the Shintō rites performed for safe diving, nor did they make regular offerings to the deities of the sea – an interesting point as fishermen are famous for being particularly active in such rituals. In fact, when a fishing household had a large catch, it was the job of the women in the household to go around to the village Shintō shrines in order to give thanks to deities. Men, on the other hand, were left with the more social task of treating all the other fishermen to a drink of sake – a role which seemed more political than ritual, but which, I later realized, was actually both. The deities do not continue to give a household large catches if the household does not share its good fortune with both the other villagers and the deities themselves. Yet, the sake drinking did have a political element as it was important for maintaining the image of being an *ii hito* or 'nice guy', an important quality which all village leaders were supposed to possess.

The grandfathers of the village, however, did participate in one Buddhist rite, at the vernal equinox, in which they recited sutras for their household dead in the village Buddhist temple. Thus, in my first months in the village, I was convinced that the model of Shintō for women and Buddhism for men was an accurate one.

However, the first large village Shintō ceremony soon managed to confuse me. On 1 July, the 'great day' in which the doors to the inner sanctum of the deity were opened, all the village men participated. The grandfathers were awarded gifts for their work in making the sacred food for the deities at the sacred Shintō shrine of Ise, but not the women who dived for this food! The village shrine was full to the brim with the political leaders of the village – grandfathers and middle-aged men who were representing their households, while, except for the grand-mothers who squeezed into the small hall, most women stood outside the shrine, peering in, as the masked male shaman called down the deity and the doors to the sanctum were opened.[12] This pattern continued in the other large village festivals; women might prepare the food for the feast which generally followed the ceremony, but in general the men played the main roles in the ceremony and each of the men's age grades had a specific role in the ceremony.

Thus, in the November Shintō festival called *Nifune*, the grandfathers made sacred implements for the young deity housed on an island outside the village; the political leaders participated in a ritual in Ise shrine and brought back sacred sake for the young deity; the men from the young men's club rowed the boats which took the sake and implements to the deity; while the men in their thirties trained and advised the younger men.[13] Women remained very much in the background, floating per-sonal offerings to the deity as part of an evening feast and ceremony as well as preparing the food for the various events which marked the male participation in the festival.

It was during the *bon* festival that I learned that while Buddhism was for men, grandmothers had the most important role in the care for the village dead (as well as the household dead). Since care for the dead falls into the category of Buddhism, I was clearly faced with real problems in understanding the villagers' model.

It was noted above that something can be learned about ritual from the way in which different people at different stages in their lifecycle participate and that the village model 'Buddhism is for men and Shintō is for women' is, at some level, true. How is this so?

If we look at men first, as would the Japanese, and as have most ethnographers, we might argue that the men are the core of the ritual performers in Kuzaki. It does not matter whether it is a Shintō or

Buddhist village festival, men have the central roles. And while these roles are organized in a hierarchal way, they also emphasize co-operation between the various age grades. I want to argue that this is definitely true for the men between the ages of twenty-five and sixty. Yet, on another level, we can ask just what is it that the young men and old men are doing?

The young men organize the dancing at the *bon* festival which, according to the villagers, is a dance to see the dead off. They also row in dangerous leaky boats out to the forbidden sacred island to leave implements for the young deity during the Nifune festival. During the Hachiman festival, which I have not described, they set up the sacred area where the deity will appear and act as servants to the men who come dressed as the feudal lord and his court. In the autumn, the young men must treat the village grandfathers to a special feast in which they serve and prepare all the food. Thus, at the bottom of the male hierarchy we get the young men who serve both the elders and the deities, doing dangerous and sacred work. At the other end of the scale are the grandfathers who make the implements for the young deity, who make the sacred food for the Ise deities, who pray for their household dead during the equinoxes and for the village dead during the *bon* festival. After the age of sixty, the men of the village have the role of Shintō lay priests and it is the young men who complement the work of the old men by serving them and performing the more dangerous rites. In between are the married men whose ritual task seems to be to act out the role of household head: they must be present at rituals, they must do the social drinking and eating which goes along with village festivals. Thus there is a continuum in which the young serve the elderly at one end, the men in the middle serve their family and the wider community in public roles, and the elders at the other end serve the ancestors and deities who protect the community. In fact, it could be argued that in Kuzaki ritual, the young men and grandfathers are doing the work which will protect the village, while the men in the middle stand for that which is being protected: the stability, hierarchy and harmony of village life.

Protect the village from what? This is a question which most analyses of ritual in Japan never seem to ask – just what is all this boundary defining and urging of cooperation and harmony all about? Only the anthropologist Bernier ever seemed to ask this question and his answer was:

[village] conceptions make a full circle from undefined suprahuman power to natural power, a circle which includes a unique deity,

personified deities, human beings both living and dead, and natural objects and processes. This continuity between the deity, natural process, men, either living or dead, and natural objects leads to a peculiar conception of the relation of man to nature . . . [and it is by] maintaining the proper relations with the other constituent parts of the universe, [that] men can help maintain the order and functioning of this universe. In fact, they periodically recreate the universe which was threatened by negative forces, namely pollution and evil.

(Bernier 1975:131)

If we substitute 'village' or community for 'universe', I think we come close to the Kuzaki conception of the world – and this is a concept which I admit is changing and dying out, so that younger villagers view festivals in a more functional way, but I want to concentrate on the traditional village conception of the world. It is a dangerous and fearful place, yet wonderful; the Shintō deities are everywhere: in cut trees, in unusual rock formations, living on islands, the sea deity is a dangerous dragon who loves to eat eggs and the dead are powerful beings – Buddhas all – who, if not properly honoured, might become hungry ghosts. The village men, the individuals who, ideally, live their whole lives in the village, are constantly defending and defining their world, maintaining both a social and ritual balance which, in Bernier's words 'keeps the circle closed'. But if men do this, both for the Shintō deities and Buddhist dead, what is it that women do?

As you can see from Table 8.1, in Kuzaki, a woman does not begin to do anything until she is married. Her exclusion from a formally organized age grade after the age of sixteen and before her marriage indicates how liminal she is to village life. She will, according to the patrilineal model, marry out. The women who live in the village, then, are mostly strangers; and in the case of village women who marry into other Kuzaki households, they are strangers to the household.[14] The common model for a married woman in anthropological literature is that she only fully becomes part of the household when she becomes the mother-in-law – when it is her turn to train a daughter-in-law in the ways of that household (Masuda 1975). Along the way are stages in which a woman has her first child, or her first male child, and is seen to become more and more a part of the household. As mother, worker and household member she too has a role to play, mediating for the Shintō deities for good luck, good health and protection for household members. However, I think it is symbolically important that she is not immediately allowed to care for the household ancestors. She may prepare the food, but learning to say the sutras (*nenbutsu*) is something she does not do until her forties when she will probably have a daughter-in-law of her own and will thus feel more established in the household.

In her 1984 book on urban Japanese women, Takie Sugiyama Lebra also notes the fact that the older women become, the more likely they are to take up reciting sutras for the household ancestors who are not, in literal fact, their own blood ancestors. She believes that as women grow older, they feel more a part of the household and that they look forward to dying because it will finally and forever unite them with the patriliny which they entered as strangers. In this sense, we can say that Buddhism is for men, for it is about the dead of the household who are truly (in most cases) their ancestors, but who are not the ancestors of the women of the household. Further, the village ancestors as a whole are also patrilineal ancestors and so their care should not be left to outsiders. Shintōism, in contrast, is not just for women but can be for anyone – even foreigners, as I learned – and, in contrast to what the household is about, is more accesible to women than is the worship of the ancestors. Thus, as young women, Kuzaki wives maintain and protect the household through their rituals, but as they grow older and become more of the household and of the village, their innate power makes it possible for them to take a role in public festival, that is, in caring for all the village dead, especially the newly dead during *bon*. So we could say that Shintō is for anyone, even outsiders, while Buddhism is for insiders only.

I have mentioned women's innate power – of what does this consist? At a macro level there is the power historically associated with women in Shintō as shamanesses and mediators, a power which represents a female affinity with Shintō deities who can be unpredictable and dangerous as well as beneficial and important to fertility. On a micro level we could say that if men have the power to recreate, protect and define the village (a power which is manifest when they are older), it seems that women have a complementary power which, when they are young and strangers to the village, must be subsumed in caring for the household. I would argue that women's power originates in their menstruation which is generally viewed as polluting. If a woman does not marry or have children, as Yoshida and Ueda (1968) have pointed out, there is a danger that she may become possessed, a 'werefox', a witch or, when dead, a demon.

In point of fact, I may seem to be arguing for a model similar to one found in many societies, where women are involved with the inside and domestic and men with the outside and public world.[15] Yet the grandmothers of the village break this pattern, and perhaps a better model for Japan might be that insiders, men who live in the village all their lives, are involved with the outside and public world as are old women. Young women, who as strangers are potentially polluting and dangerous, first must become part of the household and, by extension, part of the village.[16] Initially, then, their power to mediate for deities can be used only for the individuals to whom they have ties: their husbands and children. It takes longer to become part of the village and have ties to other villagers. Thus we have an interesting reversal, that is, the insiders (men and older women) perform outside, public rituals and the outsiders (young women) are given charge of inside rituals. As women's status changes from outsider to insider, their ritual duties change.

In Kuzaki this growing closer to the village is symbolized by the woman's initiation into the 'sutra group' (*nenbutsu-kai*) – this is a formal, Buddhist rite of passage, which is followed by a feast in which the eldest son gives a speech outlining the hard work and persistence which made it possible for the sixty-year-old woman to enter the group of grandmothers. This speech, highly formalized, is meant to describe the work which went into learning so many sutras, but could well be a description of the woman's life.

In short, ritual participation for women in Kuzaki can be discussed as a progression – as indeed can men's participation – but the important progression for women is not from symbolic protector of village to that of lay priest serving the deities; it is from the role of outsider who might be dangerous to household and village stability to that of an insider who can help maintain that stability. This progression resembles in part a man's: from servant of the elders to servant of the community (see Figure 8.1). Women, however, because of their innate power, always have the potential to mediate directly for the deities. What we have is a series of complementary oppositions of young/old, male/female, inside/outside which make up the whole fabric of everyday religion. Finally, the opposition and complementarity of male and female roles is subsumed in death when all household dead become Bodhisattvas at first, and then finally unnamed sexless ancestors.

## WOMEN AND NEW RELIGIONS

That this village model has its drawbacks when it comes to urban Japan I am willing to admit. I doubt whether modern city dwellers conceptualize the outside world as full of deities and demons at least in the literal sense: as Bestor notes, their neighbourhood rituals are often a sort of 'invented tradition' which have clear political and social functions (1989). As Nakamaki's chapter in this volume makes clear,

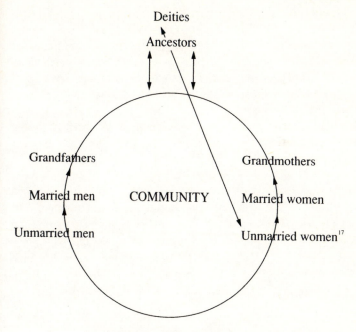

*Figure 8.1* Gender and ritual power relations in Kuzaki-chō

many men now participate in company rituals which appear to have taken over from community rituals. Many community rituals also have some sort of company sponsorship these days; and young women and children are now frequently included in large urban festivals, often carrying a portable deity's shrine (*mikoshi*), a task once reserved solely for men.[18] Urban Japanese also consult mediums, fortune tellers and horoscopes with a frequency which gives the lie to the idea that modern Japan is a purely secular society (see Lewis 1986; Davis 1980). In the new religions which appear to be largely an urban phenomenon, 60 to 80 per cent of their members are women who act as healers and preachers.[19] Sociologists of Japanese new religions such as Hardacre (1984) connect the high percentage of women members to the unhappiness and alienation these women often feel in an urban environment. What seems rarely to have been recognized is that this is an adaptation of an important feature of Japanese life – the power of the woman to protect and maintain her household. So, while men are now taking part in company rituals and urban community-based rituals (which can have much stronger political flavour than did village rituals); women involved with the new religions still seem to be

concerned with the same things as village women: subsuming potentially dangerous power, harnessing it to the need to care for the health
and well-being of their family and household ancestors.[20] An interesting
change, or, as some might argue, a throwback to an early era when many
women were powerful shamans, is the way in which women in some of
these religions acquire the power to heal others who are not necessarily
related to them.

Thus, a new situation may require a new religion, but the high profile
of women in these religions need not necessarily be because they are
more marginalized and unhappy in modern urban society than in
traditional or rural society. Rather, religious life in rural society
requires the ritual activity of both men and women, and urban women
are maintaining this role albeit in a slightly different manner. The
insistence by the new religion, *Reiyūkai*, that dangerously polluting
women can also be powerful healers is not a new idea in Japan – nor
in the anthropology of religion. It is our ethnocentrism perhaps, which
keeps us from perceiving the importance and meaning of such ritual
roles.

## NOTES

1  The research on which this chapter is based was supported by a Monbushō
   Studentship which I held at Tokyo University and a Philip Bagby
   studentship from the Institute of Social Anthropology, Oxford. Many thanks
   to various discussants at the 1990 JAWS Leiden Conference as well as the
   participants at a London School of Economics anthropology seminar in
   1992. Special thanks to D.N. Gellner, Jan van Bremen, and Susan Napier.
2  Only 10 per cent of the Japanese population are supposed to live in rural
   areas. Of this percentage, the number of Japanese who can still be held to
   follow 'traditional' religious practices may very well be smaller. Given the
   radical changes to religion during the Meiji Restoration, it could also be
   argued that there are no traditional religious practices left in Japan. For a
   clear discussion of this, see Smith in this volume.
3  Kuzaki is actually a ward (*chō*) of Toba City, but it maintains its autonomy
   in many ways as well as being geographically distant and distinct from the
   city. Thus, I refer to it as a village; villagers, however, were always careful
   to call the place Kuzaki-*chō*. As a still functioning fishing and diving village
   (local catches included abalone, shellfish and seaweed as well as prawns
   and lobsters), Kuzaki may appear unusual (see note 8 below). For a
   description of its history and 1980s social structure, see Martinez 1988.
4  I have outlined some of this relationship in a brief article entitled 'Women
   and religion in Japan' (1994, Holm and Bowker, eds.)
5  Yoshida's (1990) work on the feminine is representative of a long-standing
   Japanese interest in female pollution; this large body of work differs
   somewhat from my approach in that women's religious roles are often
   categorized as being part of folk religion, and are therefore, not analysed

in conjunction with male and community life. Yanagita was interested in the power of the sister within the household (1948), while Miyata has written about women and household deities in a more general way (1983).

6 I am not arguing here for a coherent Shintō religion in pre-Buddhist Japan (see Kuroda 1981; Grapard 1984), but find the term useful to describe whatever religious practices were prevalant at the time. I have discussed my position on this in a separate article (Martinez 1990).

7 An excellent description of the importance of individual roles within household ritual is given by Bachnik in this volume. This is, to my knowledge, one of the only attempts to analyse the importance and meaning of ritual for sets of individuals.

8 See for example Hagiwara's *Kamishima* (1973) for New Year rituals; Yanagita on islands and fishermen's rituals (1981); Davis (1977) on fishermen; Bernier (1975) on an archery festival similar to Kuzaki's Hachiman-san festival which is held in the interior of Mie prefecture; Hori (1968) on the importance of *nenbutsu*; Stefánsson in this volume on *bon* rites for just a few examples of how typical we might regard Kuzaki rituals.

9 See Reader 1990 for a discussion of this attitude.

10 It also belied the distinct symbolism of offerings made in Shintō and Buddhist rites (see Cobbi in this volume).

11 The name of this mountain and its associated Sengen cult are extremely difficult to disentangle. There is a Sengen cult on Mount Fuji for another deity, while in Kuzaki villagers were clear that Sengen was the deity itself. As Plath has noted, for the *ama* village where he worked, 'Sengen-san is clearly the most important single god for the *ama* today' (personal communication).

12 This is a rather significant point. In the pre-Meiji past, or so the grandmothers told me, Ise brought no shaman of their own. Instead, unmarried village girls dressed as traditional shrine attendants (*miko*) and filled the ancient role of shamanesses. The male shaman represents the changes made on the part of pre-war Shintō-state cult which, of course, emphasized the male and patrilineal.

13 I was told that a 'young deity' lived on the small 'island' (the villagers called all piles of rock which rose above the ocean '*shima*') called Kaminoshima. He was a young deity, apparently nameless, because the shrine on that island had been newly made for him after a typhoon in 1935 destroyed the shrine of an older deity who had dwelt on an island further out from the shore. This older deity is identified in one text as Haku-Hatsu-*daimyō* (Sakai, n.d.:15), who appears in some village legends as the man who established Kuzaki-Ise relations (Kurata 1974).

14 I was frequently told that there are more adopted sons-in-law (*yōshi*) in diving villages than elsewhere in Japan, and this would contradict many of my points if true for Kuzaki. Very few households, however, had *yōshi* in the village and what was interesting was not changes in the wife's role of incorporation into the household, but the emphasis on the husband's political participation in village life as necessary to be regarded a full member of village life.

15 This has also been argued, in terms of *uchi* (inside) and *soto* (outside) for women in Japan; see, for example, Hendry 1984, Smith 1988 and Kondo 1990.

16  This association of women with strangers, outsiders, reaffirms an affinity with Shintō deities who may come visiting in the guise of strangers. These visitors, in myth, must be well treated in order to reap some benefits, but should not overstay their welcome as this can be dangerous (see Hori 1963; Yoshida 1981).

17  See note 12 above for a historical example of how unmarried village women once enacted the symbolic role of mediators who could cut across this hierarchy.

18  In the Tokyo area where my family and I lived during the spring of 1991, the Shintō shrine, Tomioka Hachimangū, had the first portable shrine built for them since 1923. According to the *Japan Times* (5 June 1991) it was presented by the Sagawa Kyūbin Company which had close connections to that area of Tokyo, Fukagawa. The 'portable' shrine (*mikoshi*) weighed over 4 tons, was covered with 34 kilograms of gold, diamonds and rubies, cost one billion yen to build and required 400 men and women to carry it.

19  I am not discussing the new religions, such as *Agonshū* (see Reader 1990), which attract the young Japanese.

20  In her work on the alien, the fantastic and the other in modern Japanese literature, Napier finds that some of these themes still cohere around the portrayal of the female (personal communication).

## BIBLIOGRAPHY

Ackroyd, Joy (1957) 'Women in feudal Japan', in *Transactions of the Asiatic Society of Japan*, third series, 7:31–68.

Bachofen, Jacob J. (1967) [1861] *Myth, Religion, and Mother Right*, trans. Ralph Manheim, Princeton: Princeton University Press.

Bell, Rosamund J. (1984) 'Women in the religious life of the Ryukyu islands: Structure and status', *Journal of the Oxford Anthropological Society* (JASO) 15(2) 119–36.

Ben-Ari, Eyal (1991) 'Posing, posturing and photographic presences: A rite of passage in a Japanese commuter village', *Man* 26(1): 87–104.

Bennett, Lynn (1983) *Dangerous Wives and Sacred Sisters: Social and Symbolic Roles of High-caste Women in Nepal*, New York: Columbia University Press.

Bernier, Bernard (1975) *Breaking the Cosmic Circle: Religion in a Japanese Village*, New York: Cornell University East Asia Papers no.5.

Bestor, Theodore C. (1989) *Neighborhood Tokyo*, Stanford: Stanford University Press.

Davis, Winston (1977) 'The Miyaza and the fisherman: ritual status in coastal villages of Wakayama Prefecture', in *Asian Folklore Studies*, 36(2):3–29.

—— (1980) *Dojo, Magic and Exorcism in Modern Japan*, Stanford: Stanford University Press.

Douglas, Mary (1966) *Purity and Danger, an Analysis of Concepts of Pollution and Taboo*, Harmondsworth, Middlesex, U.K.: Penguin Books.

Engels, Friedrich (1971) [1891] *The Origin of the Family, Private Property, and the State*, Eleanor Leacock (ed.), New York: International Publishers.

Grapard, Allan G. (1984) 'Japan's ignored cultural revolution: the separation of Shintō and Buddhist divinities in Meiji (*shimbutsu bunri*) and a case study: Tōnomine', *History of Religions*, 23(3):240–65.

Hagiwara Hidesaburo and Hagiwara Noriko (1973) *Kamishima*, Tokyo: Ijō Shoten.

Hardacre, Helen (1984) *Lay Buddhism in Contemporary Japan: Reiyūkai Kyūdan*, Princeton: University of Princeton Press.

—— (1986) *Kurozumikyō and the new Religions of Japan*, Princeton: University of Princeton Press.

Hendry, Joy (1984) 'Shoes, the early learning of an important distinction in Japanese society', in *Europe Interprets Japan*, Tenterden, Kent: Paul Norbury Publications.

Holden, Pat (ed.) (1983) *Women's Religious Experience*, London and Canberra: Croom Helm.

Hori Ichirō (1963) 'Mysterious visitors from the harvest to the New Year', in Richard Dorson (ed.) *Studies in Japanese Folklore*, Indiana: Indiana University Press.

—— (1968) *Folk Religion in Japan: Continuity and Change*, Joseph M. Kitagawa and Alan L. Miller (eds), Chicago: The University of Chicago Press.

Hugh-Jones, Christine (1979) *From the Milk River: Spatial and Temporal Processes in Northwest Amazonia*, Cambridge: Cambridge University Press.

Jeremy, Michael and M.E. Robinson (1989) *Ceremony and Symbolism in the Japanese Home*, Manchester: Manchester University Press.

Kendall, Laurel and Mark Peterson (eds) (1983) *Korean Women: View from the Inner Room*, Cushing, Me.: East Rock Press, Inc.

Kerns, Virginia (1983) *Women and the Ancestors, Black Carib Kinship and Ritual*, Urbana and Chicago: University of Illinois Press.

Kondo, Dorinne K. (1990) *Crafting Selves: Power, Gender and Discourses of Identity in a Japanese Workplace*, Chicago: University of Chicago Press.

Kurata Masakuni (1974) 'Noshi awabi no yurai' ('The origin of *noshi awabi*') in *Nihon no Ninwa*, vol. 13, *Ise Shima*, Tokyo: Rengō Insatsu Kabushiki Kaisha.

Kuroda Toshio (1981) 'Shinto in the history of Japanese religion', trans. James C. Dobbins and Suzanne Gay, *The Journal of Japanese Studies*, 7(1):1–21.

Lebra, Takie Sugiyama (1984) *Japanese Women, Constraint and Fulfillment*, Honolulu: University of Hawaii Press.

Lewis, David C. (1986) '"Years of Calamity": *yakudoshi* observances in a city', in Joy Hendry and Jonathan Webber (eds) *Interpreting Japanese Society: Anthropological Approaches*, Oxford: JASO Occasional Paper Series no. 5.

Martinez, D.P. (1988) 'The *ama*: tradition and change in a Japanese diving community', Unpublished D.Phil. thesis, Oxford University.

—— (1990) 'The dead: Shintū aspects of Buddhist ritual', *Journal of the Oxford Anthropological Society* (JASO), Special issue on the Anthropology of Buddhism, ed. by D. N. Gellner, 21(2).

—— (1994) 'Women and religion in Japan', in Jean Holm and John Bowker (eds) *Women and Religion – Themes in Religious Studies*, London: Pinter Publishers.

Masuda Kōkichi (1975) 'Bride's progress: how a *yome* becomes a *shutome*', in David Plath (ed.) *Adult Episodes in Japan*, Leiden: E.J. Brill.

Miyata N. (1983) *Onna no reiryoku to ie no kami* (The spiritual power of woman and the household deities), Tokyo: Jinbun Shoin.

Ooms, Herman (1976) 'A structural analysis of Japanese rites and beliefs', in William H. Newll (ed.) *Ancestors*, The Hague and Paris: Mouton.

Paulson, Joy (1976) 'Evolution of the feminine ideal', in Lebra *et al.* (eds) *Women in changing Japan*, Stanford: Stanford University Press.

Ranke-Heinemann, Uta (1990) *Eunuchs for the Kingdom of Heaven, the Catholic Church and Sexuality*, trans. Peter Heinegg, London: Penguin Books.

Reader, Ian (1990) *Religion in Contemporary Japan*, Basingstoke: Macmillan.

Sakai Teikichirū (n.d.) *Kyōdoshi, Nagaoka mura ōasa Kuzaki (The Village Land Records of Kuzaki: a Major Section of Nagaoka Village)*.

Smith, Robert (1988) 'Gender inequality in contemporary Japan', *Journal of Japanese Studies*, 13(1):1–25.

Smyers, Karen A. (1983) 'Women and Shinto: the relation between purity and pollution', in *Japanese Religions* 12(4):7–19.

Thompson, Catherine (1983) 'Women, fertility and the worship of gods in an Indian village', in Pat Holden (ed.) *Women's Religious Experience*. London and Canberra: Croom Helm.

Turner, Victor W. (1957) *Schism and Continuity in an African Society: A Study of Ndembu Village Life*, Manchester: Manchester University Press.

Wilson, Brian (1983) 'The Korean Shaman: image and reality', in Laurel Kendall and Mark Peterson (eds) *Korean Women: View from the Inner Room*, Cushing, Me.: East Rock Press, Inc.

Yanagita Kunio (1948) *Imo no chikara* (The power of the sister), Tokyo: Sōgensha.

—— (ed.) (1981) [1950] *Kaisan seikatsu no kenkyū* (Research on the customs of coastal villages), Tokyo: Kokuji Kankōkai.

Yoshida Teigo (1981) 'Stranger as God', in *Ethnology* 20(2):87–99.

—— (1990) 'The feminine in Japanese folk religion: polluted or divine?', in Eyal Ben-Ari, Brian Moeran and James Valentine (eds) *Unwrapping Japan*, Manchester: Manchester University Press.

—— and Ueda, H. (1968) 'Spirit possession and social structure in south-western Japan', *Proceedings of the VIIIth International Congress of Anthropological and Ethnological Sciences*, 2:377–8, Tokyo and Kyoto: Science Council of Japan.

# 9 Sonaemono
## Ritual gifts to the deities

*Jane Cobbi*

*Sonaemono* is a term we can understand as designating all the presents given daily, as well as on special occasions, to native deities, *kami*, and to the Buddhist entities called *hotoke*. All over Japan, *kami* and *hotoke* are the two kinds of religious entities, respectively venerated in Shintō shrines (*miya, jinja, jingū*) and in Buddhist temples (*tera*). Long-standing cult practices generally maintain a basic distinction between *kami* and *hotoke*, despite the existence of some forms of syncretism, well known within Japanese religious phenomena.

Most rural Japanese homes have, among several others, two main places devoted to domestic cults; they are located, if not in two different rooms, at least in two separate or closed spaces of the same room when the house is very small. These places called *kamidana* (the '*kami* shelf') and *butsudan* (the 'ancestors' altar') are generally dedicated, one to the protecting deities, (*kami*, belonging to the Shintō pantheon), the other one to the *hotoke*, a name designating Buddhas and ancestors as well as the spirits of the recent dead of the household, since death and funeral rites are dominated by Buddhist rites.[1]

The distinct domestic cult practices regarding *kami* and *hotoke* have been pointed out by Kon Wajiro (1958) following the terminology used by Imanishi Kinji in the field of primatology: *sumiwake* (the spatial 'living separation'). More recently Nakamaki Hirochika (1983), a specialist in Japanese religious studies, has discussed the importance of this distinction through the *yorishiro* (material support, or prop of the *kami*) in an article entitled 'The "Separate" Coexistence of Kami and Hotoke: A Look at Yorishiro'. I would like to analyse this separation from another point of view of material culture, the one concerning different food offerings to *kami* and *hotoke*.

A clear distinction between the offerings given to the *kami* and those given to the *hotoke* is not immediately obvious, but a couple of clues can at least be found through the analysis of some of these offerings.

The results of a detailed study of the offerings' sets tell us about their different compositions depending on the receiver. For example, the *hotoke* are given incense, whereas the *kami* are not. On the contrary, the *kami* are the only ones to be officially given sake.

Concerning food offerings, this special kind of food given to spiritual beings from the other-world, one might think that differences depend on the changing of seasons and on the time when rituals are performed. Actually, one can see on the home Buddhist altar (*butsudan*), green branches of fresh soya beans (*eda mame*) during the *bon* festival in the summer, exactly when the living human beings start eating soya beans as a boiled new vegetable, particularly delicious with very cold beer. No more surprising is the offering of rice ears to the Inari deity after the harvest, when peasants and some privileged citizens enjoy the taste of the 'new rice' (*shinmai*).

However, the nature of food offerings itself differs in most cases according to the addressee: it seems that *kami* and *hotoke* do not accept exactly the same kind of food. They have their own preferences and dislikes. The prohibition of meat within the *hotoke*'s world is well known, but this is not the case for the *kami*. Other questions could also be raised about the different kinds of food preparations, raw or cooked, given to one category or the other of the deities.

My contribution will only concern the offering of salted or sweetened food, the privileged presence of salt in the *kami*'s proximity and sugar within the *hotoke*'s world.

Salt is, beside sake, one of the official offerings to the *kami*, as we can find in most encyclopedias, under the entry for *shinsen* (literally 'food for deities'); *shinsen* is given the meaning of 'food and sake [read as *shushoku*] presented to deities'. Even a regular dictionary like *Kōjien* is quite precise: 'Are normally used as food for deities: paddy rice (*ine*), uncooked rice (*kome*), sake, game (*chōju*: *tori* and *kemono*), fish and shellfish, fruits, vegetables, salt, water (*mizu*)'.[2] Among the basic offerings in Shintō rituals, purse salt appears on the first tray offered to the *kami*, along with sake, water and uncooked rice. One could say that this group constitutes the vital elements of life for the Japanese.

The food offerings to the *hotoke* are called *bukku* (or *buku*). The term *bukku* is given only a vague definition, for example in the *Kōjien* mentioned above it is described as 'Things offered to the *hotoke*'. Under the term *busshō*, a popular synonym for *bukku*, we find no more information than 'cooked rice' (*beihan*, *kome no meshi*) presented to *hotoke*'. Further details about *bukku* are given by Hasegawa Kunimitsu: 'Food and drinks offered to the *hotoke*, and excluding sake, meat, and the five strong-tasting plants (*goshin*)'.[3]

We see that sake and meat, while listed among offerings to the *kami*, are excluded from food given to the *hotoke* as well as the strong-tasting plants (*goshin*), which we will examine now.[4]

In the term *goshin*, 'go' means 'five', and '*shin*' is another reading of the Chinese character used for the word *karai*, 'strong tasting'. These five strong-tasting things are well-known plants: Chinese chives (*nira*), garlic (*ninniku*), leeks (*negi*), Japanese shallot (*rakkyo*) ginger (*haji-kami*), all prohibited in a strict Buddhist diet. In contrast, they have to be present (or at least some of them) in Shintō rites, as indicated by the word *kara-na*.

The enumeration of products to be given to the *kami* is traditionally included in *norito*, invocations addressed to the Shintō deities; among these products come inevitably *ama-na* (sweet vegetables) and *kara-na* (strong vegetables). Examples of the use of these distinguishing terms can be found in the oldest kinds of *norito* we can hear, repeated in the shrines, as well as in the newest *norito* created by some village officiants. In 1975, for example, on the Island of Tobishima (Yamagata prefecture), in the north-west of Honshu, the officiant (*kannushi*) of the shrine said that he had composed *norito* by himself, using basic locutions such as 'things from the sea' (*umi no mono*) and then including *ama-na* and *kara-na*. He explained that *ama-na* could be vegetables such as tomatoes and carrots, whereas *kara-na* has to be something like radishes (*daikon*) or leeks (*negi*). These vegetables can be frequently seen among the offerings given to the *kami* in shrines.[5] It is possible, therefore, to point out an opposition between offerings to the *kami* and offerings presented to the *hotoke*, since the second ones excluded *karai* food (especially the *go-shin*) such as *negi*, which are recommended in the first ones. Concerning food given to the *hotoke*, as described by Hasegawa,

> these offerings can be different according to the Buddhist sects and the rituals to be performed, but they normally contain cakes – *mochi* and *kashi* – for big Buddhist celebrations, cooked rice and tea for daily rituals devoted to the ancestors on the altar (*butsudan*).
>
> (Hasegawa 1979:572)

Tea is often given to the *hotoke*, but not to the *kami*. The term for this specific use of tea in Buddhist offerings is *cha-no-yu* ('hot water of tea'), which yet does not refer to the tea ceremony, even though it has the same name, but insists on the specificity of the water. Since Japanese does not have a generic word for 'water', the choice is always expressed between hot water (*yu*) and cold water (*mizu*). If *yu* is generally offered to the *hotoke*, *mizu* is the only kind of 'water' given to the *kami*. In front of the *hotoke*, tea (or hot water, *yu*) is associated with cakes and cooked rice, as it is on the table of human beings.

We can also notice that uncooked rice, necessarily present in the Shintō shrines, is not generally used for the Buddhist temples and altars, while cooked rice is used for both types of deities; it seems, initially, to also be the case for glutinous rice-cakes (*mochi*) and for pastries (*kashi*), but this has to be examined.

At this stage I would like to introduce a distinction: if *kashi* is also a term used for some offerings to the *kami*, its meaning is then different. First of all, we have to keep in mind that *kashi* need not necessarily be a sugared food. For example, what is today called *mame-gashi* often means salted peas, peanuts or soya beans with seasonings such as spices, soya sauce, seaweeds, etc.[6]

For specialists in food history, there are several steps in the evolution of *kashi*.[7] In early antiquity (*jō-ko-jidai*) *kashi* referred only to fruits (*kudamono*, or *ko-no-mi*), and then began designating Chinese pastries (*kara-kashi* or *tōgashi*) when these were introduced into Japan. The *kara-kashi*, prepared with wheat flour or rice flour, are sometimes steamed, sometimes boiled and often fried, but always made without sugar, as indicated by Inokuchi Shōji (1958:271). Occasionally we can find them in shrines among other offerings, beside the fruits also named *kashi*. The meaning of *kashi* changed later with the development of the tea ceremony, and with the arrival of Portuguese, bringing new types of sweets and pastries. Then its general meaning became sweet cakes and pastries, made from cereals or red beans (*azuki*) mixed together with sugar, such as *yōkan*, sponge-cakes (*kasutera*), or *manjū* (balls of wheat or blackwheat flour stuffed with sugared beans or chestnut paste). These sweet kinds of *kashi* are often given as offerings to the *hotoke*, on ritual days (*bon*, equinoxes, etc.), as well as sweetened *mochi* – *bota-mochi* (balls of glutinous rice containing sugared red beans) or *hagi* (rice paste covered with sugared red beans). Generally speaking, we often find sweet pastries, sugared products, in the *hotoke*'s world.

In the course of my fieldwork on gift-giving habits, I noticed that for the *bon* festival, neighbours or relatives going to each other's house to give ritual salutations to the *hotoke* bring with them an offering of sweet cakes such as *manjū* (stuffed with heavily sugared bean paste). These cakes are piled up on the ancestor's altar until they are eaten by the family.[8]

If sweet cakes are common offerings to the ancestors, better yet is the pure sugar which is given to the participants of a funeral as a return gift (*kōdengaeshi*). So sugar and sweets are obviously present within the Buddhist world, including the funeral rituals. If salt recently has started to appear in these rituals, it is only to better separate the world of the living from the world of death. Salt is what purifies and brings back to the world of the living that which was polluted by contact with death. In rural places it is an old tradition, when coming back from a funeral, to purify oneself before entering one's home by throwing salt over one's shoulder. Today, since citizens often do not go home directly from a funeral, but go back to work, they cannot easily procure salt unless it is provided at the end of the ceremony. This introduction of salt in the funeral rite normally exclusively dominated by sugar is an adaptation to modern society of the rule strongly separating the world of death and the world of life, which is the domain of the *kami*.

In ceremonial offerings to the *kami* salt is always present, but not sweetened preparations or any product with sugar added, as noted by Tsuji and Takahashi in their description of the Ise Jingu Festival (1985:51). Following the public disclosure of the imperial rituals after the Second World War, Matsudaira Narimitsu (1955) was able to publish, in French, an analysis of the imperial premises. He provided a long list of different foods offered to the deity: several kinds of fish and shellfish, seaweeds, vegetables, dried fruits, millet and rice gruel, with sake of course, but nothing sugared (1955: 12).

Whenever the *kami* are given *kashi* it consists of dried fruits or Chinese unsweetened pastries called *buto* (fried dumplings). When they are given *mochi*, there are also normally unsweetened (although this could be misunderstood in the English translation 'rice-cake') and are made only from glutinous rice, without any seasoning, often shaped in the form of mirrors and called *kagami-mochi*.

So, *kashi* means fruit (fresh or dried fruit) and sometimes fried dumplings in Shintō rituals, but sugared pastries in Buddhist rituals; *mochi* designates simple preparations of glutinous rice when given to the *kami*, and elaborated combinations of glutinous rice with sweetened paste of beans in the case of offerings to the *hotoke*.

If we consider, on the one hand, that most rituals concerning *kami* acquired their basic structure in the past, and used only products gathered from the immediate environment, and on the other hand, that Japanese Buddhist rituals have integrated many elements imported from the Continent (such as incense), it is not surprising that sugar, unknown in Japan until its introduction from China by monks, has been adopted for their rituals, and kept in that use until today.

We can examine now the status of salt and sugar in secular society.[9] Living in a country very rich in sea salt and relatively poor in sugar producing plants, the Japanese give a huge role to salt, their most important food seasoning. Salt also functions as the main preservative of all sorts of edible products and, as such, is the base of one of the most important food groups, *tsukemono*, which is the main complement to cooked rice.

In Japan the taste of salt is classified as a strong taste (as are hot, spicy and alcoholized foods) labelled *karai*, as opposed to neutral or soft tastes (which include the sweetness of sugar) called *amai*.[10] So we have, on the one hand, sake and whisky, ginger, radish, *miso* (fermented and salted soya beans) in the category of *karai*, and on the other hand lettuce, tomato, honey, sweet wine (for example Porto and Akadama wine) in the category of *amai*, with rice as well, since it is normally cooked without salt or any seasoning.

According to a popular saying, the Japanese classify themselves in the 'soft-taste party' (*amatō*), or in the 'strong-taste party' (*karatō*), meaning they like either eating cakes (in the case of *amatō*) or drinking sake (in the case of *karatō*) which always implies eating salted dishes, called *sake no sakana* ('side dish for sake').

This opposition between drinkers and non-drinkers seems to be quite an old one, since it is already expressed – in different terms – in some fifteenth-century scrolls: *Shucharon, Shuhanron, Shuheiron*, 'disputes' (*ron*) between sake (*shu*) and tea (*cha*), between sake (*shu*) and cooked rice (*han*), between sake (*shu*) and rice-cakes or *mochi* (*hei*). These documents highlight a difference between 'those who like sake (*jōgo*), and those who do not (*geko*), preferring something sweet' (Yoshida 1989:111). What should be noted here is not only the opposition, but also a kind of hierarchy between *jōgo* and *geko*. Since *jō* refers to what is up and *ge* to what is down, these terms suggest that, as non-drinkers, rice-eaters or cake-eaters (soft-taste amateurs) have a lower status than sake-drinkers (strong-taste amateurs), at least in these literary texts . . . and probably in the surrounding society as well.

This leads us to the sexual division between the world of *karai* (salted, spicy, alcoholized), and the world of *amai* (soft, sweet, discreet). The first one is highly appreciated by most men, the second one perceived as suiting women, who will more easily confess that they have a sweet tooth.[11]

A preference for sake, salted dishes, and other 'strong tastes' goes with the image of a strong man. Warriors used to subsist on salted food; we have evidence from the Edo period through the kind of dried food such as balls of *miso* (*misodama*) which the soldier would take with him while on campaign. During the Second World War, a soldier's typical meal was *hi no maru bento* (literally 'national flag lunch-box'), consisting of a very salted, red and round plum, put in the middle of a square box of white rice.

Women, like children, love eating sweets. They have been the first ones to adopt the Western notion of 'desert' (*dezā-to*) whereas men still show resistance to this ending of a meal, which is not a traditional food habit in Japan. If, in a man's world, food called *karai* seems to play a fundamental role, weak people, in contrast are provided with energy through sweet food. This is true not only for women and children, as mentioned above, but for sick people as well: most of the gifts given to an ill person fall under the category of *mimai*, or *byōki-mimai*, and are made of sweet products such as cakes and fruit juice.

It is clear that Japanese representations separate men and women, vigorous and weak people, and finally the world of life and the world of death through salt and sugar, and extensively through strong and soft tastes. I have tried to point out how these products played the same dividing role in the cults of *kami* and *hotoke*. It would seem that the *kami* are *karatō* and *hotoke* are *amatō*.

One wonders whether this distinction is not one of the basic representations of the Japanese since it dominates the human world as well as religious practices, in other words, the profane as well as the sacred.

## NOTES

1  As I witnessed it over ten years of fieldwork in rural Japan, particularly in the prefectures of Nagano, Ibaragi, Akita, Shimane, etc.
2  The same enumeration is given in the *Fūzoku jiten* (Dictionary of customs) under the entry '*shinshu*' (gods' sake), p. 361.
3  The encyclopedia *Nihon fūzokushi jiten*, p. 572.
4  This prohibition rule, expressed for Buddhist offerings only, can of course be broken: a bottle of sake can be seen on the altar to a grandfather who loved to drink sake when alive. If sake is ever given to monks (and not to the *hotoke*) despite the prohibition of alcoholic drinks in a Buddhist temple, it is then called under a special name, hiding its true nature: *hannyatō* ('hot water for the sutra reading').
5  This was confirmed by recent fieldwork I carried out on Japanese 'peas and beans' (*mame*).
6  Old *norito* can be found in the book *Kojiki-norito*, by Kurano and Takeda (1958); see page 387 for one read as 'Toshigoi no matsuri', which was translated into French by J.P. Berthon. I have recorded some old *norito* from the end of the 1960s in several shrines of Nagano and Akita prefectures, and through 1983 in shrines around Kyoto.

   The information collected from the officiant in the island of Tobishima was confirmed thanks to the notes taken by Jacqueline Pigeot, who was present during this interview.
7  Tada Tetsunosuke (1979:102); Sekine Shinryū (1969:118); see also Yanagita Kunio (1970 (24):178).
8  While they should be emptied by sharing between members of the family,

it is impossible to finish them. Around 1981 I noticed an attempt to eliminate this custom seen as a 'source of waste', in the community of Kaida-mura, in Nagano prefecture (Cobbi 1987:162).

9  This aspect has been dealt with in more detail in my article 'Le doux et le fort' (1988).

10  In connection with the food given to the *hotoke*, *amai* can mean extremely sweet, whereas it only means soft-tasting when concerning the *kami* (as seen above for *amana*).

11  When I was a student I angered one of my Japanese professors simply by saying to him, with no hesitation in my voice, "you are *amatō*". I did not know then that is was derogatory for some men to be seen as loving sweets!

# BIBLIOGRAPHY

Cobbi, Jane (1987) 'Don et contre-don: une tradition à l'épreuve de la modernité', in A. Berque (ed.) *Le Japon et son double*, Paris, Masson.

—— (1988) 'Le doux et le fort (Japon)', JATBA, XXXV *Le sucre et le sel*, numéro spécial (April 1990):267–79.

Frank, Bernard (1980) *Leçon inaugurale, chaire de Civilisation japonaise*, Collège de France, (29 February 1980).

—— (1986) 'Vacuité et corps actualisé', *Le temps de la réflexion* VII, *Corps des dieux*, Paris: Gallimard, pp. 142–70.

Hasegawa Kunimitsu (1979) 'Bukku', in Izutsu *et al.* (eds) *Nihon fūzoku-shi jiten*, Tokyo: Kōbundō.

Hirai Tadafusa (1971) 'Sonae-mono', in Oshima *et al.* (eds) *Nihon o shiru jiten*, Tokyo: Shakai-shisō-sha, pp. 530–2.

Imanishi Kinji (1980) *Shutaisei no shinkaron*, Tokyo: Chūō Kōronsha.

Inokuchi Shōji (1958) 'Shokuhin' (Nourritures), in Ōmachi *et al.* (eds) *Nihon minzoku-gaku taikei*, vol. 6, Tokyo: Heibon-sha, pp. 253–72.

Katō Katsuhisa (1982) *Nihon daisai-jiki*, Tokyo: Kōdansha.

Kon Wajiro (1958) 'Jūkyo no hensen' (History of habitation), in Ōmachi *et al.*, (eds) *Nihon minzo-kugaku taikei*, vol. 6, Tokyo: Heibon-sha, pp. 3–20.

Kurano, K. and Takeda, Y. (1958) *Kojiki-norito, Nihon koten bungaku taikei*, Tokyo: Iwanami Shoten.

Matsudaira Narimitsu (1955) *Le Rituel des prémices au Japon*, Paris: PUF ('Bulletin de la Maison Franco-Japonaise', IV, 2).

Matsumoto T. and Yokoyama S. (1979) *Muromachi jidai monogatari taisei*, vol. 7, Tokyo: Kadokawa.

Nakamaki Hirochika (1983) 'The "Separate" Coexistence of Kami and Hotoke. A look at Yorishiro', *Japanese Journal of Religious Studies*, 10 (1): 65–86.

Ono Susumu *et al.* (eds) (1974) *Kogo jiten*, Tokyo: Iwanami.

Ooms, Herman (1967) 'The Religion of the Household, a case study of ancestor worship in Japan', *Contemporary Religions in Japan* VIII (3–4) 201–334.

Oshima T. *et al.* (eds) (1971) *Nihon o shiru jiten*, Tokyo: Shakai-shisō-sha.

Rotermund, Hartmut (1988) *Religions croyances et traditions populaires du Japon*, vol. I, Paris: Maisonneuse & Larose.

Sakamoto Tarō *et al.* (1957) *Fūzoku Jiten*, Tokyo: Tōkyō-dō Shuppan.

Sekine Shinryu (1969) *Nara-chō shoku-seikatsu no kenkyū*, Tokyo: Yoshikawa-kōbunkan.

Tada Tetsunosuke (1979) 'Kashi', in Izutsu, G. *et al. Nihon fūkozu-shi jiten*, Tokyo: Kōbundō.

Yanagita Kunio (1970) [1931] 'Meiji Taishō-shi', in *Teihon Yanagita Kunio Zenshū* (complete works), 24, Tokyo: Chikuma-shobō, pp. 129–414.

Yoshida Mitsukuni (1989) *Naorai, Communion of the Table*, Hiroshima: Mazda.

# 10  The ritual of the revolving towel[1]

*Joy Hendry*

In this chapter I would like to take up the analysis of several apparently mundane aspects of Japanese domestic life and examine their value from a ritual point of view. In the process, I hope to bring together into a single conceptual framework a number of practices which I have for some time observed and pondered upon, with the aim of demonstrating an internal logic joining them into a unity which I have often intuitively felt that they ought to have. The research on which the paper is based has been carried out over a number of years: in Tokyo, in an agricultural village in Kyūshū, in a fishing community in Chiba prefecture, and, probably the most useful period was in 1987 amongst a group of housewives in the provincial town of Tateyama, Chiba prefecture, some two hours from Tokyo.

The research topics of these visits were rather different, but on each occasion I tried to insinuate myself into as many and varied situations as possible so that I could observe, as a regular participant, all kinds of interaction between the people concerned, and this gave me a broad base of experience in their lives. During the time I was in Tateyama, my children attended the local school and there were various events here and elsewhere to attend obligatorily as a mother. As will be seen, some of these contributed in an interesting way to the subject in hand.

## THE PROBLEM

As the title of the paper implies, my concern here is with 'towels' – in the first instance, the type of towel which is generally described in Japanese as *taoru* – although the use of the word there is somewhat different to the use of the English word 'towel' elsewhere, at least in Britain and the US. A thoughtful Japanese host, with experience abroad, may provide Western visitors with a large, soft bath towel of the kind to which they are accustomed, and this is the kind also found in expensive international hotels. In a less cosmopolitan environment, however, whether house or hotel, guests are expected to manage with one very small towel, hardly more than a large flannel. Indeed, in public bath-houses these 'towels' are used both as flannels and, once rung out, as surprisingly effective towels.[2]

The towels with which we are particularly concerned here are of a very specific type, both in size and shape. Their dimensions are around 76–80 cm long and 29–32 cm wide. People do have and use larger towels, but usually in addition to, rather than instead of the standard ones, and they may, at least in the provinces, be found in uses quite surprising to a Western eye, such as for wrapping babies. Huge towels, sometimes actually referred to as 'bath towels', or *basutaoru* are also used as bedding, as if they were sheets. Most households have a plentiful supply of towels, particularly the small standard ones, and, once their initial freshness has worn off, they are doubled up to be used as floor cloths, an interesting expression of parsimony (or value) in a society where washing machines and other electrical goods are often thrown away at the first mechanical hiccup.[3] Evidently the category of 'towel', despite the apparent English origin of the term, has, like many other foreign words adopted into other languages, and the objects adopted into other cultures, taken on a rather different range of meanings.

This, however, is barely the beginning of the story of 'towels' in Japan, for the standard objects described above have a multitude of other roles to play, far beyond their mundane lives in the service of cleanliness. Indeed, rather as a Japanese housewife might, during my research I found myself often dealing with towels of one sort or another. It is, for example, a widespread practice for shops and other commercial ventures to present towels to their customers, perhaps regularly, as at New Year, or simply in recognition of a substantial purchase. The towel used here is much like any other towel except for the fact that it will have the shop's name and address clearly marked upon it.

Hotels are also inclined to have a supply of such towels, particularly if they offer hot-spring water in their baths, although they seem increasingly likely to charge for them rather than handing them out as gifts, just as the public bath-houses do. Either way, the towel is taken home and probably used and washed frequently – the advantage for the business concerned being that of reminding the recipient of the location where it was acquired. It thus serves as a form of advertising, effectively reaching the potential client in the very heart of the home, at a relaxed, comfortable moment, perhaps touching a cord of nostalgia which will ensure renewed custom in the future.

That this practice is not simply a form of advertising, however, can be seen by comparison with another common custom involving towels, namely, that of presenting them to new neighbours. In this case, the towels have no name and address on them, but simply offer an opportunity for a family to initiate relations with neighbours when they move into a new district. There are one or two other possible gifts used at such a time, but in deference to the practice, informants often refer to the items as *taoru toka* (a towel or something like it). In both these cases the hope is expressed that the relationship signified by the movement of the towel will continue to exist, and the recipient may thank the donor for their politeness in making the presentation.

In a kind of reverse way, the tennis coach for a class of housewives to which I was attached during the 1987 period of research, gave me a towel as a token parting gift after my last lesson before I left for England. I'm not sure whether he did this for any of his pupils who left his group, or just for the extraordinary foreign one, and, indeed, I have no further examples of towels being used as leaving presents, although in connection with sport, more generally, I have received a towel for taking part in a tennis tournament, and I understand a special towel may be presented to someone who gets a 'hole-in-one' in golf.

Sheets, too, may be used as a form of ritual currency in this way, whether in the form of Western bath towels or not; indeed, their similarity in this sense may help to explain the degree of conceptual overlap. They are not given away quite as lightly as towels, but on the other hand, they may express a closer relationship. At a funeral, for example, those who present a sum of money to the family of the deceased, usually receive a gift as a sort of token return. The sum of money depends on the proximity of relationship, as does the gift received.[4] Distant acquaintances and well-wishers are usually offered a handkerchief, perhaps with a small packet of salt for purificatory purposes, but the closest relatives may well be given sheets. Packets of paper handkerchiefs are, of course, another popular object used for advertising.

An event which enables one to bring these household gifts into a single category is a school or kindergarten bazaar. This is the occasion for turning out things which have accumulated in one's house, and many 'gifts' find their way onto the local equivalent of the white elephant stall. Handkerchiefs, towels and sheets are usually available in abundance, at prices considerably reduced from those found in stores, and these are accompanied by other common gifts such as sets of bowls or glasses. None have been used, but their packaging has lost the pristine quality which makes them presentable as gifts, so their value is now merely domestic, evidently much less in that form than it was as they made the rounds as gifts. This time, however, the money paid for them goes into school funds, so these important objects have acquired another, charitable value on the way.

An interesting variation on the theme was something I observed and experienced in an association acquired, through one of my sons, with the Cub Scouts of Japan. The mothers of our particular pack had been asked to hold a stall at the annual bazaar, and some of us gathered to make a few items to brighten up the usual arrangement of worn-out gifts. The raw material – none other than an assortment of towels – probably in most cases again received as gifts. We spent several hours pulling, twisting and sewing them up, attaching bows and buttons, and lo and behold we had created a collection of charming little animals – dogs, lions and, most time-consuming of all, kangaroos.

These were to be sold at a price virtually identical to the original cost of the unadulterated towel, although when the day arrived they were actually priced at twice as much. In any case, they were worth more as little animals than they would have been in battered cellophane bags, which was the state of most of the towels brought by the other participants. As yet unaccustomed to these occasions, I had put all the towels I had received as gifts into use in the bathroom, so I had to go out and buy new ones. On the other hand, for me the four hours or so we spent in the production of these objects was also an excellent opportunity for simultaneously carrying out my research, whereas for the others the time was totally unproductive from an economic point of view. This was, of course, entirely beside the point, since the activity had the charitable purpose of raising funds for the Cub Scouts of Japan, and therefore, indirectly, to help their own sons. It did also have the incidental effect, since each participant could have worked alone, of providing an opportunity for members of the group to socialize amongst themselves.

## THE RITUAL FACTOR

The towels and sheets in question here would appear, in fact, to have become a kind of currency in the way they are being used. These objects have very clear functions in a domestic situation, but this main function is only a small part of the story of their lives. Eventually, they may be used by someone for their ostensible purpose, but they may also first have been on a round of presentations, especially if one person was able to pass them on to another before the packaging became too creased. In this way, they can be compared with money, which is also often presented as a gift in Japan, but their use is limited to certain appropriate occasions and they would probably also represent too small a sum to be presented as cash. The school bazaar provides an occasion for redistribution of these goods, and, indeed, their ultimate conversion into cash, since some families will have accumulated more of these objects than others, but this only offers a way of raising funds for the school.

The towels, sheets and handkerchiefs evidently also have an important ritual function, however, since they are used in ways which would be most inappropriate for money. Their intrinsic value is very little indeed, their functional value only very domestic and personal. In being presented by one person, or an entity such as a household or a shop, to another, their ritual function is to represent the relationship between those persons, or groups of persons. As Marcel Mauss (1974) demonstrated years ago, prestations of any sort usually involve three obligations: to give, to receive and to repay. What is particularly interesting about the rounds towels make, however, is that while it is clear that they are given, and indeed, received, what should be repaid is less evident.

In this case, the presents have such little intrinsic value that it is almost as if they are regarded as objects without any monetary value at all, and the significance of this would perhaps be that their receipt calls for no reciprocal gift – they do not need to be repaid. In some cases, they are actually returns for gifts given by others, as in the case of the sheets and handkerchiefs at a funeral, token immediate returns not intended to replace any future repayment, which will usually involve waiting for someone to die in the family of the donor. Elsewhere they have commercial value, in encouraging customers to return to a shop for future purchases. It is possible in the case of the tennis coach that he had expected me to give him a parting gift – if so this was an expectation which I failed to fulfil, but for which the towel would have been a token return.

In the case of the visit to new neighbours, the custom offers an opening of relations without burdening the recipient with obligations they may not want to take on. Here the importance of Mauss's second obligation is seen. If one is presented with a gift, one is under an obligation to receive it, on pain of breaking off or rejecting the relationship. However, the option is, at least theoretically, there, and it is quite possible to return a gift, unopened, in order to express a rejection of the relationship it implies. It is thus inappropriate, and somewhat risky, to make a substantial presentation to someone with whom one has as yet no relationship, for it immediately burdens that person with decisions about whether or not to accept it. An insubstantial gift, such as a towel, is merely an overture, its acceptance little more than a polite gesture, so that its lack of value is entirely appropriate in this case.

Another point which emphasizes this aspect of the towel as a gift is that it does not even require the layers of wrapping commonly associated with presents. It may be handed over, encased only in a plastic bag; indeed it would be inappropriate again for the contents of the bag to be further obscured since it would not immediately be clear that this was such an insubstantial prestation, rather than a gift, proper. Usually, the wrapping of a gift anyway provides some sort of indication about its contents, and in this case, the lack of opaque wrapping paper must, I feel, have some significance of its own, a point to which I will return.

## WHY THE TOWEL?

Why then, we may ask, has an apparently Western object with such small monetary value become so versatile in its ability to take on different sorts of ritual value, allowing the expression of various forms of human relationships and allegiances? As far as I know, the archetypal *taoru* is a Japanese version of the Western object, or a Westernized version, in its texture, of a similarly shaped Japanese object called a *tenugui* (literally, hand-wiper). The fact remains, however, that the word used in the circumstances mentioned is the foreign loan-word (*gairaigo*), as is the case for sheets (*shiitsu*), handkerchief (*hankechi*), and bath towel (*basutaoru*). All these objects do, of course, represent new forms of domestic appliance, involving new technology, but then so do oven (*ōbun*), cooler (*kūlā*), and fork (*fōku*), and none of these seems to have found any ritual value.

There are one or two practical answers concerned with each of the objects: for the towel, for example, as for packets of handkerchiefs, the convenient size and weight allows it to be slipped into a shopping bag, or presented with little fuss; and the towel's porous texture allows the successful printing of colours, signs and advertising. It is also a useful size for tying and wearing in one way or another, which makes possible another ritual function of towels in their use as *hachimaki*, a cloth of some sort, which is tied around the head, particularly during work of a ritual nature. On the first day of a housebuilding, for example, every friend and neighbour who turns up to help may be presented with a towel dyed red at one corner. These are to be used throughout the day to mop the sweaty brows of the participants, but the red corner symbolizes the auspicious nature of the occasion, as indeed does the tying of such an object around the head at all.

*Hachimaki* are worn on various occasions when work of some sort is ritualized, and they may have a further symbolic value. At some festivals, for example, members of a particular neighbourhood will wear *hachimaki* of a special colour while they pull their float around the vicinity. As the different floats meet at a central shrine, or at another location, it is immediately clear from which area any participant hails. These *hachimaki* are not necessarily towels, of course, but their size is very similar, and this object could offer us a clue towards beginning to understand the logic behind attributing ritual value to such a mundane object. *Hachimaki* have for some time been associated with festivals; they are also used to wipe the sweaty brow, when the sweat is generated in pursuit of ritual aims. In fact, according to Segawa Kiyoko (1979:572), the association of the *hachimaki* with ritual occasions would seem to precede its association with labour, so perhaps this could be an antecedent for the ritual association of both the *taoru* and the *hankechi* – in its use in Japan for mopping the forehead – and a possible explanation also of the size and shape of the former.

The *tenugui* is another obvious forebear of the *taoru*, and, indeed, the above-mentioned *hachimaki* used for festivals would appear to be a specific example of the use of *tenugui*. According to Segawa, again (1979:474), the *tenugui* has long been worn on the head for various types of labour, and a new one would be given at New Year to anyone who helped to pound the *mochi* (pounded rice, for cakes). The housewife who went out for the first water at New Year would also wear a new *tenugui*, and, in both cases, this would symbolize the sacred nature of the work being done – hence its use also as a *hachimaki* at festivals. A legend even tells of the miraculous powers of a *takaratenugui* (treasure *tenugui*). This object evidently possesses plenty of potential ritual value.

A glance into some of the other folkloric literature on Japan would suggest, however, that there are some further interesting antecedents for the use of a towel to express social links. First of all, in this case, however, we have to establish a link in the argument by discussing briefly an object which was previously used as a towel, but which is now better known for other purposes. This is the *furoshiki* (a cloth used to wrap objects for carrying around). According to Yamada Yōko (1989), this object is an excellent example of Japanese flexibility since it was originally a combination of a bath towel, a bath mat and a clothes basket. It would be used, first, to carry clean clothes to the bath house, second, as a bath towel, third, as a bath mat, and finally, to wrap and carry the soiled clothes home again.

This item is now to be found in a variety of sizes, used predominantly to carry things about. Its use has lapsed somewhat in recent years, apparently, with the introduction of a huge number of purpose-built bags and cases, but *furoshiki* are still to be seen on the streets, and, in my experience in the country, they are used particularly to envelop and carry a present from one house to another. This serves the dual purpose of containing the item in a way convenient to transport, and concealing its precise contents from the eyes of curious passersby. On arrival at its destination, the *furoshiki* is removed, and the present handed over in its own wrapping.

This practice would appear to have given to the *furoshiki* something of a ritual function which it probably lacked in its role as an all purpose bath mate, but it would seem that there is definitely a precedent for this too. In Kyūshū the *furoshiki* has a special form known as a *mino-furoshiki*, reported until recently at least in islands of Nagasaki prefecture (Tanakamaru 1987). This *furoshiki* seems to have formed an important part of a woman's trousseau, used again at several ceremonial occasions throughout her life. Consisting of three pieces of cloth sewn together, it would bear the crest and the name of the woman's house of birth. It was presented after the wedding, symbolizing the link being set up between the families.

The *minofuroshiki* was used to cover the boxes to be sent with the bride to her new home and to carry presents back to her natal family when she returned to visit. It was kept carefully amongst a woman's most valuable possessions. In some poorer families, the bride's trousseau would be sent in parts over the years after the union was initially set up, and the *minofuroshiki* would cover the last load, symbolizing the bride's complete separation from her former home. After this had arrived, the marriage was formally cemented, and the bride was treated with new respect since, until that time, there was always a possibility that the arrangement might break down. The *minofuroshiki* was thus a status symbol, standing for the security of the bride in her new home, but also for the link she retained with her former family. It was laid on the woman's coffin when she died, and passed on down through the family, thus keeping alive for several generations the memory of the family ties created by that particular marriage.

Similar traditions seem to have been found in the prefectures of Saga and Fukuoka, as well as Nagasaki (Tanakamaru 1987), although the *furoshiki* was there known simply as a *yomeiri-furoshiki* (*furoshiki* for the entry of a bride), an item still reported until the present day in the Karatsu district of Saga prefecture, where old women are said to bring them into hospital with them, and handle them tenderly as if for comfort. These *furoshiki* have been described as a combination of a *furoshiki* and a *noshi* (an emblem attached to a gift) (Tanakamaru 1987), indicating also the status and position of their owners, but whatever they are in this respect, they certainly serve a very clear symbolic function in representing links between individuals and households again.

An amusing discussion of *furoshiki* by the Korean commentator, Ii Oryon (who calls himself O'Young Lee in English), suggests that this item, found in other Eastern countries besides Japan, is far from representing outmoded traditions. He sees it, rather, as a model for the future (Ii 1989). In his book, *Furoshiki bunka no posuto modan* (The postmodern in furoshiki culture), he first makes a contrast between the easy-care, adaptable *furoshiki* and the rigid inconvenience of the *kaban* or suitcase, and then draws up a series of oppositions between other flexible aspects of Eastern lifestyle and the more fitted ones of the West. For some time, examples of the latter represented modernity as they were introduced from the West, but he goes on to argue that in the postmodern world the advantages of the *furoshiki* style of life are becoming appreciated again.

One example he gives for this argument is related to the origin of the *furoshiki* in Korea, where it seems to have had ceremonial features for many centuries. Its name in Korean is *pojagi*, where the first character '*po*' has the possible readings of *okurumi*, a wrap for a baby, or *mutsugi*, which sounds closer to modern ears to the word in Japanese for nappies or diapers, and which is, indeed, how the character in question is used. Nevertheless, the soft *okurumi* is contrasted by Lee with the Western cradle, as is the custom of carrying one's baby *onbu* (on the back) style with pushing it around in a pram. Since the practice of carrying babies around is currently spreading to the Western world, now into a postmodern phase, Lee argues that this is one way in which the old-fashioned characteristics of *furoshiki* culture are being revived.

The use of the so-called *basutaoru* for wrapping babies does of course become quite logical now, since in the country, at least, babies were certainly secured to their mothers' backs with *furoshiki* in Japan too, so that it would seem to be a simple transfer of flexibility. Again according to Lee, it was common practice in Japan to print patterns and the household crest onto *furoshiki*, from the time (Muromachi period) of the *shōgun* Yoshimitsu, who apparently introduced this idea to avoid confusion at bath houses (Ii 1989:2). It was a short step, then, to use them for advertising, which is indeed what happened; Daimaru department store was apparently the first to profit from the idea by using them to envelop their goods, thus displaying their name all the way down the Tōkaidō route from Edo to Kyoto. The carrier bag has undoubtedly effectively taken over this function for the large department stores, but it is also easy to see why towels, too, have acquired that particular role.

Lee's argument includes discussion of several differences between Japan and Korea, but one of the themes he continues to develop is that of the apparent Eastern preference for flexibility. This *furoshiki bunka* (*furoshiki* culture) is illustrated, again, in the use of screens instead of walls, where he refers to the subtle and welcoming nature of the latter as opposed to the repressive characteristics of the former, clearly expressed in Russian literature as hard and terrible. Screens prevent drafts, provide privacy and can be covered, divided and decorated to control and manoeuvre the surroundings, thus having the advantages of walls, but with much greater flexibility. He identifies some of the same principles in modern architecture, citing the University of Caracus as an example where there is built-in flexibility in the use of movable panels. Further examples of this flexibility are to be found in the use of chopsticks, as opposed to knives, forks and spoons, and *zabuton* cushions rather than chairs. In the last case, Lee pursues the theme of flexibility more generally into a discussion of the use of space, naturally involving the comparison of beds and *futon*, and in the light of the current Western interest in the latter, predicting that *zabuton* will not be long in joining post-modern Western culture.

This argument begins to get a little out of hand, at times, but there is an interesting section drawing together this apparent preference for flexibility into something which Lee describes as *kagen* culture. This Japanese word is rather difficult to translate into English. It is composed of the two characters for addition and subtraction, suggesting immediately one of its meanings, namely 'to adjust', as in *yukagen*, or the adjustment of the bath water to an appropriate temperature; but another usage, which is rather different in English, is when a person is exorted to *iikagen*, or stop talking, in the sense 'leave it at that', or 'that's enough'. The implication here is that some things should be left deliberately unclear, and talking too much closes off the possibilities for flexibility.

Lee brings in the notion of *yutori* (room, latitude) at this point, mentioning a Chinese practice of serving soup with a round ladle from a square container, always leaving some behind for others. He sees this as symbolic of a general preference to leave things open for interpretation, or new ideas. With clothes, he contrasts the tidy fit of Western tailoring with the looser, more flexible cut of Korean and Japanese garments, which again leaves room for expansion, or shrinkage. At the level of language, he in fact chides the Japanese for what he sees as too much concession to Western logic, and too much simplification which, he argues, leaves no room for nuance, discussion or argument. Language, in Lee's view, should not be clear cut.

## BACK TO THE TOWEL

This brings us neatly back to the towel, though it may not be immediately obvious quite why. First of all, we have offered various precedents for aspects of the use of the *taoru* in their more traditional manifestations. If Lee's argument is to be credited at all, the *taoru*'s flexibility also evidently gives it great strength, and, even if it was not particularly flexible in Western eyes, it has certainly become so in Japan. From a more strictly anthropological point of view, however, it has also acquired a great deal of symbolic value in expressing relationships and allegiances of one sort or another, and in this way I suggest that it is also helping to make possible the kind of communication which Lee is struggling to describe.

True, the spoken word should not be too clear. It has often been pointed out that various aspects of the Japanese language, and undoubtedly Korean, too, leave open the possibility of making adjustments, or of retracting without losing face. In a negative way, it has been described as vague and ambiguous, even unsuitable for scientific communication; but all this is water long under the bridge, and Japanese is proving equal to most tasks imposed upon it by the world at large. The value of the towel, on the other hand, is something which has less clearly been evident to innocent outsiders stepping into the Japanese universe of discourse.

Here, in fact, the towel becomes just one of a number of possible objects, for its role is plainly to communicate at a level beyond that of words, to convey meanings which may actually be quite hard to put into words. In considering the *hachimaki*, *tenugui* and the *furoshiki*, we have provided several examples of fairly clear symbolic communication of this sort, as precedents for the value of the towel in this respect. There are, of course, any number of other objects used in comparable ways, and it would be labouring the point to provide further examples of objects. At this stage, I would like to say a little bit more about the importance of this type of communication in a cross-cultural perspective.

The value placed on non-verbal communication of one sort or another is of course by no means limited to Japan. In fact, there are several other areas around the Pacific Rim where it is, as in Japan, very bad form to express oneself directly, particularly on negative subjects. It is perhaps no coincidence then that many of Mauss's examples in *The Gift* (1974) came from this very ethnographic region. The work of Malinowski (1972) on the Trobriand Islanders, for example, made very clear how much value the ceremonial presentation of gifts has for the people as a whole, as well as for the expression of differences of status within specific groups. A more recent study of the same people by Annette Weiner (1983) has revealed even more information about the symbolic value of objects in that society. Here it is taboo to mention directly any kind of negative feelings one may have about other people, and the anthropologist herself recounts with some clarity an occasion of near disaster when she began to upbraid a local person whom she felt had damaged her bicycle. The individual left immediately, warning her to *iikagen* – to put it into Japanese terms – – before she caused him to break off relations altogether. Her mistake was clarified in subsequent discussions with other people, and she learned that a more suitable moment to express smouldering dissatisfaction with someone is by the speed and efficiency– or, rather, by the lack of it – used when helping them to pick yams. An annual occurrence, when neighbours turn out in force to help one another, is also the occasion for measuring one's popularity or otherwise, apparently, and this is plain for all to see in the size of the pile of yams one is able to accumulate.

In Japanese villages, the traditional way of expressing community dissatisfaction with a particular household was a kind of ostracism known as *mura hachibu*, when neighbours agreed together to withdraw all but an eighth part of their co-operation with that household, leaving its members alive, but very little more, since all communication beyond that necessary for survival was withheld. This is of course an extreme case, however, and in everyday life, people express satisfaction and dissatisfaction with each other in various ways, very often using material objects as vehicles for doing this. Any number of small symbolic gestures may be required to ensure the mutual goodwill of parties engaged in a social relationship, and their mode of presentation may offer a means of qualifying the meaning of the symbol.

My experience as a housewife in Japan involved a great number of small gestures of this sort, using a variety of objects other than the towels we have already discussed, and even a series of negative messages during a very unfortunate rift in relations with a long-standing friend. Fortunately, relations never broke down completely, and a series of the usual objects exchanged between friends and neighbours passed between our houses, – food, parts of gifts received, flowers sometimes – but their manner of presentation became much more formal, and their accompanying messages clearly less intimate and friendly. It would be tedious here to labour the details of this particular encounter, especially one so polluted with Western incompetence – but there is evidently a clear difference between sitting down together over a cup of coffee and a chat to share a gift received and leaving a parcel of fruit in the porch with a polite note. Happily, most of my attempts to blunder into the system of communication through objects in Japan were more pleasant, though I still cannot pretend that I have perfected my understanding of all the subtle possibilities.

## THE ROLE OF THE TOWEL

To return, finally, to my question about how a simple object like a towel can have become caught up with all this ritual meaning, I would like to venture one last suggestion of an order rather different to those thus far proposed. This is at the level of symbolic association, and is concerned with why the task of establishing and maintaining relationships through the use of objects such as *taoru toka* should seem more often than not to fall to women such as the housewives with whom I was working. Towels are concerned with cleanliness, and keeping the house clean is another basic activity of women in this role, although the towels we have been discussing would seem to go beyond that – or do they? From one perspective, cleanliness is simply concerned with order (see Douglas 1970), with removing things, including dust and dirt, from places where they should not be, and putting things back into places where they should be. And order is also very much concerned with classification, with knowing where things should and should not be, with knowing where they belong.

This is the crux of the matter, because my argument ultimately is that these little towels, along with a number of other material objects, have a nice role to play in helping people to keep their relationships in order. In the traditional Japanese house, the *ie*, there were several adult members to get involved in the exchanges necessary to maintain relations between *ie* (see, for example Bachnik's chapter in this volume), but in nuclear families most of this role falls to the housewife. It is thus no small part of her life to ensure that the right objects are moving at the right time between the right people. Towels rank fairly low in the hierarchy of material value of such objects, but since they are actually serving in some cases to open up new links, they are obviously quite vital in this respect.

In Japanese villages no one doubts the high value attached to maintaining good relations with one's neighbours. Apart from the general benefits to one's prosperity and comfort, there are also special occasions to consider. Funerals have traditionally been occasions for much neigh-bourly assistance, as has the reconstruction of all or part of the house. Another good example is to be found when the time comes for the younger generation to be married, for it is very likely that members of the families of prospective partners will come round asking the neigh-bours about the kind of family they are considering joining. At this point neighbours and local shopkeepers are apparently usually fairly honest, for they would not want to be responsible for a marital disaster. In the village where I did my initial fieldwork, three families who were widely known to be difficult were reduced to finding partners amongst them-selves instead of setting up the more preferable exogamous marriages.

The role played by shopkeepers here, as well as neighbours, perhaps contributes to an explanation of why shops use towels to sweeten their customers a little. In Japan at large, it is thought preferable to do business with insiders, with people with whom one shares other social relations, perhaps with whom one drinks. It may be a little difficult for shopkeepers to drink with all their customers, but the presentation of an occasional towel makes it possible to express a little more than an impersonal business transaction. Many traders also make it an annual practice to present their regular customers with a New Year gift such as a calendar.

Walter Edwards's book (1989) about weddings in Japan demon-strates very clearly the way each element of the ceremony has ritual meaning about the future lives of the couple and the associates they have invited to share in the nuptials with them. He argues that these express not only the mutual complementarity of the individuals being joined into marital union, but also their need to rely on others around them. A presentation of bouquets to the parents of the bride and groom mark off these people as due for gratitude for the past, but also serves as a request for benevolence in the coming years. Similarly, a candle ceremony brings everyone into this network of future relations which the couple hopes to nurture and maintain.

Thus, at the very creation of the family unit, in the case of the nuclear family, objects are already being used to anticipate relations which will be important to the couple in the coming years, and which they will certainly need to follow up with further objects, presented in a prescribed ritual fashion, in order to keep them alive and dependable. In case anyone doubts the importance of this principle, perhaps in the case of close relatives, it might be interesting to recall a family in the community in Kyūshū where I worked, where first cousins who lived within a few paces of one another, denied the existence of their kinship at all, on the one hand, and described the relation as 'very distant' on the other. I did not enquire about the movement of objects between the houses, but I suspect that, if I had done so, I would have discovered something of interest. In that community, every small event involves the distribution of cakes and other consumables between the houses of relatives and neighbours, the size of the parcel reflecting the degree of proximity of the relationship, and the denial of such close kin is almost certainly expressed in some way in material form.

In the traditional community, houses maintained long-standing relationships with one another, based on a complicated network of exchanges of various sorts. These were understood by the older generation and explained and passed on to their successors. For a while in the modern period, such exchanges, and other ritual activities in which houses had for long engaged, were regarded as outmoded relics of a previous age, and people tried to cut out some of this ritual in their lives. Recently, however, it has begun to increase again. Sociological predictions about the demise of the *ie* and its replacement by nuclear families have actually been proved in need of modification, and the housewives of the post-modern nuclear family are very much aware of the importance of maintaining good relationships with family, friends and neighbours. During my research it became clear that a not insubstantial part of a housewife's life is spent procuring suitable objects for the expression of these relationships, and planning and executing their presentation.

Of course, most people are aware of the importance of gifts in Japan – every foreigner knows that they must travel there armed with a good supply – but how many of us are also aware of the precise meaning of every little towel and handkerchief we have acquired during our time there? In my view, the towel may be regarded as a vitally important present, for though of little monetary value, it serves a subtle function in allowing people actually to establish, from scratch, relations with previous strangers, and to express just a little more than the usual businesslike impersonal thanks to customers who come regularly to the same shop. It thus offers a way to maintain order and therefore a symbolic cleanliness with people we are likely to meet, but whom we yet know only slightly.

Finally, to return to the point left open earlier about the lack of wrapping required for *taoru toka*, the towel actually seems almost to be a present and its wrapping all rolled into one, as long as it is encased in some way, and it looks new and clean. Meaning usually expressed by the wrapping of a gift is there in this case in the object itself, and in the fact that it has changed hands. Further meaning may be printed onto it by the donor. The presentation of towels, or *taoru toka*, is simply to open a relationship, or express the hope that it will continue. Because of the low monetary value, the recipient is obliged only to acknowledge this relationship, although those presenting the towels may well be hoping for more. In the postmodern world of new nuclear units moving at short notice to different parts of the country, or even the world, this would seem to be an important mechanism indeed – even, perhaps appropriately Western!

## NOTES

1 Information in this paper was gathered during various spells of fieldwork in rural and provicial areas of Fukuoka (1975–6, 1979, 1981, 1987–8) and Chiba prefectures (1981, 1986–7, 1988), as well as during residence and travel in Tokyo, Kyoto and many other parts of Japan.
2 Objects regarded in the West as flannels are used, on the other hand, as *shibori*, provided in restaurants, airlines and so forth, for freshening up before, and sometimes after a meal.
3 This makes an interesting contrast with current British practice, where electrical goods are generally repaired at least once, whereas dishcloths and floorcloths are nowadays very often the disposable 'J-cloth' type.
4 This practice illustrates the thesis of Parry and Bloch (1989:9) that the Western notion of money as a signifier of 'economic' relationships 'inherently impersonal, transitory, amoral and calculating' breaks down in other societies, where it may be used as an intimate gift, quite appropriate to represent bonds of kin and friendship.

## BIBLIOGRAPHY

Douglas, M. (1970) *Purity and Danger: An Analysis of Concepts of Pollution and Taboo*, Harmondsworth: Penguin.
Edwards, W. (1989) *Modern Japan through its Weddings: Gender, Person and Society in Ritual Portrayal*, Stanford: Stanford University Press.
Ii O. (1989) *Furoshiki bunka no posuto modan* (The postmodern in *furoshiki* culture), Tokyo: Chūō Kōronsha.
Lee (see Ii O.)
Malinowski, B. (1972) *Argonauts of the Western Pacific*, London: Routledge & Kegan Paul.
Mauss, M. (1974) *The Gift*, London: Routledge & Kegan Paul.
Parry, J. and M. Bloch (1989) *Money and the Morality of Exchange*, Cambridge: Cambridge University Press.
Segawa K. (1979) *Minzokugaku jiten* (Folklore dictionary), Ōtsuka Minzokugakkai (ed.) Tokyo: Kōbundo.

Tanakamaru K. (1987) *Mono no shōchōsei: Iki no minofuroshiki*, (The symbolism of *mono*: *minofuroshiki* of Iki Island) *Nihon minzokugaku*, 171:99–115.

Weiner, A.B. (1983) 'From words to objects to magic: hard words and the boundaries of social interaction', *Man* (n.s.) 18:690–709.

Yamada Y. (1989) *Tsutsumu: Nihon bunka no katachi* (To wrap: the form of Japanese culture), *Shosai no Mado*, 381:20–25.

# 11 Cleaning floors and sweeping the mind

## Cleaning as a ritual process[1]

*Ian Reader*

It is important, when discussing ritual and ceremony, to look not only at formal ritual performances which have set and ordained (often both in terms of the ritual and in terms of prior initiation processes) participants, ritual implementa and formulae, but also at actions that, whilst not overtly designated as rituals, appear to express and contain many of the implicit themes, messages and meanings of formal rituals. Our understanding of ritual as a whole can only be enhanced by paying attention to the processes and nature of ritualization itself and to the ways in which this may occur, and by looking at how actions which appear, at least on the surface, to be ordinary and everyday ones, may assume the status of rituals endowed with inner symbolic meanings. Certainly in Japan, at least, the widespread structuralization of the modes of everyday behaviour, in which such matters as sending greetings cards and bowing may be placed, by the presiding rules of social etiquette, in a formal and ritualized framework, provides ample scope for such examinations.[2] It is my intention here to pursue such an examination by looking at one activity that, on the surface, appears to be functional, practical and everyday in nature, but which often assumes a ritualized format that endows it with meanings other than the apparently practical.

Clearly in this context I am treating ritual as something which provides or creates defined codes of action that regulate and structural-ize individual behaviour and action, placing them in a social context whereby the behaviour of individuals can be fitted into or co-ordinated with that of others for the purpose of shared goals or aims by the participants acting either as a communal social entity or for an implicitly understood social goal. It is irrelevant whether those goals are desired or even cared about by separate individuals; what is important is the form the action takes, and the manner in which it is done. At the same time, however, the very actions which take place, and their form itself, contains, and in theory at least should express, an inner meaning that is of value to the individual performing the action and, through that individual, to the social group as well.

In order to demonstrate these points, and to illustrate my point about the applicability of the processes of ritualization to everyday actions, and the resultant transfiguration of such actions onto a plane beyond the ordinary, I will examine the seemingly mundane activity of cleaning in Japan. No matter in what context it occurs, cleaning appears to be little more than a fairly basic, functional activity that, whatever the medium – whether a broom on the floor, or a bar of soap on the face – aims to transform the unclean into the clean. Of course, it involves far more than simply removing the unclean for, as Mary Douglas (1984) has amply demonstrated, what is classified as clean or unclean is itself a matter of great cultural and ritual significance. Consequently, cleaning itself is innately connected with ideas of restoring or establishing a sense of order in the surrounding environment. In so doing it thus signifies the preoccupations and attitudes of the social milieu in which it occurs.

In Japanese terms the apparently simple action of cleaning, whether of an external environment such as a park, or a personal one such as one's face, can incorporate a whole series of metaphors which have spiritual significance which is, in turn, related to the conduct and nature of everyday life. This is most overtly true in the religious context and, since my own primary area of interest and research is in the world of religious behaviour and activity, the main focus of this chapter will be on ritualized cleaning processes which occur in religious environments, and the ways in which they are imbued with and express specific religious symbolisms and meanings.

I will, however, attempt to broaden my perspectives a little and try to relate what occurs in religious terms to the wider world of everyday Japanese behaviour, for I consider that the borderlines between religious and cultural actions are virtually inseparable in many respects. There are, as I shall suggest in the latter part of this chapter, many resemblances between the formalized manner in which people in overtly secular situations (housewives sweeping the area outside their homes is an example that comes readily to mind) may take part in ritual, or at least ritualized, cleaning activities and the more clearly religious forms of cleaning with which I shall begin. Housewives sweeping outside their houses are not, unlike the members of new religious groups who will be described later, taking part in explicit religious actions. They are, however, performing actions that have an identifiably ritualized (and, I would add, implicitly religious) content whose meaning and nature clearly transcends the simple act of cleaning.

# SIX MONKS, FIVE BROOMS AND FOUR LEAVES: ZEN AND THE RELIGIOSITY OF WORK

The first year I spent in Japan, in 1981–2, was spent in Zen Buddhist temples, and perhaps my fondest memories of that year were of the autumn, when I was living at a temple in Sendai. During the autumn the morning routine was fairly constant: arise at 4:00 a.m., go to the main hall of the temple for an hour and a half of meditation and chanting, followed by a long period of *samu* (a Zen Buddhist term meaning work, the inner meaning and importance of which I shall shortly discuss).[3] In the autumn at this temple, as at many others throughout Japan, the most common and pressing *samu* was sweeping the autumnal leaves up from the temple grounds and from the grave-yard. This would occupy me, and occasionally a Japanese monk also staying there, until 8:00 a.m. which was time for breakfast. The simple act of sweeping up the leaves and carefully heaping them into piles ready for burning gave me a sense of tranquillity and made me feel I was doing something useful and practical to help justify the food and accommodation the temple priest provided for me.

After my happy broom-sweeping experiences in Sendai I later stayed at a Zen temple in Kanagawa prefecture. The temple routine again involved rising at 4:00 a.m. and doing meditation for some hours, followed by a morning service and then breakfast followed by a period of *samu*. On one particular day I, along with five others, was assigned to sweep up the leaves in the garden. Being a visitor to the temple, and hence not knowing the set-up well, I was the last to get to the shed where the tools were kept and hence found myself broomless, for the temple clearly possessed only five brooms, and there were six of us. In reality, in terms of the assigned task of sweeping up the leaves, I did not need a broom for there was hardly a leaf in sight; it was, after all, late winter and those who had swept the garden on the previous day had done a thorough job. In fact I could have picked up what leaves there were by hand.

My suggestion that we might as well go in and have a cup of tea (rational enough from the stance of my British work experience) fell upon shocked ears. We were there to clean the garden and sweep the leaves during the period, which normally lasted for around forty-five minutes or so, so clean it we must, and clean it we did. In actuality we went through a rather theatrical performance of work that was as much concerned with its avoidance as with its enactment. Those with brooms found it easy to go through the motions; I, broomless, had a more uncomfortable time and was confronted with a situation that perhaps was more akin to a Zen *kōan* than anything else. How does one sweep the leaves up without a broom when there are no leaves to sweep?

I was, however, the only one who appeared to question the logic of the operation of cleaning that which was already in a state of considerable order. As a result I came to reflect on the extent to which *samu* was not simply a functional procedure. It also made it clear to me that the importance of work, in this respect, was in the performance of an action rather than with its practical ends, and that, for those of us in the garden, or at least the lucky five with brooms, the central issue was of going through the motions, with a ritual performance that stated both to themselves and to all around that they were doing the right thing in the proper way at the correct time. Cleaning and sweeping the garden was a ritual performance and hence, as with ritual in general, its importance need not primarily, or at all, be with the external actions involved but with the inner meanings they symbolized.

The concept of work, is intrinsic to the whole of Zen Buddhist thought and practice. Although Zen, as its very name implies, is centred on the practice of meditation, the life of Zen monasteries has, from the outset, incorporated various other activities as well, all of which may be seen as forms of meditation in their own right.[4] In Zen terms any activity when pursued purely and totally is the same as, indeed is no other than, meditation, and is equally a gateway to the enlightenment which is embedded in, rather than separate from, everyday life. Since, in Zen Buddhism, enlightenment also is considered to be the basic human condition and hence, logically, is a matter of the everyday, Zen has always tended to emphasize basic, ordinary and menial activities such as sweeping floors and cutting wood, as suitable activities not just to provide an alternative to seated meditation, but as forms of meditative action in their own right.

The routines and life patterns of Zen temples thus traditionally incorporate periods of work – which are treated as meditations in themselves – in which all those at the temple have to participate. In earlier ages before the onset of modern plumbing, electricity and gas, such activities included cutting and carrying wood from the mountains, and drawing water from the river, as well as other tasks, such as cleaning, which are still performed today. In performing these tasks trainees were expected to maintain the concentrated mind of the meditation hall, and to use the periods of work as a form of moving, physical meditation. Like all spiritual exercises in the Zen temple, which stress the importance of the community of monks and hence of the idea of enlightenment itself as a social as well as an individual event, work was as much social as individual. By contributing to the life of the temple, by working with one's fellows, and by improving oneself, one is considered to help and contribute to the lives of others – a social contribution that brings further benefit to the individual.

It is difficult, though, to avoid the feeling that *samu* is often work created for its own sake, a view that is especially pertinent in the case of Zen temples which do not (unlike their Christian monastic counterparts) as a rule carry out economically productive work such as growing vegetables and producing goods for trade. Such mercenary activities have never found favour in the Buddhist monastic system and have been actively proscribed in Zen monastic rules. Temples instead depend for their economic support on donations and, more importantly, on the provision of religious services and rituals, the most widespread of which in Japan is the series of rites that follow a death. As a result, work in the Zen context tends to signify something that is, in economic terms, non-productive. More often than not, in contemporary temples at least, this involves some form of cleaning of the temple grounds and environment, such as sweeping the *tatami* floors of the halls of worship, meticulously dusting the Buddhist altars, washing out the toilets and scrubbing and polishing the wooden corridors, cleaning up the grave-yard and sweeping up leaves. In the year I spent at Zen temples the work I performed was invariably one or more of these activities.

Zen texts and treatises have constantly stressed the importance of such work as the grounding for enlightenment. The founder of the Sōtō Zen sect (it was at temples of this sect that I stayed) in Japan, the thirteenth-century monk Dōgen, laid down guidelines for the performance of and for the manner in which the practice of cleaning should be carried out in such writings as the *Tenzō kyōkun* (rules for the temple cook), as well as in his magnum opus the *Shōbōgenzō* (the eye and treasury of the true law).[5] Yet the importance of cleaning, and of cleaning as a metaphor for enlightenment, is not limited in Dōgen's view to external performances of work, or of cleaning corridors, but relates also to the cleansing of one's personal environment.

In Dōgen's view even the most basic everyday actions, such as washing the face, took on formal, ritual significance as meditative acts. One chapter of the *Shōbōgenzō* is entitled *Senmen* ('Washing the face') and is precisely that, a treatise on how to wash the face, and the meanings of this rite. Thus he writes:[6]

> Purifying the body and mind with fragrant oil and washing away impurities is the first principle of the Buddhist Law. Thoroughly washing and annointing the body . . . purifies the inside and outside. When the inside and outside are purified everything around us is purified.

> (Nishiyama 1983:1)

The act of cleansing is synonymous with the true law of the Buddhas (Nishiyama 1983:3). Indeed, Dōgen further states that 'It is not merely a way of removing dirt and oil – it is the lifeblood of the Buddhas and Patriarchs' (Nishiyama 1983:4).

After this he proceeds to give detailed instructions on how to wash the face and how to clean the teeth, showing that these processes are metaphors for cleansing the entire world, for removing impurities on all levels and attaining enlightenment. The detailed instructions form the text of a ritual of personal hygiene, a point further emphasized by Dōgen's statement that the method of washing the face has been pre-ordained by the Buddhas and hence should be followed exactly (Nishiyama 1983:3).

Clearly, in Dōgen's writing, as in the life of Zen temples, cleaning processes are strictly formalized and made into ritual practices with specific religious meanings that transcend the physical function of simply making place and face clean. Polishing the floor, brushing the teeth and washing the face are rituals that metaphorically polish the mind and open the way to enlightenment.

The ritualization and transformation of everyday actions into meditative disciplines is not, however, solely limited to the Zen monastic sphere. Indeed much of the contemporary literature produced by the Sōtō Zen sect for its lay members manifests a similar focus and emphasis, talking in particular about cleaning in metaphorical as well as pragmatic terms, as the following comments by Fujimoto Kōhō (1977:22) in a recent Sōtō publication show: 'Zen practice starts and finishes with cleaning. By doing excellent cleaning this in itself purifies the spirit.' Fujimoto further expands on this theme by talking of the importance of developing a 'cleaning spirit' (*sōji suru kokoro*) (1977:22) and seeking a 'cleaning of the spirit' (*kokoro no sōji*) (1977:23).

The various rites associated with the ancestors (which are, of course, a major area of Buddhist concern and activity in Japan) also bring into play the idea of cleaning as a religious activity. At various points in the year, such as the equinoctial *higan* festivals, it is considered obligatory for the family to clean the graves of their dead ancestors; indeed, failure to do so may, according to commonly held folklore, cause offence to the spirits of the dead and lead to various forms of spiritual retribution.

Cleaning the family Buddhist altar (*butsudan*) at regular intervals is another action that involves filial obligation as well as the pragmatic necessity of keeping a household item free of dust. Yet such actions are, according to the popular literature that Buddhist sects in Japan produce for their members, more than just pragmatic and obligatory performances: they are religious actions that show veneration and service to one's ancestors, and as such should be performed with the 'cleaning spirit' that 'cleans the spirit' of the performer while bringing solace to the ancestors. This point is demonstrated by the *Shinkō jūkun* ('ten articles of belief'), a short treatise produced by the Sōtō sect to outline the actions and attitudes expected of good Sōtō members. The first article of the ten stresses the importance of cleaning the *butsudan* on a daily basis as an act of devotion towards the ancestors (*Sōtō-shūshūmuchō* 1981a: 4; 1981b: 28–9). Cleaning thus, for lay people as well as monks, is more than just an everyday physical action performed out of pragmatic necessity or social need. It is a distinct and ritualized religious practice in its own right.

## THE RITUALIZATION OF CLEANING IN THE NEW RELIGIONS

It is not, however, Zen Buddhism alone which elevates mundane work into a spiritual practice and which transforms cleaning into a symbolic and ritual performance in Japan. Similar motifs are seen in many of the Japanese new religions as well. Members of the new religion Agonshū, for instance, regularly take part in what they term *shugyō*, a word that generally refers to religious training or austerities, but which has come to be widely used by new religions when referring to the religious practices they ask their members to perform. One of the most common forms of *shugyō* performed by Agonshū's lay members involves helping in some way at the various offices and centres of the religion. As with Zen temples, this often means cleaning, usually of the floors and corridors which, although seeming quite spotless to the outside observer, may be polished vigorously and frequently by groups of Agonshū members wearing special headbands and Agonshū jackets.

They perform the task with a joy that is evident to all around them. Members I have interviewed at Agonshū centres in Tokyo and Kyoto, affirmed that taking part – indeed being able to take part – in such voluntary religious practice brought them great happiness and helped them cultivate a sense of gratitude.[7] Gratitude is an important emotion in Japanese religious terms and is a necessary concomitant and indeed component part of the process of hardship and suffering inherent in the notion of austerities or *shugyō*.[8] In performing a task that normally might be seen as arduous and menial, such as scrubbing a floor, Agonshū members learn to see beyond its menial nature and inconveniences; by performing such *shugyō* as polishing the floor they are metaphorically 'polishing their souls', a term widely used (see, for example, Hardacre 1986:11–21) to describe the nature, structure and meaning of religious practice in the new religions.

This practice is not simply individual. Indeed, in its very nature it is, as with the cleaning practices in Zen temples, innately social as well. Without the idea of service to others the action would be simply selfish; thus one cleans the floor (or indeed performs any religious practice) not just to polish one's own soul, but for the benefit of others as well, and for the good of the community. Thus one element in religious practice, and hence in such ritualized performances of cleaning is the notion of charity and giving to others. One of many ways in which Agonshū expresses this sense of charity is through organized cleaning activities in which a group of members dressed in Agonshū shirts and headbands bearing Agonshū slogans cleans up a public area such as a park or some similar open space. Such activities are conducted on a regular basis, and members are not only encouraged to participate in them, but also to organize their own cleaning groups. The joyous manner in which they carry out these activities not only helps Agonshū members 'polish their souls' while performing acts for the public good, but also of course is intended to attract new members, presumably through the suggestion that a religion whose members can be happy in the simple task of sweeping up public parks must have something going for it!

The cleaning motif is prominent also in Tenrikyō, one of the oldest and largest of all Japanese new religions, as anyone who has visited the city of Tenri will be aware. The main Tenrikyō hall of worship is flanked on all sides by long wooden corridors, all of which are shiny and extremely well-polished. Indeed it is rare, when walking along these corridors, not to have to manoeuvre one's way around Tenrikyō members wearing special jackets emblazoned with Tenrikyō motifs and diligently polishing the smooth and seemingly spotless floorboards.

These members are performing this task voluntarily, and do so normally with the joyously positive feelings of those who do the task not because it is a job that has to be done, but because it is an action of religious practice and social service. They are performing *hinokishin* a term and concept central to Tenrikyō meaning voluntary work or service to and for others that is simultaneously helpful in one's own development. While *hinokishin* can refer to all type of actions (for example, missionary work) done for others, one prominent expression of it is in the voluntary work members put in at Tenri centres to keep the place running smoothly and, as with the ritualized polishing activities in Tenri corridors, clean.

Again, as with Zen temples, it seems not to matter all that much whether the surface that is swept and polished actually, in purely practical terms, needs cleaning. The corridors at Tenri, because of the hordes of people who glide in along them in their socks (shoes of course having been removed at the entrance) and because of the constant armies of volunteers polishing them are rarely other than bright and clean. Behind the action of cleaning, and working in conjunction with the notions of active service to others and joyous participation in organized group and social activities, there is, as with Zen, a definitively metaphorical dimension to such ritualized cleaning, and one which relates not just to the idea of 'polishing the soul', but, in Tenrikyō, to the religious interpretation of the causes and healing of illness.

Tenrikyō teaches that although the mind in origin is clean and pure, it becomes clouded because of spiritual dust (*hokori*), which settles on the mind as a result of bad deeds and thoughts. This spiritual dust gradually builds up and clouds the mind, and as this happens all manner of problems may arise, such as illness.[9] Becoming ill is a sign that the mind has been allowed to become cloudy and needs cleaning.

Thus both the solution and the prevention of illness revolve around removing this spiritual dust and stopping it from accumulating. *Hinokishin*, in which the performer learns gratitude and attains joy through selfless actions, is such a practice which metaphorically polishes the soul and cleans the dust from the mind. Often, too, as we have seen, it involves the physical action of sweeping dust away. Cleaning is thus a ritualized religious practice with both pragmatic and metaphorical meanings. Tenrikyō religious literature frequently refers to the processes of cleaning and sweeping that are necessary for cleaning the mind and, like the physical action of *hinokishin*, such references often allude to the actual processes of cleaning. In a discussion of Tenrikyū's view of the nature of this dust and the ways of removing it, Tanaka Kikuo (1982) affirms the importance of constant and daily spiritual practice as a form of cleaning mechanism, and uses, as an example of the necessity of constant practice, the following metaphor from daily life:

> We can keep our rooms clean only when we clean every day. We know through our daily experiences that, if we are negligent in our cleaning, dust will pile up in the meantime until we cannot easily clear it away merely by sweeping and wiping.
>
> (Tanaka 1982:5)

In such ways, Tanaka continues, 'man can keep his mind clean only when he sweeps it every day' (1982:28), using the power of Tenrikyō's God the Parent who serves as the broom that clears away the dust. This image of God as the broom is a common image in Tenrikyō literature, deriving originally from the *Ofudesaki*, the writings of Tenrikyō's foundress Nakayama Miki, that form the basis of Tenrikyō's scriptural and theological tradition, in which there are numerous references of the following type: 'Sweeping clean people's hearts throughout the world I, God, act as a broom' (*Ofudesaki* Part 3, Section 52, in Inoue and Eynon 1987:45).

In such respects the actions of Tenrikyō members as they religiously and ritualistically polish the floors become externalized expressions of the religion's internal processes of sweeping the dust from the mind, and may even be seen as a manifestation of the workings of Tenrikyō's chief deity, God the Parent.

## ITTŌEN: CLEANING THE LAVATORY AS A RITUAL PRACTICE

In at least one case a religious group has become widely known because of its emphasis on cleaning rituals. I am referring to the utopian religious movement Ittōen, whose communal centre is located a little way out of Kyoto. The daily routine at the commune commences with a ritual period of cleaning in which members scrub, sweep and clean the precincts and buildings of their commune for around twenty minutes (Davis 1975:292). Besides this communal cleaning rite, however, Ittōen members perform a ritual practice known as *gyōgan* (literally 'seeking austerities'), and it is for this practice, which usually involves some form of cleaning, generally of lavatories, that Ittōen has become widely known. In *gyōgan* members are expected to go out and seek tasks that they may perform without reward for the benefit of members of the public.

While *gyōgan* theoretically can involve any task, in reality it largely centres on cleaning toilets. The practice of cleaning latrines was strongly advocated by Ittōen's founder Nishida Tenkō because he saw in it a way of overcoming the self and eradicating the ego. Nishida was especially strongly influenced by Zen thought, and espoused the apparently demeaning process of toilet cleaning as a means of liminalizing and depriving the practitioner of status, and hence of ego, much in the same way that Zen uses the performance of menial work activities and the traditional begging round (*takuhatsu*) (Davis 1975:284–302).

Ittōen also runs special spiritual training sessions for outsiders in which they are expected to follow the same practices. Many of those who participate in these sessions have been sent by their companies, often because they are new employees, as part of the general company training and induction processes. The participants are told to go out to various housing estates and knock on doors asking permission to clean the toilets. They are expected to persevere all day no matter what response they get and, if they are lucky, to be able to clean a few toilets. Not surprisingly, however, their requests are often unsuccessful, for many people are not particularly pleased with the implication that their toilet needs cleaning, or with the idea of letting a stranger come in the house to do it. Failure to enter houses does not mean failure in the task, however, for the very process of rejection is, as many religious organizations which send their members out on door-to-door evangelizing expeditions will affirm, a further aspect of spiritual training that tests the mettle and helps polish the soul just as does the action of cleaning itself. Ittōen members also take part in periodic cleaning campaigns on public lavatories – which have, anyway, lagged somewhat behind private ones in terms of hygiene in general (Davis 1975:303–4).

Ittōen's focus on (or perhaps obsession with) cleaning, especially of the toilet, has been ritualized into a religious practice whose focus is clearly – as with my Zen temple experiences – far less concerned with the efficacy of the activity in its overt manifestations (i.e., actually cleaning something for utilitarian purposes) than with the internal spiritual dimensions of the task. It has also involved a very definitive process of ritualization just as the formalized structures within which cleaning practices are carried out in Zen temples, with its own ritual title (*gyōgan*). Winston Davis has commented on Ittōen's cleaning activities with the following words: 'Work itself, especially the perfunctory morning cleaning routine, seems often to have more importance as a ritual than as a means of keeping up the community's property or increasing its wealth' (Davis 1975:318).

In fact – as we have seen already – the economic dimensions of work are not of primary importance in Japanese religious situations. Work in the religious context is seen not so much as a means of enabling a temple or community to prosper, as a formalized religious practice with symbolic meanings relating to the expected goals of the religious group both in individual and social terms. Consequently, it may be ritualized to the extent that the practical effects of the performance may be secondary to the meaning of the rite itself.

## CREATING GOOD EMPLOYEES: SPIRITUAL TRAINING AND CLEANING RITUALS

The use of ritualized cleaning activities as a form of spiritual training is not limited just to overtly religious organizations in Japan. The numerous ethical or moral welfare training organizations (*shuyō dantai*) which have flourished in Japan in recent years and which exhibit many of the qualities and practices of religious organizations, even while eschewing their legal form, also make use of spiritual training sessions that manifest many of the practices and concepts used in Zen temples and the new religions (Numata 1988:227–78).

Such spiritual training sessions are, like those run by Ittōen (and also increasingly by Zen temples in Japan), often patronized by business companies who send their members to them to learn determination, discipline and obedience. Dorinne Kondo (1987:250), in an interesting description of one such training session, which she attended, notes that 'cleaning is a standard ingredient of spiritual education in Japan'.[10] It is not, however, as she notes, enough to just perform the task; to have the correct attitude is equally important. Thus Kondo and her fellow participants were expected to demonstrate enthusiasm for the task, even being encouraged to chant slogans in unison as they did so (1987:251).[11] As Kondo reports, one of these chants contained the phrase 'Polish the floor! If you polish the floor your heart too will shine!' (1987:251). When the participants came to the end of the corridor they were asked to turn round and do it all over again – an affirmation, if one were needed, of the extent to which the aims of the task itself were not primarily concerned with cleaning the corridor. I am interested to note, too, that, just as I did in the face of the apparent futility of the Zen garden cleaning cited earlier, Kondo found it hard to come to terms with the logic of the situation, and admitted to anger at what she saw as a waste of energy, although none of her fellow participants expressed similar sentiments.

## SELF, OTHERS AND RITUAL INTENT

In all the accounts I have given above of instances where the activity of cleaning has been harnessed for spiritual ends, cleaning some external object has served as a metaphor for the potentially more vital goal of polishing the soul. Although such spiritual training seeks to enhance each individual it also, at the same time, is a social activity, a point I have made earlier when talking of the new religions. In her description of the ethics retreat Kondo shows that activities were organized on a group basis, with each person being considered to belong to a particular group, with the group being responsible for the actions of each of its members (1987:248–9). In such circumstances responsibility to others is a spur to the individual's spiritual practice.

Hence, as we have seen in the practices of Agonshū members and in the concept of *hinokishin* in Tenrikyō, acting for others is an integral part of acting for and polishing the self; it also is an intrinsic part of the creation of a sense of group cohesion, belonging and identity which provides the individual with a framework in which s/he can feel at home. The humble attitude that one should take in performing such menial tasks as cleaning helps to subliminate the ego and bring all members of the group into a feeling of community and harmony in which all strive for a communal good that is equated with the individual good – which of course helps explain why companies are so keen for their employees to go on such courses! Even the suffering that is felt in some of the more ascetic practices in the ethics retreat (and in all ascetic practices) is also a gateway to joy, for it teaches one endurance and helps one realize the importance of humility. Thus, through suffering, as with all such communal acts of voluntary work, one can develop the sense of gratitude which, as I have previously mentioned, is so important to self-development.

## COMMUNITY CLEANING RITES: OBLIGATORY ATTENDANCE AND ENFORCED JOY

Although I have concentrated on cleaning as a ritual activity largely in religious contexts, and always with some spiritual significance, I should like to conclude by drawing attention to the ways in which communal cleaning activities may occur in the day-to-day flow of life, and to suggest that in these there may be some close parallels with the spiritual nature of cleaning.

It is hard to avoid the overt, potentially obsessive, concern with ordering the personal and spatial environment in Japan. The various acts by which people remove the dirt of the outside by removing their shoes, wiping the soles of their feet, gargling, etc. (Ohnuki-Tierney 1984:21); the actions of shopkeepers who dutifully and regularly sweep the street before their shops, often sprinkling it also with water; and the frequency with which taxi drivers dust down their taxis while waiting for customers are but a few of the examples that one could cite.

Often such activities have a socially coercive side to them: those who have lived for any amount of time in Japan may well have shared the sense of shame and discomfort my wife and I acquired on realizing that ours was the only house in the street before which the road had not been neatly swept each morning. Occasionally such cleaning is organized on a communal basis in the area around one's house or apartment, and announced by a circular sent round to all households. At such times attendance, at least for one representative of each household, appears obligatory: failure to turn up may give rise to a general feeling amongst one's neighbours that one does not have the desired and expected sense of community.

Certainly one can be made to feel guilty about failing to attend. In February 1984 my wife and I had to inform the administrative committee in charge of the apartment block where we lived in Kōbe that we would miss the semi-annual clean-up of the grounds because of other commitments. The muttered acceptances of this apology let us know that, although they would be able to manage, our absence would cause problems. The response, as it was intended to, caused us some unease and shame. We had, after all, only recently moved in, and it was clear that our failure to attend – indeed our self-centred decision to go travelling at such a time – brought into doubt our commitment to the community living in the apartment block.

We subsequently attended, dutifully and religiously, the next communal clean-up and, as a result, spent two boring hours doing very little – the area was relatively clean, there were few fallen leaves, and the drainage ditches had unfortunately remained clear of refuse and hence did not require attention. In fact, much of the activity consisted of trying to find something to do, and in exerting energy to manifest one's enthusiasm for the task. The most enthusiastic participants even competed with each other to pick up the few bits of rubbish lying around. The committee member in overall charge kept a close eye on his watch and, when a suitable time had elapsed, he decided we could all stop.

Again, as with my earlier temple experience, it was the time spent, the fact that it had been spent with and for others, and the attitude involved that was paramount, rather than the concept of a task accomplished. Certainly the cleaning session served to impose a sense of order on the external environment in terms of making sure everything was in its correct place, but underneath this physical exterior the rite imposed a further, and probably more vital, sense of order on the social environment. Obligatory attendance itself confirms a form of order, of people and households in their correct place in social terms, performing the role which is socially expected of them. The ritual of spending a couple of hours going through the motions of sweeping and gathering up (non-existent) fallen leaves allowed us to demonstrate our commitment to be in the right place at the right time and hence to uphold and reinforce the social order of the community. The very inconvenience of the process (at 9:00 a.m. on a Sunday morning when many of the participants would have preferred to be in bed seeing off the effects of Saturday night) enabled us all to demonstrate and make a sacrifice (in time and comfort) for this end. The sacrifice itself encouraged us to demonstrate the joyous attitude that was part of the process. After all, we were (or should have been!) grateful to be able to take part and help out.

The obligatory nature of organized cleaning is found elsewhere in Japanese society. In schools, for instance, students are expected to take care of their classrooms (homerooms), sweeping the floor and tidying it up every day after school (Rohlen 1983:179). While this is intended to make class members feel part of the social community and to develop a sense of shared responsibility it also has the practical and economic function of saving money that otherwise would have been spent on cleaning staff.

## CONCLUDING REMARKS: PURITY, ORDER AND A NICE HOT BATH

I think it is reasonable to raise the question of whether we can view all such processes in which cleaning takes place in any ritualized form, from the apparently secular occurrences of periodic community clean-ups to the overtly religious discipline of *samu* in Zen temples, in a similar light. Can we thus relate the housewives taking part in their ritual street sweeping to members of new religions as they perform their *shugyō* with cloths and buckets, and to the followers of Ittōen as they clean public lavatories?

In social terms there are many common threads: cleaning as a rite serves to generate a sense of community, belonging and social identity whether in a religious institution, a school or a housing estate. It demonstrates a commitment to the social milieu, a commitment that is strengthened by the apparent futility of the action when there is seemingly so little matter out of place to deal with. In individual and social terms the prevailing attitude which should be adhered to when performing the actions (and which is equally one of the aims of the action) are the same in all cases, whether in a temple or on a housing estate: endurance, service, gratitude and joy. Moreover the manner, form and the way in which this ritual process is performed are invariably more essential than the actual practical task that is carried out.

A further common area of relationship for all such forms of cleaning – a relationship that would point to the enduring sense of ritualism and to the implicit religiosity to be found in Japanese everyday behaviour – is their concern with definition, order and purification, issues that are, of course, vital components of the Japanese religious system, and of Shintō in particular. In fact I feel that it is probably the deep Japanese religious concern (expressed most strongly in Shintō) that concepts of purity and of definition should be expressed and reinforced through action which is at the heart of the obsession that Japanese Zen temples have with ritual cleaning. Certainly I have yet to find any evidence to suggest that such an intensive focus on cleaning, in ritual and religious terms, exists at Buddhist temples outside Japan.[12] Indeed, interviews I have had with Japanese Buddhist priests who have visited other Buddhist countries frequently show that they often remark on this matter and that they are often disturbed by the fact that, in their eyes, temples in other Buddhist countries are invariably 'dirty'.[13]

The notions of cleanliness as hygiene (which one might consider to be the primary intent of sweeping the streets) and as a moral state of purity (which is certainly the primary intent of religious cleaning) are overlapping concepts in Japan. Commenting on the importance of 'feeling clean' Emiko Ohnuki-Tierney quotes the following description, made by the pianist Nakamura Hiroko about her music teacher: 'when I played for her I felt as though I had *had a nice hot bath*. Everything felt clean and marvellous' (1984:34, italics in original). She goes on to comment:

> This clean feeling is not only personally most desirable and satisfying, as Nakamura notes, it is one of the most cherished moral values in contemporary Japan . . . the same expressions are used to describe cleanliness in the hygienic as well as the moral sense.
>
> (Ohnuki-Tierney 1984: 34)

Cleaning is a process of making definitions, of imposing order on an environment, and purifying it in accord with the prevailing social and cultural understandings of what such purification involves. In this essay I have been concerned with examining the relevance and nature of cleaning – beyond its merely pragmatic functions – in Japanese society and religion. This does not mean that discussions of the type I have engaged in concerning the everyday nature of ritual, of the ritualization of everyday practices, and of the religiosity of everyday actions, are limited to Japan. Indeed, much progress has been made in identifying and discussing the themes of implicit religiosity within ordinary life in other societies.[14] What I would add here is that the Japanese case, where we find a very strong religious emphasis on cleaning as a spiritual practice and ritual, certainly appears to affirm the point that the lines of differentiation between religion, ritual and everyday activity are rather fine. In such terms one could ask to what extent it is possible to differentiate between a broom wielded by a monk in a temple, and one wielded by a housewife in the street, either in act, attitude or presumed intent – especially when neither of them might really want to be wielding them in the first place.

# NOTES

1 Between April 1981 and April 1982 I did research on the Sōtō Zen Buddhist sect in Japan, during which time I lived at a number of Zen temples. The observations I made during this period form the basis from which this chapter developed.

2 The large numbers of guidebooks to social etiquette which may be found at any popular bookshop in Japan are evidence of a continuing, if not expanding, importance placed on the correct performance of all manner of actions, not merely those concerned with social interaction, but also with all manner of situations that involve some form of action or reaction. For instance, I recently acquired one such compendium which, as its title, *Seikatsu no chishiki hyakka* (1990), suggests, is a veritable encyclopedia of the social knowledge that is required in every aspect of social living in Japan. It provides, with illustrations, instructions on such diverse but socially important actions as behaviour and procedures at funerals and weddings, the way to send greetings and other such cards at different times of the year, how to wrap and give presents, how to sit down properly and put on a napkin at a French restaurant and many other things (*Shufu to Seikatsusha* 1990).

3 *Samu* has a clearly ritualized format, with a set and specific place in the temple routine. The ritual motif is emphasized by the fact that the monks don clothing (*samue*) consisting of loose cotton trousers (usually grey or black), a light cotton loose wrap-round jacket and a cloth to cover the head, all of which are worn only for this task and which thus take on the air of a ritual uniform.

4 The Japanese word '*zen*' is the Japanese pronunciation of the Chinese ideogram *ch'an* which was used to translate the Sanskrit *dhyana*, meditation: hence Zen is (or was, in its eighth-century Chinese origins) a Buddhist movement that centred almost exclusively on the practice of meditation.

5 The most complete and accessible volume of Dōgen's writings is to be found in *Dōgen zenji zenshū* compiled and edited by Ōkubo Dōshū (1969–70, 2 vols). Besides the numerous contemporary Japanese translations of his various works that are available, a growing number of translations in various European languages, notably English, have also begun to appear.

6 I have cited the translation by Nishiyama *et al.* here because it is the most accessible (if not always the most textually precise) of all the available translations of the *Shōbōgenzō* and also because of my own involvement with it. During the six months I stayed at Nishiyama's temple in Sendai (the one referred to earlier in this chapter) I helped with work on several sections of this translation including the chapter cited here.

7 I base these remarks on several visits to Agonshū centres and interviews with Agonshū members during the period from February 1987 until November 1988, in Tokyo, Kyoto, and Hirakata.

8 For general discussions of the dynamics of suffering, gratitude and asceticism see Miyake (1981:128–43) and Reader (1991:107–33). Blacker (1975), which remains the classic work on Japanese shamanism and asceticism in Western languages, also shows the close relationship between suffering, endurance, gratitude and the spiritual awarenesses that ascetics sought and achieved.

9  My explanation here is, for reasons of space, a rather generalized and simplified account of Tenrikyō teaching, for in fact Tenrikyō differentiates between eight types of spiritual dust, each caused by a particular type of misdeed or bad thought (Tanaka 1982:7–26). Ultimately, however, the treatment for all is the same and relates to the processes of sweeping the mind described in the paper.

10 I should like to thank Professor Jane Bachnik of the University of North Carolina for bringing this article to my attention.

11 One notes, however, that Rohlen, in a description of another company spiritual training session held at a Zen temple notes that his fellow workers treated the ritual period of cleaning in a manner that was less disciplined than intended. Although the priest directing operations was extremely meticulous, 'his example was ignored by many of the trainees who . . . lazily wandered about with rakes over their shoulders' (1973:1546); proof, if proof were needed, that any ritual can be undermined by the intent and attitudes of its putative performers.

12 I base my remarks on observations at Buddhist temples I have stayed at in the following countries: Thailand, India (Burmese, Tibetan and Bhutanese Buddhist), Nepal and Sri Lanka.

13 I base this remark on interviews with numerous priests during my years (1981–2 and 1983–9) in Japan. In particular I remember six young monks from a temple in Nagano whom I interviewed in December 1981, just before they left on a trip to Indian Buddhist sites, and in March 1982 just after they had returned. Before they went they had numerous images of India, mostly connected with its position as the original home of Buddhism and as a spiritual centre. On their return the overriding first impression of all of them was that it was dirty and that even the temples were untidy and disordered. Consequently, it seemed, their notions of it as a spiritual centre were appreciably diminished.

14 I am referring in particular here to the numerous papers read at the annual Denton Hall conferences of the Network for the Study of Implicit Religion, and the research interests of the members of that organization.

## BIBLIOGRAPHY

Barthes, R. (1982) *Empire of Signs*, New York: Hill and Wang.

Blacker, C. (1975) *The Catalpa Bow: A Study of Shamanistic Practices in Japan*, London: George Allen and Unwin.

Davis, W.B. (1975) 'Ittōen: the myths and rituals of liminality', Parts I–III, *History of Religions*, 14 (4):282–321.

Douglas, M. (1984) *Purity and Danger: An Analysis of the Concepts of Pollution and Taboo*, London: Ark Paperbacks.

Fujimoto Kōhō (1977) *Gasshō no seikatsu*, Tokyo: Sōtōshūshūmuchō.

Hardacre, H. (1986) *Kurozumikyō and the New Religions of Japan*, Princeton, NJ: Princeton University Press.

Inoue Akio, and M. Eynon (1987) *A Study of the Ofudesaki*, Tenri: Tenrikyō Dōyūsha.

Kondo D. (1987) 'Creating an ideal self: theories of selfhood and pedagogy at a Japanese ethics retreat', *Ethos* 15 (5):241–72.

Miyake Hitoshi (1981) *Seikatsu no naka no shūkyō*, Tokyo: NHK Books.
Nishiyama Kōsen *et al.* (trans.) (1975–83) *Dōgen Zenji: Shōbōgenzō*, Tokyo: Nakayama Shobō.
Numata Kenya (1988) *Gendai Nihon no shinshūkyō*, Ōsaka: Sōgensha.
Ohnuki-Tierney, Emiko (1984) *Illness and Culture in Contemporary Japan*, Cambridge: Cambridge University Press.
Ōkubo Dōshū (ed.) (1969–70) *Dōgen zenji zenshū* (2 vols), Tokyo: Chikuma Shobō.
Reader, Ian (1991) *Religion in Contemporary Japan*, Basingstoke: Macmillan.
Rohlen, T.P. (1973) '"Spiritual education" in a Japanese bank', *American Anthropologist* 75:1542–62.
—— (1983) *Japan's High Schools*, Berkeley and Los Angeles: University of California.
Shufu to Seikatsusha (ed.) (1990) *Seikatsu no chishiki no hyakka*, Tokyo: Shufu to Seikatsusha.
Sōtōshūshūmuchō (ed.) (1981a) *Sōtōshū no nenjūgyōji*, Tokyo: Sōtōshū-shūmuchō.
—— (ed.) (1981b) *Sōtōshū hōreki*, Tokyo: Sōtōshūshūmuchō.
Tanaka Kikuo (1982) *Dust and innen*, Tenri: Tenrikyō Overseas Mission.

# Conclusion: The rituals of urbanity

## Temporal forms and spatial forms in Japanese and French cities

*Augustin Berque*

### RITES, FORMS, TOWNSCAPES

I do not intend here to relate the question of rituals to that of cities by showing that there exists a wide spectrum of rituals in present-day Japanese cities, and that some of these rituals, e.g. the ceremony of setting up the framework of a house (*muneage*), may have direct implications in the making and management of the city. The rite of *muneage*, for example, is strongly linked to the existence of powerful corporations of carpenters, which fact, in its turn, bears a close relationship with the architectonics of the city. Such an approach would certainly be apposite to our present topic (rituals and ceremony), but it would remain on an anecdotal level, only adding some more samples to the already superabundant catalogue of Japanese rituals, and considering the city as a mere locale or container of some of these rituals.

What I shall try to do instead is to search for the common ground from which stem, on the one hand, the behavioural performances that rituals are and, on the other hand, the environmental performances that townscapes are. In other words, I will strive to search for the common cultural matrices from which issue the former, mainly temporal forms, as well as the latter, mainly spatial forms. By so doing, I shall try to shed some new light on the old question of form.[1]

That the temporal forms of the body (behaviours, rituals, and so on) and the spatial forms of the city must have some common ground is suggested, in the first place, by the etymological connection of the words, behave, habit, inhabit (Latin *habere/habitus/habitare*). These words are all related with the idea of propriety, as both possession and pertinence; which, in its turn, is linked to the notion of ritual. A ritual is indeed a codified pattern of behaviour, appropriate to certain times and certain places, expressing that one belongs to a certain community, but it also possesses the mastery of the practices which give this community its formal setting; e.g. taking off one's shoes when 'climbing' (*agaru*) into the house, a ritual in which architecture and politeness form a single integrative pattern.[2]

Such a pattern is not only both temporal (the rite) and spatial (the house); it is also both active and passive, individual and collective, symbolic and ecological. Indeed, taking off one's shoes is a voluntary act of the subject, but the individual actor is compelled to do so by politeness (a collective form) on the one hand, and on the other hand by the architectonics of the house. In this process, the house is not a purely passive object, or formed form (having been built by human actors in a certain way), it is also a matrix which, by compelling the individual actor to behave in a certain way, 'actively' partakes in the ritual process of *agaru*.

In this process, a social matrix (usage) coincides with a physical matrix (the house). The distinction between subject and object is blurred, as Bourdieu has shown in his analyses of habitus.[3] But habitus is not only a 'second nature' for social actors.[4] If one extends the physical setting of a habitus from the house to the city and thence to the whole environment, one clearly sees that it is the distinction between culture and nature in general (not only as 'second nature', but also in an ecological sense) which is blurred in such a process.[5] The ritual of *agaru* is but one particular expression of the general process of the Japanese mediance (*fūdosei*) – i.e. the physical/phenomenal tendency, feeling and meaning of the relationship of Japanese society with space and nature – just as Japanese cities also are, on another scale, both in space and time, both passive (formed) forms and 'active' (forming) forms.[6]

In other words, space is both organized by society and organizes society. As I argued some time ago:[7] it is fraught with numberless habitus (which Bourdieu defines as 'structured structures predisposed to function as structuring structures').[8]

Hereafter I shall make use of the word urbanity as meaning an expressional process at city scale, in the course of which the actors' behaviour and the setting of their action interplay between the subject and the object, the active and the passive. In this sense, urbanity may be understood as the mediance of a city, or of the cities belonging to the same medial relationship of a given society with space and nature (i.e., to the same milieu).

When dealing with architecture, it is essential to take into account this ambivalence of urbanity, in order to avoid, on the one hand, the illusion – to which the modern movement in architecture was particularly prone – that one can transform society only by transforming material forms, and on the other hand the illusion that society is not affected by environmental change (this latter way of seeing can be frequently found in sociological writings of the 1960s and the 1970s). Urbanity is indeed a much more complex set of relations than can be apprehended in these two simplistic stances.[9]

## JAPANESE AND FRENCH URBANITY

Following Maisonneuve's classification (1988), we can broadly divide rituals in two categories:[10]

1 magic/religious rituals, such as have been described by generations of cultural anthropologists in traditional societies, and
2 secular and everyday rituals, e.g. polite salutations in the morning, such as have been described in our present modern societies by sociologists like Goffmann or Maffesoli.

I shall consider here primarily the second category, while setting the question at a level (that of the above 'common ground', or the problem of form in general) where any clear-cut distinction between the two categories would be absurd.

The data has been gathered during a co-operative research programme of the Maison Franco-Japonaise (Tokyo), 'La Qualité de l'environnement urbain au Japon', which was initiated in 1985 and concluded in 1989 with a symposium held at Royaumont, following an intermediary one held at the Maison Franco-Japonaise in 1987. On these two occasions, a total of nearly one hundred papers was submitted, three-quarters were on Japanese cities, and the rest on French cities. About one-third of the papers were presented by Japanese authors. Though all these papers have provided the material of the present analysis, for practical reasons I shall quote here only those (about half of the total) which have already been published in the first of the two volumes of the proceedings.[11]

A first consideration reveals that what the French and the Japanese conceive as a proper behaviour – namely, politeness – does not have the same referents. In the French tradition, the referents of politeness pertain, for the most part, to the realm of human relationships and especially to the city, as the words *urbanité* (L. urbs: Rome) and *civilité* (L. civis: citizen of Rome) show. Even *politesse* (L. politus: polished) paronymically evokes the Greek *politês* (citizen of a polis) which indeed is the root of *policé* ('having civilized manners').

In the Japanese tradition, on the other hand, no clear relation appears between good manners and the city as such. On the contrary, the old word *miyabi* ('elegant manners'), though stemming from the same root as *miyako* (the capital, i.e. Heian: Kyoto), designated an appropriate way of appreciating nature. Tea ceremony, to name but one of many ritual performances related with good manners and still widely practised today, is fraught with metaphors of nature, e.g. the *roji* (the garden of a tea arbor, *chashitsu*) with its stepping stones representing a mountain path, or the pavilion itself, which is a metaphor of a mountain hut. But, inferring that good manners, in Japan, do not refer to the city at all, would be too hasty. In fact, it seems rather that the sacred referents of the idea of city itself, as the place (*ko*) of a *miya* (Shintō shrine/imperial palace/imperial prince), are anchored in nature, as the use of the term *miya-no-mori* (a shrine's sacred grove) still shows.

It appears, thus, that urbanity, as the quality of what is urban/urbane (in behaviours as well as in townscapes), is not founded on the same grounds in the Japanese and in the French traditions. In France, it seems to be founded on the political relation between men; in Japan, on the aesthetical relationship of man with nature, which correlatively blurs the political side of the link between men. This also implies, of course, that 'the city' is a much less consistent figure in Japanese than in French minds. A well-known illustration of this uncertain substantiality of the Japanese city is given by the heart of Tokyo, which is occupied by a forbidden forest (the Imperial Palace) – so to speak a giant *miya-no-mori*, with its frontiers and its rites of passage.

## FIGURE AND GROUND

Analysing the above data shows that the French – e.g. Michel Butor – are prone to conceive, as an archetypical image of the city, a figure neatly detached from the ground, which is either nature or the country-side.[12] This distinct form is both material and symbolic (urban values contrasting with those of nature, to which the French texts do not often refer).

In the Japanese texts, on a symbolical as well as on a material plane, this distinction between the city and its environment is much fuzzier: not only do they often speak of nature (though the topic is the city), but they explicitly insist on the morphological continuity between city and country, and on the indecision of figure/ground (the city/nature) patterns in the Japanese culture. Especially so in the case of Tokyo in the Edo period, as stressed by Maki Fumihiko.[13]

The recent trends of urbanization have indeed attenuated this contrast between France and Japan: French cities tend to be more diluted (i.e., less distinct from their environment on both formal, demographical and sociological grounds) than in the past. This phenomenon, at a higher degree, is developing in Japan as well (if one excepts central areas). It can be measured in physical terms (e.g. a declining density in Paris). Yet it seems that this development has not yet much affected our phenomenal patterns or perceptual schemata.

## VISIBLE AND INVISIBLE FORMS

Beyond such evidences, it appears that the notions of form and of morphology do not have the same value in both cultures.

It seems that, for the French, urban forms are endowed with an intrinsic reality, which confers on them a relative independence *vis-à-vis* the observer. They are the forms of objects which possess a proper outline and substance; which entails the possibility of a positivistic semiological approach to these forms.

In contrast to this, the concreteness of the forms of Japanese cities is questioned by several authors. There is no clear difference between actual urban forms, materially disposed in space, and the processes of urbanization – as Manuel Tardits (1987) stresses, that is the temporal layout of virtual forms.[14] Japanese architects – and this is explicitly stated by Andō Tadao (1987) – visibly attach more importance to the expression of the essence of things, rather than to design their sole visible forms (*katachi*).[15] It is also stressed, on the Japanese side – e.g. in Fujimori Terunobu's work (1987) – that the city is, for its inhabitants, less a world of objects (it appears as such only in the eyes of a foreign visitor) than a 'space', that is, a symbolic field, the invisible reality of which tends to dissolve the materiality of urban forms as well as the distinction between the inside and the outside of buildings.[16]

Such a relativization of material forms is expressed in many ways in the Japanese tradition. For instance, on a verbal and conceptual plane, the notion of *ba* (of which Andō profusely makes use), a word which can mean a situation or a scene as well as a field in modern physics (e.g. a magnetic field) is important. In the traditional house, the utilization of space depends on the situation and on the ritual fulfilment of certain sets of action (e.g. laying the *futon* at night), rather than being determined by concrete and stable forms (e.g. a bed in a bedroom). Thus, a single room can be multifunctional. Today, this prevalence of dynamic or temporal forms over static or spatial forms is well expressed, among many possible examples, by the use of the *jūbako* (nest of boxes) principle in organizing the space of the city. Take, for example, a room (closed with a sliding door) in a restaurant, the front of which opens on a street which is on the tenth floor of a building opening on an underground commercial street that runs directly into a railway station. When proceeding along the path from table to train, or the reverse, you never see an architectural form, in the sense of the external envelope of a substantial object, but only the sunken forms of the functional entrails of an invisible city. A more general aspect of the same tendency is that function overwhelmingly prevails over form in present day Japanese townscapes.

## FORM AND RITE

French urbanity has been, from a long past, prone to privilege material forms, as shown in the Parisian façades of Rivoli street, Haussmannian ordering, or the monumentality of the Louvre-Défense axis. Instead of this, Japanese urbanity may be characterized by the precariousness of tangible forms and, on the contrary, the structuring stability and the transmissibility of such intangible forms as traditional skills and the various rituals of sociality (e.g. a festival). The Bunka-chō (culture agency) officially recognizes and protects these intangible forms, as much as it protects tangible monuments (see Claire Gallian 1987).[17]

Let us briefly analyse the apparently paradoxical case of Ise Shrine. For about fifteen centuries, this temple has been ritually rebuilt in an identical shape (at least in principle) every twenty years, on alternating sites. Thus, it seems that we have in Ise a stable or even immutable tangible form, in contrast to what I have said above. But in fact, what is stable here is the perennial performance of a rite. The form of the temple only expresses this stability, in a literally insubstantial way because the material of the building changes every twenty years. Ise is indeed a monument, i.e., something which reminds (*monere*) the community of its existence as a community; but its monumentality is expressed through the ritual of rebuilding rather than through the building itself. Form perdures as such both temporally and spatially; it depends very little on matter (substance). This has little to do with the monumentality of Notre-Dame or of Julian's Thermae in Paris, where, on the contrary, form is so inherently attached to matter that, in the extreme case of the Thermae, the substance of the building (brick) may be almost shapeless, and devoid of any function linked to the form.

Such considerations lead us to think that Françoise Choay (1987), when stating that monumentality may be founded on the symbolical permanence of either form in space or matter in time, takes a very French or European stance, in which form evokes substance and thus tends to be predominantly spatial.[18] In the Japanese way of seeing, form does not rely on substance to the same degree, and thus it can tend to be predominantly temporal, as is a rite.

In a more prosaic mode, one can notice that, in Paris, relatively stable material forms can successively shelter variable functions, whereas in Tokyo the forms of the buildings readily change according to their function. This is but another way of saying that, in Japan, temporal or dynamic forms prevail over spatial or static forms.

Yet this contrast seems to become questionable. In reaction to the solitary and substantial forms of modern architecture, we see a French architect like Henri Gaudin (1987) profess that the object in itself does not exist, and a French sociologist like Michel Maffesoli (1987) speaks of the city as being also a *cosa mentale*.[19,20] It seems that we are not far, here, from the 'invisible city' (*mienai toshi*) which the architect Isozaki Arata announced more than twenty years ago – that city woven with mediatic functions and relationships.[21] Would postmodernism, beyond its formal games, tend to desubstantialize the object? This would mean to put on a same plane both tangible (or spatial) and intangible (or temporal) forms.

## ACTING FORMS AND ACTED FORMS

Confronting the texts and the discussions in the two symposia reveals that such a tendency is still limited on the French side. More than one French participant rejected the notion of forming form, or, in other words, the idea that human behaviour can be determined by the environment. This shows that in France, unlike Japan, there remains a clear distinction between the tangible and the intangible. Indeed this question is related to that of the correspondence (or lack of correspondence) between social forms and material forms. From the French side, it is stressed that, on the one hand, there may occur numerous disconnections and disharmonies between these two categories of forms, and that, on the other hand, only the former (i.e. social actors) are acting, whereas the latter (i.e. the forms of the city) are acted upon. Such a distinction is evidently none other than that of the subject and the object. As is well known, the subject/object relationship is quite differently conceived of in the two cultures: the so-called Cartesian tradition opposes the two terms (while according the subject an absolute pre-eminence), as much as the so-called Oriental tradition seeks to unite them. In fact, only one text, on the Japanese side, considers problematically the relationship between the forms of the city (the hardware) and those of society (the software); and yet even that concludes that the former conditions the latter.[22] The other Japanese texts implicitly apprehend the city as both a material and a social being, and they slip smoothly and evenly from the morphological to the sociological. More precisely, the second term (social determinations) does not seem, in these texts, to create much of a problem. This is particularly pronounced in Kawazoe Noboru's contribution (1987), as contrasted to Henri Raymond's (1987) – the same theme was initially proposed to the two authors: 'Define urbanity, as both a type of sociality and the reality of the city'.[23,24]

This Japanese propensity, as can be seen, is not only antipodal to the socially and politically critical standpoint which authors like Henri Lefebvre (1968, 1970, 1974) or Manuel Castells (1972) illustrated during the 1960s and the 1970s in urban studies; more fundamentally, it is anti-positivistic.

## POSTMODERNISM, POSTPOSITIVISM?

It becomes clear that what is at stake in the theme of postmodernity is much more than the so-called postmodernistic liberation of form in architecture. At this juncture, 'modern' does not refer only to the *mouvement moderne* in architecture or to the avant-garde in painting, but well and truly to the question of modernity in the sense of an abstraction of the subject out of its environment – an environment henceforward objectifiable and workable as such (i.e. as a mechanical arrangement of discrete and passive objects), as Bacon, Galileo, Descartes, etc. formulated it.

Effectively, some of the texts on the French side reveal that the positive distinction between the actors and their environment is, at least, questionable. The notion of *mémoire corporelle* (body memory, i.e., inveterate ways of acting which the subject is not conscious of) leads Françoise Choay (1987), for instance, to place in the same category of urbanity some types of human behaviour and some material aspects of the city (e.g. street-walking and traditional pavements).[25] In another perspective, Henri Raymond (1987) stresses the importance of such immaterial forms as the rules, norms and practices which constitute a specifically urban sociality, and which he subsumes under the notion of *policé*.[26] Going further, Michel Maffesoli (1987) speaks of an 'accentuation of the spatial', that is, a tendency to think of the environment as participating of the practices which constitute a given sociality.[27] Such a position clearly questions the articulation of social forms with material forms, although Maffesoli's (1987) text does not treat of this problem as such: to be sure, he speaks of proxemy and of situations – that is, of something in which the material organization of space influences social relations – but the latter remain his central focus of interest. Moreover, Maffesoli's (1987) stance about 'matricial forms' (a notion which was criticized on the French side) relate to other considerations than urban morphology proper.

The preceding examples open two perspectives. On the French side, in spite of the qualitative gap which separates the world of the subject (here social actors) from the world of the object (here the forms of the city), this alternative tends to be questioned, and questioned in terms which have nothing to do with scientism (which conceives the relationship between environment and society only in terms of objects), but such a tendency is a minor one. On the Japanese side, on the contrary, this is a major tendency, but this is not a reappraisal, as it is on the French side. A massive underflow, alien to positivism, never ceased in Japan to connect tangible forms to intangible forms; which poses in a peculiar way the question of relating the subjective to the objective, and consequently of relating the forms that are performed by a subject (e.g. a behaviour, a rite) to the forms which pertain to the objects of an environment (e.g. the morphology of a city).

## RITUALS AS A LOGIC OF IDENTIFICATION

What I have tried to show is, in a phrase, that in Japan an emphasis is put on temporal forms, whereas in France an emphasis is put on spatial forms. Of course, this must be related to the evidence that Japanese society has not only remained much more ritualistic (or formalistic) than Western societies have become in the long process of their modernization, but that it is much more ritualistic even after having modernized to at least the same degree as its Western counterparts in terms of material civilization. To put it simply, Japan performs a comparatively formalist version of modernity, whereas Western societies perform a comparatively substantialist one.

But, then, how can the Japanese society be at the same time formalist and so highly functional in achieving its material goals? This is a paradox only if one retains a conception of forms as mainly spatial, thus static, as seems to be the prevailing tendency in France, but it ceases to be a paradox if one conceives forms as mainly temporal, thus dynamic, as appears to be the case in Japan.

Yet, if considering rituals as temporal forms sheds some light on the question of form and function, it does not explain why the Japanese tradition has chosen to put an emphasis on temporal forms instead of spatial ones; in other words, to privilege behaviour over things, and becoming over substance (being).

This problem is in fact only the reverse of the problem of the rise of modernity in Europe, and of its pre-modern roots in Greece. As has often been stressed by Japanese philosophers, European thought has been dominated by a logic of the subject, or of identity of the subject, which privileges substance and being.[28] In such logic, *A* is *A* in any circumstance – an abstract idea of which modern Western individualism is a sensible expression. Being in principle (since Descartes' *cogito ergo sum*) certain of his own identity as the subject, the modern Western individual is relatively unlikely to feel that anguish or exaltation of change, the conjuration of which is one of the main functions of rite. Hence (among many other factors, of course) the progressive debasement of rituals which, in Europe, accompanied the process of modernization.

By the same token, it is understandable that rituals are more important in a society such as Japan, in which the intellectual tradition has been dominated by relation instead of intrinsic substance, by becoming or transformation instead of being, and especially – to borrow Nakamura Yūjirō's (1989) expression – a logic of the predicate instead of a logic of the subject; in other words, a logic of metaphor, or of identification, by dint of which, according to the circumstances, *A* can become *B*, the self can identify with what (in Western terms) is not the self (i.e. the other or nature), and the subject can identify with the object, as the well-known expression *mono no aware* suggests.[29]

In a word, the Japanese society values rituals because it values change. Formalizing the performance of a set of human actions in the natural flow of time is indeed a way to identify symbolically these actions to the action of time, i.e., change, and thus to identify culture with nature, which is a permanent longing of the Japanese culture. This is, needless to say, completely opposite to the modern-classical European worldview, which asserted the pre-eminence of Man's action upon nature, and correlatively favoured substance over form.

If such a hypothesis is valid, then one can forecast a recrudescence of rituals in postmodern Western societies as well. This is indeed what some sociologists like Michel Maffesoli (1988, 1990) are insisting upon.[30] Maffesoli argues that rituals – some of them a revival of ancient religious ceremonies, but mostly on untraditional, often ludic grounds – are a symptom of postmodernity. One is reminded here of the cosmogenetical significance which Eugen Fink (1966) has shown in the link between play, magic and religious ceremonials.[31] One may indeed surmise that in the course of postmodernity, play – and correlatively rites – should in some way regain this cosmogenetical significance, which modernity had debased.[32] In this respect, it is also relevant to notice that

Japan, since the Kyoto School (*Kyōto Gakuha*), and after a forty years parenthesis, is again overtly posing itself as a challenger of the (late?) modern Western paradigm. Will the city of tomorrow be a city of rites?[33]

## NOTES

1 For a recent synthesis, see Raymond Ledrut, *La Forme et le sens dans la société*, Paris, Librairie des Méridiens, 1984.

2 On this 'active' social role of the traditional Japanese house, see Jacques Pezeu-Massabuau, *La Maison japonaise*, Paris, Publications Orientalistes de France, 1981.

3 Pierre Bourdieu, *Le Sens pratique*, Paris, Editions de Minuit, 1980.

4 François Heran, 'La Seconde nature de l'habitus. Tradition philosophique et sens commun dans le langage sociologique', *Revue française de sociologie*, 1987, XXVIII (3): 385–416.

5 As I have tried to show in *Le Sauvage et l'artifice. Les Japonais devant la nature*, Paris, Gallimard, 1986. (Japanese translation: *Fūdo no Nihon. Shizen to bunka no tsūtai*, Tokyo, Chikuma, 1988.

6 On this process, see note 5 and also Augustin Berque, 'Some traits of Japanese *fūdosei*', *The Japan Foundation Newsletter*, 1987, XIV (1): 1–7.

7 Augustin Berque, *Vivre l'espace au Japon*, Paris, Presses Universitaires de France, 1982. (Japanese translation: *Kūkan no Nihon bunka*, Tokyo, Chikuma, 1985).

8 Bourdieū (1980:89).

9 To apprehend urbanity, or more generally mediance, one has to consider reality as intertwining the phenomenal and the physical, as being between the two theoretical poles of the real of the thing in itself and the unreal of representations for oneself. See note 6.

10 Jean Maisonneuve, *Les Rituels*, Paris, Presses Universitaires de France, 1988. (*Que Sais-je*, nº 2425). See also, about everyday rituals, Michel Maffesoli, *La Conquête du présent. Pour une sociologie de la vie quotidienne*, Paris, Presses Universitaires de France, 1979.

11 See Augustin Berque (ed.), *La Qualité de la ville. Urbanité française, urbanité nippone*, Tokyo, Maison franco-japonaise, 1987 (hereafter quoted as QV). Second volume, *La Maîtrise de la ville*, Paris, Éditions de l'École des hautes études en sciences sociales (1994).

12 Michel Butor, 'Comment parler de la ville', QV, 3–7.

13 Maki Fumihiko, 'La Construction des lieux', QV, 112–18.

14 Manuel Tardits, 'Tokyo: des éléments', QV, 28–34.

15 Andō Tadao, 'Sumiyoshi, Rokkō, Sanjō Kobashi', QV, 97–102.

16 Fujimori Terunobu, 'Le Problème de la Tour de Tokyo', QV, 130–8.

17 Claire Gallian, 'Le Système de protection du patrimoine de la ville japonaise', QV, 139–49.

18 Françoise Choay, 'Mémoire de la ville et monumentalité', QV, 121–130.

19 Henri Gaudin, 'Des Poches hospitalières', QV, 94–6.

20 Michel Maffesoli, 'Post-Modernité affectuelle', QV, 249–58

21 The idea of *mienai toshi* is discussed in Ichikawa (1987).

22 Tanabe Hiroshi, 'Le Centre-Ville et la banlieue de Tokyo du point de vue des migrations', QV, 177–86.

23 Kawazoe Noboru, 'L'Urbanité comme expression des pratiques et des liens sociaux', QV, 211–16.
24 Henri Raymond, 'L'Urbanité: socialité et fait urbain', QV, 202–10.
25 See note 18
26 See note 23
27 See note 20
28 Most clearly in Nakamura Yūjirō's recent book, *Basho/topos*, Tokyo: Kobundo, 1989.
29 I have insisted on these identificational processes in 'Identification of the self in relation to the environment', in Nancy Rosenberger (ed.), *Japanese Sense of Self*, Cambridge: Cambridge University Press, 1992, 93–104.
30 Michel Maffesoli, *Le Temps des Tribus. Le déclin de l'individualisme dans les sociétés de masse*, Paris, Méridiens Klincksieck, 1988; and also, *Au creux des apparences*, Paris, Plon, 1990.
31 In the French translation: *Le Jeu comme symbole du monde*, Paris, Minuit, 1966.
32 This is correlated with the fact that modernity has debased identification and extolled identity, which entails that play is not cosmogenetical, i.e. a source of reality, but only a copy of a higher reality (as Plato put it). On this question and its link with the relation of our postmodern society with space and nature, see Augustin Berque, *Médiance. De milieux en paysages*, Montpellier, Reclus (diff.: Documentation française, Paris), 1990 (Japanese translation: *Fūdo toshite no chikyū*, Tokyo, Chikuma, 1994).
33 I propose an interpretation of this question in *Du Geste à la cité. Formes urbaines et lien social au Japon*, Paris: Gallimard, 1993 (Japanese translation: *Miburi kara machizukuri e*, Tokyo: Chikuma, forthcoming).

## BIBLIOGRAPHY

Andō Tadao (1987) 'Sumiyoshi, Rokkō, Sanjō Kobashi', in Augustin Berque (ed.) *La Qualité de la ville*, Tokyo: Maison franco-japonaise.
Berque, Augustin (1982) *Vivre l'espace au Japon*, Paris: Presses Universitaires de France. (Japanese translation, *Kūkan no Nihon bunka*, Tokyo: Chikuma, 1985.)
—— (1986) *Le Sauvage et l'artifice. Les japonais devant la nature*, Paris: Gallimard.
—— (ed.) (1987) *La Qualité de la ville. Urbanité française, urbanité nippone*, Tokyo: Maison franco-japonaise
—— (1987) 'Some traits of Japanese *fūdosei*', *The Japan Foundation Newsletter*, XIV (1): 1–7.
—— (1990) *Médiance: De milieux en paysages*, Montpellier: Reclus (diff.: Documentation française, Paris).
—— (1992) 'Identification of the self in relation to the environment', in Nancy Rosenberger (ed.) *Japanese Sense of Self*, Cambridge: Cambridge University Press.
—— (1993) *Du Geste à la cité. Motifs de l'urbanité nippone*, Paris: Gallimard.
—— (ed.) (1994) *La Maîtrise de la ville*, Paris, Éditions de l'École des hautes études en sciences sociales.
Bourdieu, Pierre (1980) *Le Sens pratique*, Paris: Editions de Minuit.

Butor, Michel (1987) 'Comment parler de la ville', in Augustin Berque (ed.) *La Qualité de la ville*, Tokyo: Maison franco-japonaise.

Castells, Manuel (1972) *La Question urbaine*, Paris: Maspéro.

Choay, Françoise (1987) 'Mémoire de la ville et monumentalité', in Augustin Berque (ed.) *La Qualité de la ville*, Tokyo: Maison franco-japonaise.

Fink, Eugen (1966) *Le Jeu comme symbole du monde*, Paris: Minuit.

Fujimori Terunobu (1987) 'Le Problème de la Tour de Tokyo', in Augustin Berque (ed.) *La Qualité de la ville*, Tokyo: Maison franco-japonaise.

Gallian, Claire (1987) 'Le Système de protection du patrimoine de la ville japonaise', in Augustin Berque (ed.) *La Qualité de la ville*, Tokyo: Maison franco-Japonaise.

Gaudin, Henri (1987) 'Des Poches hospitalières', in Augustin Berque (ed.) *La Qualité de la ville*, Tokyo: Maison franco-japonaise.

Heran, François (1987) 'La Seconde nature de l'habitus: tradition philosophique et sens commun dans le langage sociologique', *Revue française de sociologie*, XXVIII (3): 385–416.

Ichikawa Hiroshi (1987) 'Possibilité du lieu (*basho*) – postmoderne et sensibilité collective', in Augustin Berque (ed.) *La Qualité de la ville. Urbanité française, ubanité nippone*, Tokyo: Maison franco-japonaise, pp. 237–45.

Kawazoe Noboru (1987) 'L'Urbanité comme expression des pratiques et des liens sociaux', in Augustin Berque (ed.) *La Qualité de la ville*, Tokyo: Maison franco-japonaise.

Ledrut, Raymond (1984) *La Forme et le sens dans la société*, Paris: Librairie des Méridiens.

Lefebvre, Henri (1968) *Le Droit à la ville*, Paris: Anthropos.

—— (1970) *La révolution urbaine*, Paris: Gallimard.

—— (1974) *La production de l'espace*, Paris: Anthropos.

Maffesoli, Michel (1979) *La Conquête du présent. Pour une sociologie de la vie quotidienne*, Paris: Presses Universitaires de France.

—— (1987) 'Post-Modernité affectuelle', in Augustin Berque (ed.) *La Qualité de la ville*, Tokyo: Maison franco-Japonaise.

—— (1988) *Le Temps des Tribus. Le déclin de l'individualisme dans les sociétés de masse*, Paris: Méridiens Klincksieck.

—— (1990) *Au creux des apparences*, Paris: Plon.

Maki Fumihiko (1987) 'La Construction des lieux', in Augustin Berque (ed.) *La Qualité de la ville*, Tokyo: Maison franco-japonaise.

Maisonneuve, Jean (1988) *Les Rituels*, Paris: Presses Universitaires de France, 1988. (*Que Sais-je*, no. 2425.)

Nakamura Yūjirō (1989) *Basho/topos*, Tokyo: Kobundo.

Pezeu-Massabuau, Jacques (1981) *La Maison japonaise*, Paris: Publications Orientalistes de France.

Raymond, Henri (1987) 'L'Urbanité: socialité et fait urbain', in Augustin Berque (ed.) *La Qualité de la ville*, Tokyo: Maison franco-japonaise.

Rosenberger, Nancy (ed.) (1992) *Japanese Sense of Self*, Cambridge, Cambridge University Press.

Tanabe Hiroshi (1987) 'Le Centre-Ville et la banlieue de Tokyo du point de vue des migrations', in Augustin Berque (ed.) *La Qualité de la ville*, Tokyo: Maison franco-japonaise.

Tardits, Manuel (1987) 'Tokyo: des élements', in Augustin Berque (ed.) *La Qualité de la ville*, Tokyo: Maison franco-japonaise.

# Index

260 *Index*